Feminism

Film

Fascism

Feminism
Film
Fascism

WOMEN'S AUTO/BIOGRAPHICAL FILM

IN POSTWAR GERMANY

Susan E. Linville

UNIVERSITY OF TEXAS PRESS, AUSTIN

Requests for permission to reproduce material from this work should
be sent to Permissions, University of Texas Press, Box 7819, Austin,
TX 78713-7819.

∞ The paper used in this publication meets the minimum requirements of American National Standard for Information Sciences–Per-
manence of Paper for Printed Library Materials, ANSI Z39.48-1984.

Library of Congress Cataloging-in-Publication Data

Linville, Susan E. (Susan Elizabeth), 1949–
Feminism, film, fascism : women's auto/biographical film in
postwar Germany / Susan E. Linville.
p.   cm.
Filmography: p.
Includes bibliographical references and index.
ISBN 0-292-74696-2 (cloth : alk. paper).—
ISBN 0-292-74697-0 (pbk. : alk. paper)
1. Motion pictures—Germany—History.   2. Women in motion
pictures.   3. Women motion picture producers and directors—
Germany.   4. Motion pictures—Germany—Psychological aspects.
5. Guilt—Psychological aspects.   I. Title.
PN1993.5.G3L56   1998
791.43′0943—dc21   97-3076

This book is dedicated to Kent, my partner in love and work, to Laurie,

who taught me how to laugh, and to the "part-timers."

Contents

Acknowledgments

First and foremost, I would like to thank Kent Casper, without whose scholarly knowledge, tireless patience, generosity of spirit, humor, and wisdom this book would have been unthinkable. I also owe thanks to many other scholars who provided me with invaluable input, materials, and encouragement or who fed my thinking at various points in the development of this work. They include Richard McCormick, Susan McMorris, Elihu Pearlman, Shirley Johnston, Catherine Wiley, Bruce Kawin, James Palmer, John Davidson, Janet Lungstrum, David Bathrick, Anton Kaes, Eric Rentschler, Sandra Frieden, Teresa de Lauretis, and Tania Modleski. While many students have enlivened my ideas about German cinema, three women—Deborah Levitt, Lyle Nelson, and Francesca Prada—deserve special acknowledgment. Additional thanks go to the two insightful, anonymous readers for the University of Texas Press, as well as to humanities editor Ali Hossaini, Jr., for his professionalism and *Menschlichkeit*, to director Joanna Hitchcock for her initial interest in the project, to Lois Rankin, and especially to Mandy Woods for her expert editing. I am also grateful to the University of Colorado at Denver for a faculty development grant and other forms of institutional support.

My gratitude goes as well to Jutta Brückner, Marianne Rosenbaum, and Gérard Samaan for providing me with photo illustrations, and to Elaine Beemer, Mary Ferrell, Brigitte Hauptman, and Mary Ann Hult for helping me obtain additional photographs. Photo illustrations are reproduced here courtesy of: Nourfilm, Munich (*Peppermint Peace*); Jutta Brückner Filmproduktion, Berlin and Pahl-Film, Tübingen (*Hunger Years*); New Yorker Films (*Germany, Pale Mother* and *Marianne and Juliane*); Auraria Film Collection, Auraria Higher Education Center (*Malou* and *Germany, Pale Mother*).

Some portions of this book have appeared elsewhere in different form. A version of chapter 2 was first published in *New German Critique* 55 (Winter 1992); a version of chapter 3 first appeared in *Perspectives on German Cinema*, eds. Terri Ginsberg and Kirsten Moana Thompson (New York: G. K. Hall, 1996); and an earlier version of chapter 4 was first published in *PMLA* 106 (May 1991). I gratefully acknowledge these sources.

Feminism

Film

Fascism

Introduction

Seeing Through the "Postwar" Years

Innovative West German women filmmakers of the late 1970s and early 1980s such as Marianne Rosenbaum and Margarethe von Trotta created films that focus on the three *K*'s of women's traditional sphere in German culture—*Kinder, Kirche, Küche*—children, church, and kitchen—in order to reinterpret the politics of the "postwar world" they experienced in their childhoods. While these films embrace an auto/biographical and often intensely personal focus, they neither conceptualize female identity as separate from public politics nor skirt the issue of the Nazi horrors; instead, they demonstrate in diverse ways how the triad of *Kinder, Kirche, Küche* is politically inflected and enmeshed with the process of understanding the Nazi past. These films develop distinctive critiques of the conventional social gender order that the postwar era furiously struggled to reinstate; in the process, they create narrative structures and cinematic styles that implicitly oppose the hierarchic and matrophobic dimensions of the postwar discourse on the authoritarian personality. Women's auto/biographical films reflect back on how daughters growing up in the 1940s and 1950s were taught to see and not to see; how food and consumption worked as mechanisms to deflect and confound their *Wisstrieb* (epistemophilia) and their *Schaulust* (scopophilia);[1] how schooling and religious training at best fell short in educating young people about the Holocaust, at worst remained hypocritically complicit with fascist practices from the past; and how traditionally structured families and gender identities, far from leading to a radical break from authoritarianism and xenophobia as experts claimed they would, helped perpetuate their hold on the culture, exacerbating Germany's amnesiac tendencies and undermining forces for change. Concurrently, the films recall and sharply reprove the unequal access to the channels of public discourse and memory authorized by media apparatuses and cultural tradition.

At one level, this book is an examination of the diverse ways in which women's auto/biographical films of the late 1970s and early 1980s contradict, critique, and enlarge the postwar theories on authoritarianism, melancholy, and mourning that have centrally shaped our understanding of postwar Germany and the New German Cinema. Their detractors have used postwar psychosocial theories to fault German feminist films. In sharp contrast, my aim is to demonstrate the varied means by which women auto/biographical filmmakers shed new, critical light on the intersections among the authoritarian, patriarchal, and oedipal dynamics that absorbed postwar theorists, and to reveal how these filmmakers augment spectatorial desire for alternatives to the postwar vision of the "restored family"—a vision which "restored" women to their traditional sphere within German culture—*Kinder, Kirche, Küche*. The original and diverse contributions of these films can be appreciated only against the backdrop of those postwar conceptual frameworks, which also metaphorized fascism as secretly female—and not patriarchal after all.

This introduction sketches and historicizes postwar psychosocial research on mourning and the authoritarian personality—in particular, the work of Alexander and Margarete Mitscherlich—as a prelude to an appraisal in the chapters that follow of the aesthetic and political contributions of Marianne Rosenbaum's *Peppermint Peace* (*Peppermint Frieden*, 1983), Helma Sanders-Brahms's *Germany, Pale Mother* (*Deutschland, bleiche Mutter*, 1979), Jutta Brückner's *Hunger Years* (*Hungerjahre*, 1979), Margarethe von Trotta's *Marianne and Juliane* (*Die bleierne Zeit*, 1981), and Jeanine Meerapfel's *Malou* (1980). Fredric Jameson notes the gap between individual experience rendered through the aesthetics of a work of art and the scientific or cognitive models that map the social structure of existence.[2] Yet just as autobiography is both the invention and the discovery of selfhood, so too are the biological and social sciences as much tools for the construction of natural and social reality as they are a means to its discovery. Although the politics inherent in an auto/biographical work are necessarily tethered to the anecdotal and limited, auto/biography can usefully be juxtaposed in a contrapuntal relationship with "scientific" modes of interpretation. Self-portraiture can comment on the hidden fictionality of science—for example, its unacknowledged debts to "universalist" master narratives of the "Western" humanist tradition. Moreover, insofar as the autobiographical subject's self-representation requires situating the self in its cultural embeddedness and giving that embeddedness aesthetic expression, self-portraiture can transcend the purely idiosyncratic or idiopathic. It can provide a figuration and critique of the social realities that structure lived experience. As I show, the continuum that exists between West German auto/biographical films by women and (for example) the contemporary antihierarchic essays of science historian Donna Haraway illustrates the ties that bind the seemingly disparate fields of autobiography and social-science writing.

According to the postwar psychosocial research of the Mitscherlichs, German authoritarianism and avoidance of both mourning and *Vergangenheitsbewältigung*—coming to terms with the past—are rooted in the prototypical German son's failure to accept or identify fully with patriarchal authority. Both *Society without the Father* (Alexander Mitscherlich, 1963) and *The Inability to Mourn* (Alexander and Margarete Mitscherlich, 1967) depend upon this concept of the underoedipalized son, and both point toward a corollary scientific-political position—namely, that in the wake of World War II, a forceful reinstatement of the traditional patriarchal family and social gender hierarchy offered the only possible antidote to fascism, a politics they metaphorized as "effeminate" and "regressive."[3] Much like their cold-war counterparts in the United States, the authors validated patriarchist policy by linking the need for traditional sexual identities to issues of a viable national political identity.[4]

Its masculinist politics notwithstanding, *The Inability to Mourn* has remained a privileged text in analyses of German cultural expression, including New German Cinema. Indeed, despite some acknowledgment of limitations in the Mitscherlichs' work, its general validity has remained largely unchallenged. Andreas Huyssen, for example, uncharacteristically misses the misogynistic inflection of the Mitscherlich texts and contexts and attests to the authors' persuasive power.[5] Thomas Elsaesser filters their work through Lacan, Metz, and Baudry in order to theorize specular relations in New German Cinema generally, ultimately conflating Hitler's

gaze, the maternal (phallic mother's) gaze, and the gaze of the camera in a
dynamic defined by primary narcissism.[6] More recently, Martin Jay has
cited the Mitscherlichs not to question their work's accuracy or applicabil-
ity to postwar Germans, but rather to spell out the limits in parallels between the post-1945 and post-1989 situations in Germany. While highlighting important differences between the issues of mourning called up
by the death of GDR socialism in 1989 and those evoked by the demise of
National Socialism, Jay also emphasizes the failure of citizens of the former GDR to mourn losses suffered in 1945.[7] I want to insist, however, on
the complex status of the Mitscherlichs' work as a *cultural product*. For
while their work brings a crucial postwar problem into focus and affords
a revealing interpretive framework, its science is imbricated both with
Western humanist fictions of melancholia and with twentieth-century political narratives that naturalize male supremacy.

Like Freud's "Mourning and Melancholia" to which they are indebted,
Society without the Father and *The Inability to Mourn* participate in a masculinist discourse of melancholy and mourning historically rooted in the
universalist poetic and philosophic traditions of European Renaissance
humanism. Juliana Schiesari has drawn a detailed map of the misogynistic
gender divisions which have shaped this discourse virtually transhistori-
cally and regardless of the discipline in which they appear. From Ficino to
Freud and Lacan, and from humoral medicine, philosophy, and literature
to psychoanalysis, melancholy has been gendered and valued or disparaged
as follows: First, "when melancholia is considered undesirable it is stereotypically metaphorized as feminine or viewed as an affliction women bring
onto men."[8] Second, female depression and grieving are "seen as the
'everyday' plight of the common (wo)man, . . . quotidian event[s] whose
collective force does not seem to bear the same weight of 'seriousness' as a
man's grief"—or the same need for special comment.[9] Third, when melancholy *is* culturally valued, as it is with individual men of great accomplishment, it is deemed superior to mourning, a traditionally feminine
ritual function that has been privatized and repressed. A final character-
istic derives especially from Freud and his efforts to differentiate melancholia from conditions that are stereotypically feminine. As Schiesari explains, "A criterion of differentiation [for Freud] is found in the *narcissistic*
identification said to be carried out by melancholia. This narcissistic basis
for differentiation is consonant with an implicit masculinizing of the neu-

rosis," particularly in its culturally validated form.[10] Narcissism is gendered masculine here, because, "following Freud's logic, narcissistic identification would be effected by the child through its identity with an ego ideal, whose paradigmatic case is that of the boy identifying with the father";[11] that is, Schiesari, unlike the Mitscherlichs, reads Freud's emphasis to be on secondary rather than primary narcissism.

While the Mitscherlichs stress that no widespread melancholia set in among West Germans, they analyze "representative cases" of psychological disturbance that fit all too well the patterns Schiesari detects. The Mitscherlichs' attribution of negative "feminine" qualities and mother-dependence to "representative" male case studies,[12] their theorizing of Hitler as an internalized maternal imago,[13] their neglect of female experiences per se, and their lack of attention to traditions that identify both the capacity for sympathy and the ability to mourn as feminine illustrate their allegiance to the masculinist mythos of melancholy. By following the centuries-old practice of spotlighting male melancholia while suppressing women's experiences of loss, their work effectively reduces women and children to tropes of emasculation and guilt in a dehistoricized male psychomachia, tropes that elide the postwar experiences of German women and children as such.[14] Far from innocent, their work was made to order for the official needs of a postwar society that, into the 1960s and beyond, was still struggling to rigidify the social gender hierarchy and to exonerate patriarchy of its role in the fascist past. Their exculpation of the paternal function, moreover, occurs at the expense of that familiar postwar scapegoat, the "mother"—whatever "her" guise.[15] The Mitscherlichs' identification of Hitler as a maternal imago and their failure to consider the role of the negative stereotyping of mourning as women's work are two areas that merit more specific comment, for both are relevant to the women's auto/biographical films to be examined here.

One of the more startling theses in *Society without the Father* is the notion that the authoritarian "mass leader" resembles the "imago of a primitive mother goddess," the child's tie to whom "never reached the level, so rich in conflict, where the conscience is formed and ties with it are established"; that is, the notion of underoedipalization.[16] This gender transformation of the authoritarian leader, it should be stressed, does *not* take its cue from what might be an expected source—namely, Freud's "Group Psychology and the Analysis of the Ego." There, Freud identifies the

Hitlerian type of leader as a version of Nietzsche's *Übermensch*—as the
dreaded primal father, whose absolute narcissism is not balanced out by
any love for others.[17] Neither do the Mitscherlichs take their cue from
Nazi propaganda, with its constant idealization of the *father*land. Their
argument does, however, effectively reenact the gendered psychomachia
that forms the heart of the conventional Western mythos of melancholy.
Indeed, their "bad mother" fantasy is thoroughly bound up in the melancholic tradition, and that tradition in turn helps sustain the fiction of the
sufficiency and integrity of the classical male subject.

In the essay on melancholy and mourning, Freud asserts, "We see how
in [the melancholic subject] one part of the ego sets itself over against the
other, judges it critically, and, as it were, takes it as its object. . . . What
we are here becoming acquainted with is the agency commonly called
'conscience.'"[18] That is, Freud sees in the melancholic a strong identification with the father—in Lacanian terms, the law. Schiesari glosses
Freud's account of the object which the paternal voice criticizes as follows:
"My feminist suspicion is that this object, at once vilified, desired, and
judged by a 'superior, moral' instance, is situated *in the same way* as woman
in classic phallocentrism (that is, as a devalued object, as abject and at
fault)" [Schiesari's emphasis]—a suspicion she proceeds to confirm.[19] The
Mitscherlichs' formulation in no way contradicts Schiesari's idea. Indeed,
their argument depends upon a retrospective view that Hitler was not *really* an introjected father figure, despite innumerable testimonies about the
idealism Germans felt he represented; instead, he was a variant on the
so-called pre-oedipal, phallic mother—a figure whose guilt and lack are
retrospectively exposed in a process that empowers the father. Hence, according to the Mitscherlich view, melancholy failed to loom over the culture because the identification with the father never took complete hold.

This revisionist view of Hitler as maternal and of the narcissistic cathexis to him as primary rather than secondary (or as comprising some
tessellation of the two) seems particularly counterproductive to the process
of mourning when one remembers the negatively "feminine" stereotyping
of Jewish men during the Third Reich. Nazi propaganda deemed Hitler
the powerful father and demeaned the Jewish male as feminine, guilty,
abject. After the war, the Mitscherlichs not only identified Hitler with the
guilty mother, they also, in one case history (that of "R."), identified the
Jewish male as the paternal surrogate.[20] "Frailty thy name is woman," in-

deed. This kind of repetitious attachment of pejoratively feminine labels to whoever is currently being devalued and vilified (whether deservedly or not) suggests that it was not "feminine" psychic qualities and intrusions that impeded the Germans' ability to mourn, as the Mitscherlichs argue, but something else entirely. More likely, it was the fear and hatred of traditionally or stereotypically feminine things, one of which is mourning, both as private experience and as public ritual. The displays of emotion associated with grieving would have been seen as an unbearably painful affirmation of the German male's so-called emasculation-feminization-infantilization.

An insight close to this one, in fact, informs an essay on German melancholia that is otherwise inattentive to differences of gender—namely, Michael Schneider's "Fathers and Sons, Retrospectively: The Damaged Relationship Between Two Generations."[21] In an analysis that partly dovetails with Schiesari's findings, Schneider contends that postwar Germany failed to grieve due to the cultural prejudice against mourning as stereotypically unheroic—as women's work. He asserts that the misogyny which militated against the fathers' expressions of sorrow and their acknowledgment of pain during the postwar era is a Nazi legacy:

> The paralytic "character shield" and the resulting spiritual and psychological immobilization of the war generation can be attributed . . . to the internalization of a specific ideal of manliness which unconditionally denounced any sensitive coming-to-terms with one's emotions as a form of "weakness." . . . Mourning, sorrow, the acknowledgement of pain could not (at least in public) be reconciled with [this generation's] heroic image of humanity and masculinity as perceived under National Socialism ("as tough as leather, as hard as Krupp steel," so the slogan went).[22]

This analysis of the Nazi and postwar discourse of masculinity creates a welcome and revealing alternative to the Mitscherlichs' view of authoritarianism. Indeed, by exposing the postwar aversion to things "feminine," Schneider's argument helps explain how the culture would produce the biases and blind spots in the Mitscherlich study, such as their failure to theorize empathy or female subjectivity and their disparagement of nonclassical male subjectivity.

For all Schneider's insight, however, his essay remains caught up in the same old web that Schiesari details. He reproduces an identical symbolics of loss that elides female experience, and his discussion of prejudices against stereotypically female things serves the narcissistically restricted purpose of illuminating a male psychomachia, wherein women serve as little more than abstract tropes and precipitating or introjected causes.[23] Schneider explains, "If the generation of the fathers had manically defended against sorrows, melancholy, depression, and all the emotional problems which went along with it, the present generation is made up of little else."[24] The "feminine" emotionalism which the fathers disdained is thus recuperated in the name of male experiences of loss, specifically the sons' relationship to the "lost pasts of their fathers during the Third Reich."[25] On the other hand, women's actual experiences of loss due to their perennially devalued status within European patriarchy, including in postwar Germany and during the 1970s, their debilitating virtual synonymity with passivity, emotion, ineffectuality, and guilt, do not figure into Schneider's text.[26] Nor does Schneider pose the question of how women were to work through the process of mourning and remorse when the representational deck for doing so was so heavily stacked against them. When "feminine" passivity and maternalized guilt are posited as essentialized qualities and as essential causes of genocide, are not two likely results women's all-consuming self-loathing or their total denial? Schneider, however, identifies his generation with Hamlet and concurs with Ernst Bloch's description of the melancholic prince as a "disabled Orestes"—that is, unable to kill the mother who has arrogated his (father's) power to herself. And here, the matrophobic echoes of *The Inability to Mourn* are unmistakable. For all Schneider's insight, the Mitscherlichian image of Hitler as an evil primitive mother figure, a Clytemnestra in drag, remains a palimpsest to his text.

The sons' narcissistic derealization of women's status under patriarchy during the 1970s is of course problematic also for another reason: It can be linked back to the fathers' narcissistic derealization of Jewish suffering and to the totally erroneous view held by some postwar Germans, male and female, that they themselves were the war's principal victims. I want to emphasize that I do not in any way regard these two instances of derealization as equivalent phenomena. At no point in the history of Western patriarchy have women as a group faced the threat of annihilation, of total derealization in that sense, faced by the European Jews. Historically, however, a lack of empathy for women as subjects and the trivializing of their experiences have formed the culturally validated prototype for derealizing the experiences of other groups defined by difference.[27] Hence, though decidedly disparate, the phenomena are related.[28]

Besides the psychoanalytic context, the biosocial context is also critical to a historically grounded understanding of the Mitscherlichs' work. In an important sense, *The Inability to Mourn* is a continuation of the project Alexander Mitscherlich began in *Society without the Father*. Like the work that followed it, *Society without the Father* seeks to identify the etiology of authoritarian behavior, but through argumentation that is relatively more propped on research in the biosocial sciences, disciplines which first gained autonomy between 1920 and 1940. Whether rooted in psychoanalysis or in biosocial research, however, the assumptions that guide these two books share, first, the binary logic found within all hierarchical systems based on the polarization between feminine and masculine; and second, the dislocation of key gendered social practices into a naturalized sphere, be it the pre-oedipal or what contemporary social science took to be an objectively viewed, necessary, natural order. I will now turn from a focus on the gendering of melancholia to a consideration of the gendering of social science, especially its biologically determinist models of culture, and its relationship to mourning in the Mitscherlichs' work.

The gendering of Hitler as secretly female and maternal is linked to concerted efforts in the biosocial sciences to naturalize the social gender hierarchy. These attempts to equate dominance with nature rather than culture abetted the conceptualization of Hitler's role in German history in nonpatriarchal terms. As Donna Haraway has demonstrated, biosocial research that examined dominance hierarchies among animals held a mirror up to nature and discovered models of competition, divisions of labor, and patterns of resource allocation that were in full accord with contemporary views validating human male dominance. Such findings granted scientific legitimacy to patriarchist assumptions in a range of other fields. For example, they became the basis for anti-labor union positions.[29] Haraway expressly relates the biosocial research to authoritarian behavior studies as follows: "Throughout the period around the Second World War, similar studies of the authoritarian personality in human beings abounded; true social order must rest on a balance of dominance, interpreted as the foundation of co-operation. Competitive aggression became the chief form that organized other forms of social integration." [30]

It is illuminating to examine one example of this research in some detail, for the parallels between it and *Society without the Father* are striking. A specific instance of animal research that promoted the biologically determinist view of the social gender hierarchy is Clarence Ray Carpenter's late-1930s investigation of social organization among rhesus monkeys. Carpenter's experiment entailed removing the "alpha male" from a free-ranging society of monkeys. The resulting "society without the father" purportedly suffered from unproductive, individualistic competition among the primates and serious social disruption. Tellingly, however, Carpenter never carried out the presumably obligatory control experiment of removing animals other than the dominant male—an experiment which might have revealed that co-operation, co-ordination, and flexibility are as valuable to simian social survival as competitive aggression. This omission occurred, according to Haraway, because performing the control experiment "did not make sense within the whole complex of theory, analogies to individual organisms, and unexamined assumptions." [31]

Using floridly sexual rhetoric, Mitscherlich depicts a paradigmatic human counterpart to Carpenter's fatherless simian community: It is "a gigantic army of rival, envious siblings. Their chief conflict is characterized not by Oedipal rivalry, struggling with the father for the privileges of liberty and power, but by sibling envy directed at neighbors and competitors. . . ." The "army," he avows, ensures the success of "a mother-goddess lavish with her milk, the political conjurer (demagogue)." [32] Like Carpenter, Mitscherlich here legitimizes and naturalizes the *political* principle of male dominance, according to which females are by definition excluded from the pursuit of the father's "liberty and power" and knowledge. [33] Consequently, he is able to avoid interpreting fascistic behavior in terms that challenge the presumed naturalness and necessity—including the moral necessity—of a male-headed social gender hierarchy. Indeed, by warding off competing constructions of social reality, he precludes the emphasis on matrifocal, *non*hierarchical, and productively collaborative forms of social organization that has subsequently shaped feminist perspectives in physical anthropology and primatology, feminist studies of ancient societies centered on fertility goddess worship, and the work of various German feminist filmmakers, including Rosenbaum and von Trotta—directors who have *not* spared patriarchy the kind of radical critique that the triple catastrophe of World War II, fascism, and the Holocaust should have prompted.[34] Instead, and paradoxically, he contributes to the fortification of conventional family arrangements and gender identities as a postwar imperative, the only scientific means, given his assumptions, for averting further authoritarian personality disorders and their potentially cataclysmic social consequences.

Not surprisingly, the most recent biosocial research into the roots of fascist behavior among primates encompasses far more evidence than was available to Mitscherlich. It is equally unsurprising that this evidence lends a good deal more credence to feminist perspectives than it does to his. In particular, current research into the biological and evolutionary roots of social violence—including deliberate intraspecies murder, so-called ethnic cleansing, and imperialist expansion—has focused on the telling differences between the behaviors of two of our closest primate relatives, the chimpanzees and the bonobos. The latter resemble chimpanzees in appearance, but their social behavior differs radically.[35] Among chimpanzees, the social gender hierarchy is brutally enforced; collaboration among females is minimal; and intraspecies warfare, gang violence, battery, infanticide, and rape are within the norm of male behavior. Among bonobos, in sharp contrast, a female-policed pacifism wards off the excesses inherent in the social hierarchy; extensive female bonding serves to augment the exercise of restraint and compassion; and, as Harvard anthropologist Richard Wrangham and science writer Dale Peterson explain, "your rank depends on who you are, not what sex you are."[36] Moreover, among the bonobos, the closest bond between the sexes is that between mother and son. Wrangham and Peterson affirm that "female power is a sine qua non of bonobo life, the magic key to their world."[37] From these authors' perspective in the 1990s, female power may well also be a key to creating a future that limits human male aggression and that militates against the frenzied collective allegiance to a demonic male that commonly characterizes the politics of fascism.

Yet from Mitscherlich's quite different perspective in the early 1960s, the trend that he perceived toward a weakened patriarchy was lamentable. Moreover, his very choice of the title *Society without the Father* bespeaks a fear that it is already too late for the hierarchy to be restored. And the sense of absence, loss, or lack signified in his book's name finds its counterpart in a mood of melancholic longing for traditional European patriarchal values, norms, and labor practices that coexists with and inflects the science of his text. Mass culture, technological advancements, and the recognition of equal rights for women emerge in this narrative as a key triad of counter-fatherly forces, as modern developments that have sadly undermined authority structures founded on the civilized, Old World paternal image.[38] The result of their impact, according to Mitscherlich, is that individual men now suffer an enormous sense of inner loss, while the civilization as a whole is diminished and fragmented.[39] This phenomenon of a loss that is both in the world and in the ego, of course, fits Freud's concept of melancholia, and I am suggesting that *Society without the Father* both describes and participates in a highly problematic melancholic relationship to what its author sees as a dying paternalistic ideal. This view of patriarchy is in no small measure facilitated by the reconceptualization and splitting off of patriarchy's most horrific hour (that is, 1933–1945) from the concept of "real" patriarchy, a splitting off which, I assert, seriously undermines any genuine work of mourning, whether for patriarchy or for the German nation's fascist crimes. The reconfiguration of the Nazi past as a deviation from true paternal law and authority, which purportedly allowed men to be men and women women, simultaneously fed a postwar nostalgia for traditional gender identities, the fortification of which could be seen as serving the best interests of the state and of the individual.

Thus both the science and the sexual nostalgia that shaped Mitscherlich's *Society without the Father* were able to take a vital place in validating a body of cultural criticism, film, and West German legislative efforts from the immediate postwar era onward that furiously worked to demonstrate the social and moral urgency of pairing powerful fathers with economically dependent, supportive, privatized mothers, precisely at a time when women were challenging these roles.[40] Many of these postwar texts were popular and in some regards more retrograde than Mitscherlich's. Some, including the work of influential sociologist Helmut Schelsky, were far more overtly antifeminist—and antilesbian and homophobic—than Mitscherlich's.[41] But along with Schelsky, Mitscherlich argued for a social model that served to ward off the kind of thoroughgoing cultural self-scrutiny that the crimes committed under authoritarian patriarchy could have provoked. The Germans' inability to mourn thus not only reflected a failure to acknowledge the value of the traditionally feminine labor of mourning or to appreciate the importance of women's access to public life; it also betokened an unwillingness to face the radical social ramifications of the history that German and Western culture in general needed—and still needs—to confront.

Conversely, the films examined in this study develop markedly different concepts of the relations among authoritarian, patriarchal, and oedipal issues. Not only do they focus on the experiences of daughters—not sons—and revise received notions of authoritarian dynamics, each also visualizes the dynamics of social hierarchy in a way that illuminates gendered spectatorship, with its interrelated cinematic and sociopolitical dimensions. In these films, patriarchal social structures, such as the church and state's mechanisms of surveillance, emerge not as potential antidotes to fascism or as vehicles for remembrance and contrition but as apparatuses of authoritarianism and amnesia. Far from being a panacea, the restored patriarchy is at best a palliative or placebo whose psychological benefits come at a tremendous cost.

I begin my analysis of these films in chapter 1 with a close reading of Marianne Rosenbaum's *Peppermint Peace*. As this point of departure reveals, my order of discussion for the films does not follow the chronology of their production but instead tracks a biochronology across the films, seen at one level as a collective diachronic record of the female subjects' shifting places in language and culture—moving from childhood to adolescence to adulthood within specific historical parameters. Accordingly, *Peppermint Peace* focalizes the perspectives of a very young, very inquisitive female child, expressionistically rendering her vantage point through camera work that makes war and the female socialization process appear strange. A potent comedy, the film defamiliarizes and satirizes West German postwar social dominance hierarchies, contradicting the Mitscherlichs' position that such social ranking is the antidote to fascism. The film not only mocks the lunacies of German society during World War II and the cold-war era, it also implicitly attacks United States foreign policy of circa 1983. Simultaneously, it criticizes various forms of repression within German culture during its narrative time frame (from about 1943 to 1950), including the inhibition of healthy sexuality, the avoidance of confronting the public with the meanings of the Holocaust, and the inhibition of desires for genuine social change. The Church as an agent of repression comes under particularly acute attack.

Chapter 2 also examines a film that takes as its autobiographical subject a girl in her early childhood. This film is the far better known *Germany, Pale Mother,* the most analyzed and controversial film to be considered here.[42] While *Peppermint Peace* implicates the distanced "Antigone phase" of the mother-daughter dyad in authoritarian dynamics, *Germany, Pale Mother* recollects and affirms an intensely cathected mother-daughter dyad. Even though the mother in this film literally "shuts the blinds" on the Nazi atrocities, the film nonetheless posits the daughter's bond with her as a basis for female authorship and feminist resistance. Concomitantly, it posits a healthy female narcissism and a compassionate, though not condoning, view of the apolitical mother as an antidote to debilitating depression. Further, by focusing on the particulars of the mother's experience and by casting Eva Mattes not only as the German mother of the title, but also as a Polish peasant and a French partisan, the film deconstructs the hypostatized "Pale Mother" Germania figure announced in its title.

Hunger Years, the focus of chapter 3, validates the Mitscherlichs' view that many West Germans substituted identification with the economic system for other sources of identity. The film explores the unhealthy female narcissism that helped sustain this process. What *Hunger Years* contributes well beyond the Mitscherlichs' study, however, is an illuminating appraisal of the role of the commodified female body in promoting postwar amnesia. The film offers a stark assessment of the toll that consumerist dynamics and narrow social blinders take on an adolescent girl, who is isolated and blocked in her efforts at both coming of age and coming to terms with her nation's repressed history. In effect, the *Küche,* the site of consumption, becomes the central metaphor here and the locus for understanding the relationship between bulimic consumerism and the undigested past. In this context, the girl's psychopathology emerges as a product and expression of the pathology of her culture. Moreover, the repressive binarity that underlies, on the one hand, unhealthy narcissistic mother-daughter dyads and, on the other, the cold-war superpower "economy of the same" becomes the grounds at the end of the film for its emphasis on the need for radical change—through rejection of repressive narcissistic female positionings, through "Third World" anticolonialist revolt, and, implicitly, through a dialogization of women's movements and national liberation movements.

Chapters 4 and 5 both analyze films that dramatize the process of memory by depicting it from within the subjective flashbacks—or mind-screens, as Bruce Kawin terms them[43]—of an adult female protagonist. In each case, the protagonist's present, in the 1970s or early 1980s, is at least as much the film's focal point as is her past. And in each, the woman's attempts to remember and mourn are resisted by her liberal and well-intentioned but uncomprehending male companion. *Marianne and Juliane* explores the past in relation to present tensions and ties between sisters, one a feminist, the other a terrorist shaped loosely after Baader-Meinhof member Gudrun Ensslin, who died under suspicious circumstances in Stammheim Prison. A fictionalized biography rather than an autobiography, *Marianne and Juliane* nonetheless contains strong autobiographical resonances, as von Trotta has avowed.[44] While the film partly accords with Elsaesser's sense that von Trotta's work in general examines dramatizations "of self and other, of identification and projection,"[45] in contrast to his claims, von Trotta also joins the other women directors in treating identity politics at the level of history and auto/biography. Indeed, she dramatizes the process of retrieving both personal and public history as a critical form of feminist intervention. Further, von Trotta deviates from the patterns of traditional psychoanalytic theory by representing mourning in terms of the intersubjectivity of women, ultimately showing feminine mourning to be a mobilizing process with potentially regenerative powers. She aims to bridge the gender divide which, especially in the 1950s, but also in the 1970s and 1980s, privatized the women's work of mourning and mothering. Her film's German title, *Die bleierne Zeit* ("The Leaden Time"), a phrase drawn from Hölderlin, refers expressly to the 1950s in Germany, an era whose repressions she recalls primarily in the context of family and church.[46]

Meerapfel's *Malou*, a film named after the protagonist's mother, also addresses the ways in which female grieving has been sequestered in the private sphere and denied public forums for expression. The most multicultural of the films discussed, *Malou* inscribes mourning in relation to pluralistic subjectivities made diverse by multiple languages, cultures, religions, and ethnicities—those of the mother, a convert to Judaism who died in exile, and those of the daughter who remembers. At one level, depicting an expressly feminist version of Freud's grandson's *fort/da* game, the film insists on the cultural embeddedness, as well as on the femaleness, of the mourning ritual it represents. *Malou* reveals the disproportions in power that have cut off the incorporation of these rituals into the public sphere. Further, like the other films, *Malou* is a fictionalized life story and, just as in the other films, fictionalizing serves partly to generalize the experiences depicted and to augment spectatorial involvement in order to overcome resistance to difficult realizations.[47] Yet while this fictionalizing component concurrently functions, in accordance with Barbara Kosta's theory, as a means of demarcating a distance between present and past lives and as an acknowledgment of the distortions of time, memory, and representation,[48] it contributes only slightly to a distanciated aesthetic in *Malou*. Indeed, breaking with New German Cinema, this film turns to Latin American genres and forms in creating an aesthetics that is far more lyrical and intimate than that which typifies the strongly Brechtian-influenced New German films.

It should be added that for most, if not all, of these directors, even the term "postwar" is dubious: In Sanders-Brahms's view, as German efforts at remasculinization took place, the war moved inside, into the family, and became "domestic"—even Germany itself experienced no real "postwar" era. In a 1984 interview, at a time when the cold war seemed to be heating up, Rosenbaum stated that "there is still a thirty- or forty-year war that has been going on continuously since 1945."[49] The films of Rosenbaum, von Trotta, and Brückner overtly recall that even if Germany was no longer battling the Allies, wars continued to be waged—in Korea, Algeria, Vietnam, and elsewhere—whether they were "cold wars" between the "First World" superpowers or "hot wars" in "Third World" countries resisting "First World" colonizers. For these filmmakers, moreover, domestic and international wars were interdependent. My own choice to use the term "postwar" in this book is based on its convenience as a period designation, but the term itself should be read here as always implicitly placed in quotation marks or prefaced by "so-called."

As for the question of theorizing auto/biographic filmmaking, I am interested, especially in the last chapter, in the complex problems and pleasures of conceptualizing feminist autobiography. My general aim, however, is less to originate a theory of German feminist narratives of women's lives than it is to create a dialogue between feminist films and postwar authoritarian theory. I aim to reveal the ways in which specifically feminist film strategies for thematizing identity, the home, the family, the political, history, and the processes of mourning and remembrance create critical oppositional perspectives to influential postwar outlooks.[50] Having said that, I nonetheless wish to stress that even the historical development of the theory of autobiography provides a context that elucidates issues of postwar matrophobia. For this reason and others, some prefatory remarks on the theory of autobiography are in order.

As Nancy K. Miller has documented, 1950s theorists of autobiography valued what they saw as a differentiated, autonomous, and insular individualist—not a subject woven into a fabric of intimate human relationships or situated as part of a political collective. Underscoring the postwar theorists' need to suppress the autobiographer's attachment to others—especially the mother—and to "promote a concomitant fantasy of a separate self," Miller explains:

> In 1956, echoing what we now see as a cold-war rhetoric of autonomous selfhood, Georges Gusdorf, the founding figure of modern autobiography theory, famously posed individualism as the sine qua non of Western autobiography. Autobiography, he claimed, does not develop in cultures where "the individual does not oppose himself to all others . . . [where] the important unit is . . . never the isolated being."[51]

In contrast, during the 1970s and 1980s, feminism and feminist theorists of female autobiography valued relatedness—relatedness both to a single, select other (especially the mother) and to an oppressed collective (especially a community of women).[52] Relatedness became, in fact, a defining trait of a newly invented, purportedly universal, female subject. Without denying the enduring importance of this feminist theoretical project, Miller reminds us that women's collective experience "was (and remains) a good deal more diverse than we may have sometimes made it out to be."[53] Just as importantly, Miller discovers that key canonical and postmodern male autobiographies also conceptualize identity as an intrinsically relational process. Certain canonical texts such as Augustine's *Confessions* are far more maternally cathected than cold-war theorists allowed; and some postmodern texts, including Art Spiegelman's *Maus*, conceive the male self in relation to an oppressed collective and to "a significant other—who is

also a mother."[54] The relationship to the mother can be especially important to postmodern elegiac auto/biographical texts, whether they bear a
female or a male signature.

Alongside its valuing of connectedness to others was feminism's belief
that "the personal is the political," a position articulated by U.S. feminist
Charlotte Bunch in 1968.[55] Most memorably, the esteeming of relatedness
and the recognition that the personal is political became tightly interwoven themes in the work of Carol Gilligan, whose research throughout
the 1980s focused attention on gendered ethical development.[56] Although
Gilligan has sometimes been misconstrued as offering a simple celebration
of the traditionally feminine values of human attachment and empathy,
her work, in fact, consistently criticizes the separation of public and private—the gendered division of labor and of values that weds "masculine"
autonomous selves to public life and "feminine" interconnectedness to the
domestic sphere.

The perception that this traditional gendered division must be criticized
and dismantled strongly informs not only Anglo-American feminism but
also German feminist auto/biography; it is, as well, a cornerstone in the
work of Kosta, who has written the most extensive analysis of German
feminist literary and cinematic autobiography to date. In Kosta's words,
German feminist autobiographies are "personal histories" that dissolve the
split between public and private and displace fictions of "objective" historiography with subjective accounts. By dismantling the traditional separation of public and private, she explains, German feminist self-portraits
expose the disjunction between oppressive postwar power structures that
were condemned in the public sphere but accepted in the private.[57] Beyond that important function, I would add, woman-filmed personal histories offer compelling evidence that conventional concepts of melancholy
and mourning exacerbated the double standard that shaped the postwar
public-private split. These concepts thereby hindered rather than helped
the processes of mourning and regeneration and allowed human needs to
be instrumentalized in the name of hierarchical nationalist ideals. A related hindrance, as some of these films also reveal, was the father fetishism
of the postwar era, which saw fatherlessness as the key to all social evils—
a point of view only too similar to right-wing U.S. political discourse of
the 1990s, which has further used the term "feminazi" to dissociate itself
from fascism, to disavow fascism by gendering it female.

While Kosta's theorization of the interdependence of the public and private is compelling, her assertion that autobiography is "the most self-reflexive of literary and cinematic forms" is problematic.[58] A text's consciousness of itself does not inevitably follow from or imply its author's self-awareness. Varying degrees of reflexivity characterize the aesthetics of the films discussed here. Further, the presence of reflexivity is no guarantor of a progressive feminist text—any more than the presence of melodrama inevitably makes a film politically retrograde.[59] I also differ from Julia Knight when she goes to the other extreme by overemphasizing the "realist" and "documentarist" aspects of the films' autobiographical aesthetics. Knight asserts:

> Although drawing on one's own experiences, especially autobiographical material, would tend to identify the filmmaker as a film's author, the representation of personal experiences can be viewed as diametrically opposed to a cinema of self-expression. The former is rooted in real events and can thus be viewed as constituting a representation of "reality" rather than as an act of creative self-expression.[60]

While auto/biographical films do make important uses of documentary footage, radio broadcasts, and documentarist elements, Knight's view underestimates what Kosta rightly highlights: that German women's autobiographies are acts of self-invention, embodied in stylistically innovative—often reflexive—aesthetic forms that serve as powerful critical tools.

In addition to these characteristics and to the complex fictionalizing dynamics already identified, the following aesthetic and thematic elements typify the German feminist auto/biographical films examined here: 1. an emphasis on mother-daughter and other familial relationships, often represented through the codes of maternal melodrama, codes that are simultaneously complicated and/or critiqued by means of alienation techniques, multicultural inflections, or dialogic combinations with other aesthetic modes, including fairy-tale narratives and motifs; 2. a dismantling of the public-private split through deconstructive juxtapositions of disparate discourses, such as documentary and melodrama, and/or an emphasis on the power dynamics of media apparatuses, including the cinematic apparatus; 3. a concomitant rejection of the hierarchy that deems only public, conventionally heroic, or famous lives to be fit subjects for auto/biography; and 4. a foregrounding of subjective processes, especially memory, through the use of mindscreens, subjective flashbacks, directorial voice-over, optical point-of-view shots, expressionistic use of mise-en-scène, free-association editing, and other techniques of first-person cinema.

It is worth noting that the autobiographical impulse crystallized in key women's films is also all but omnipresent in New German Cinema as a whole. Self-portraiture, often in less overt, more distanciated and deflected form, is a constituent of the New German Cinema's auteur-ist orientation.[61] Fassbinder's various cameo appearances, acting parts, and voice-over commentaries and Herzog's emphasis on "*Herzog*'s" film-making process, both within his films and in his personal appearances, are two of the more obvious examples. The feminist auteur-biographer, how-ever, should no more be conceived in individualistic terms, as the source, guarantor, or final arbiter of meaning, than should any other auteur. To view filmmaking in such terms is naively romantic—an endorsement of masculinist myths of "seminality" and creativity.[62] From a feminist theo-retical perspective (and hence for my purposes), far more productive is Sandy Flitterman-Lewis's elegant conception of authorship as a tripartite structure of enunciation comprised of the following: "1) authorship as a historical phenomenon, suggesting the cultural context; 2) authorship as a desiring position, involving determinants of sexuality and gender; and 3) authorship as a textual moment, incorporating the specific stylistics and preoccupations of the filmmaker."[63] My focus throughout is on the per-petually dynamic interrelations among these spheres.

With regard to the second of them—authorial desire, encompassing sexuality and gender—psychoanalytic tools are commonly used to under-stand it. Although in this book I also attempt to use psychoanalytic con-cepts to explore identity and desire, I view psychoanalysis as an extremely problematic discourse, not as a heuristic system to be taken at face value. For while poststructuralism may be correct in asserting that psychoanalysis "speaks us"—produces us, creates us—feminists and others know that psychoanalysis also leaves many of us misspoken or simply unspoken al-together. The implicit blaming and silencing of women that are charac-teristic of much psychoanalytic discourse on melancholy and mourning prove this area to be no exception.

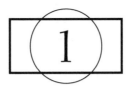

Kinder, Kirche, Kino

The Optical Politics
of Marianne Rosenbaum's
Peppermint Peace

A film unfortunately unfamiliar to most Americans, Marianne Rosenbaum's *Peppermint Peace* (*Peppermint Frieden*, 1983) is unique among the feminist auto/biographical films of the early 1980s for its playful wit and humor.[1] Shot mostly in black and white, with some tinted footage and some surreal full-color sequences, *Peppermint Peace* focalizes the inquisitive, sensuous gaze of a small child, Marianne Worlicek (Saskia Tyroller-Hauptmann), in order to expose the absurdities and hypocrisies of German culture roughly between the years 1943 and 1950. At the psychological level, the film reveals the process by which the girl's gaze is deflected and disciplined by parenting practices complicit with fascism and by a catechism of sexually repressive religious ideals. At the level of social satire, the child's look functions as a defamiliarizing mediator between the audience and the bizarre adult world of the time in which the film is set, marked by war, genocide, and cold-war hysteria.

Besides the 1943–1950 time frame, another context is indispensable to the film—namely, the West German peace movement of the 1970s and 1980s, an activist politics, born of the student movement, that intersected in important ways with the women's and environmentalist movements.[2]

To grasp the sense of urgency behind the antiwar politics that drives *Peppermint Peace* and other contemporary German feminist-pacifist films, it is crucial to recall that during the early 1980s, Ronald Reagan and his advisors were actually speaking in terms of a "winnable" and "limited" nuclear war to be waged in Europe. Germany was a likely first battleground. Among the "nuclear freeze" movement responses, especially memorable is the mobilization of the antinuclear, ecologist-oriented West German Green party. The Greens and their leader Petra Kelly made a push for peace and disarmament—most strikingly in Kelly's speech of October 10, 1981, at a peace rally in Bonn, a demonstration motivated by NATO's hotly contested decision in 1979 to deploy cruise and Pershing II missiles in Germany. And certainly more than the U.S. Republican presidents deserve it, Kelly, the European Green parties, and, along with them, the feminist pro-peace activists and filmmakers deserve credit for working to end the cold war and nuclear-arms race.[3] For the filmmakers, moreover, this contemporary context is an indelible determinant in their historiography.

Memories of World War II fueled the drive for peace, as *Peppermint Peace* documents. Yet the historical consciousness of a filmmaker such as Rosenbaum must be set apart from the pro-peace positions that an earlier generation of women came to endorse. As Annemarie Tröger explains, German women's remembrances of their suffering in the second half of World War II led them to "basic assumptions similar to those of the [1980s] peace movement," but their intense sense of victimization also crowded out their consciousness of Germany's culpability for National Socialism's Jewish victims, as well as their self-awareness about their complicity in their own victimization.[4] As I intend to demonstrate, Rosenbaum's film cannot justly be accused of any such delusions.

The film begins during World War II, with a darkly comic shot of three small children, Marianne and two friends, wearing gas masks and playing under what is soon revealed to be a grand piano. Swaying to Zarah Leander's popular wartime tune "*Der Wind*," the youngsters whisper speculations about the gas mask's amorous uses. The film's title in pink lettering appears across the black-and-white image as it freezes. A full shot then reveals two older girls about to enact a schmaltzy scene of passion and tenderness à la film star Leander, whose singing style they emulate. One is made-up and juxtaposed with jars of homemade jam on shelves; the other wears the uniform of the BDM (the *Bund Deutscher Mädel*, the girl's side of the Hitler youth). In the first shot to show the film's recurrent use of literally distanciating mobile framing (that is, backward tracks and zooms), the hand-held camera zooms out, tracks left, and zooms in slightly to a closed-in image of the children looking from under the piano. This vivid image of constraint and limitation inverts the mainstream Hollywood filmic paradigm of the camera as male gaze, granted visual access to the image, and serves as an introduction to the major themes and movements of the film as a whole.

In the following sequences, preschooler Marianne protests the departure of her soldier-father (Hans Peter Korff) for the Russian front, nervously scratching the back of her hand raw. Her beloved Jewish friend Dr. Klug (Gérard Samaan), with his funny, playful "monkey tricks" and papier-mâché rabbit mask, helps heal her wounded hand and the psychic wound it reflects—a reversal of the anti-Semitic Jew-as-crucifier stereotype. But then Dr. Klug too vanishes. "Where is Dr. Klug?" she asks her mother (Gesine Strempel). Instead of telling Marianne what she knows about his fate and that of other victims of the Holocaust—and she clearly knows something—the mother diverts Marianne by creating an imaginary radio contact with her father and, in the process, by encouraging Marianne's narcissistic preoccupation with her body, height, and favorite foods. The mother's efforts to avert Marianne's attention from the loss and the atrocities are contrasted with Marianne's endeavors to see and recall. For example, in a scene underscoring the cinema's role as a technological memory trigger, Marianne mentally interpolates Dr. Klug's death into a children's film based on "The Race between the Rabbit and the Hedgehog," a fairy tale in which the rabbit loses and dies. (And however naive, the child's active spectatorship clearly operates contrary to the intent of the fascist film apparatus that controls the screenings.) She also attempts to alert her father to the disasters that are upending her world, but the radio with which her mother had diverted her allows only for one-way communication, and Marianne's needs remain frustrated.

When the war ends, Frau Worlicek, in another narcissistic substitution, replaces the portrait of the Führer with a mirror. Immediately thereafter she and Marianne become refugees transported in a cattle car—an ironic reversal of positions with Germany's Jewish victims. The mother and daughter are reunited with Marianne's father in a socially conservative,

1. Mistakenly imagining that the radio is two-way, Marianne futilely attempts to communicate with her father through an apparatus of the disembodied male voice. (Saskia Tyroller-Hauptmann in *Peppermint Peace*. Photo courtesy of Nourfilm.)

Catholic-dominated (i.e., typical) Bavarian village. Its residents include a perceptive leftist carpenter—a kind of countertype to the biblical Joseph—who is openly critical of both the church and the Nazis, and a faux-blind veteran—a familiar postwar type who insists on his male dominance even as he feigns physical incapacity and passively depends on female support and care. The community's spiritual leader is Herr Expositus (Hans Brenner), a grotesque, gaze-driven, proto-fascist priest who is clearly meant to typify the dubious role which the Bavarian Catholic church played in the process of denazification.[5]

While the villagers make half-hearted gestures toward denazification and, in another ironic reversal, the father burns pages from school books containing the Führer's portrait, American forces introduce the heady, sensuous pleasures of peace and the commodities that come to connote it—peppermint chewing gum and jazz. The amiable GI Mr. Frieden (Peter Fonda) embodies the new trinity of peace, love, and freedom for Marianne and her young friends, who take hilarious oral delight in chewing the *Kaugummi* he gives them.[6] (As Gabriele Weinberger notes, the children accept the sticks of gum on their tongues "very much like they receive a wafer during holy communion"!)[7] They relish, as well, going for rides in his enormous phallic car, and they imaginatively participate in his amorous relationship with Nilla, a young German woman (Cleo Kretschmer). The film accompanies the children's experiences with whimsical forties-style jazz music, often played on an organ.

But the pleasures are short-lived. All too soon, Herr Expositus, the embodiment of what is oppressive in religion, terrorizes Marianne and her classmates by collecting their gum (evidently saving it for his own surreptitious enjoyment) and admonishing them that gum and kisses are forms of carnal desire, and carnal desire is a mortal sin—*eine Totsünde*. Thus the children's postwar world becomes fallen. Herr Expositus then singles Marianne out for an illustrative lesson in God's all-seeing gaze: He leads her back and forth before a kitschy likeness of Jesus, whose eyes seem to follow her every move. In a quick mindscreen, Marianne imagines Mr. Frieden and Nilla dead. A soundbridge couples the father's voice from the next scene with the priest's voice in this one. The father's warning about not using "their toilet," gives rise to Marianne's question, "What is syphilis?" Left by her father in the dark about the disease, the girl begins to worry not only that Mr. Frieden's lovely nose will go rotten, but also that her own will.

Marianne now tries to become a saint. She fakes stigmata first with jam and later with bur scratches on the backs of her hands. She plays the role of her name saint, the Virgin Mary, both in a tableau vivant staged by Herr Expositus and in her own playtime fantasies and dreams. When MPs take Mr. Frieden away for fraternizing with Nilla,[8] Marianne's mother diverts the girl's attention, just as she did when Dr. Klug disappeared; her father also attempts to evade the issue of the American's fate, and gets a spirited debate from his daughter, reflective of the film's early 1980s context, as to the meaning of *Frieden*—namely, peace and, to her mind but not to his, "freedom"—as if to say the two are inseparable. In an extended surrealist dream sequence, Marianne conflates memories and scenarios

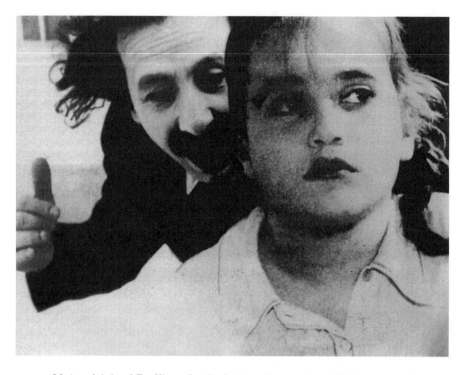

2. Marianne's beloved Dr. Klug, a Jewish physician taken away by the Nazis, reappears in Marianne's guilt-ridden dreams. (Gérard Samaan and Saskia Tyroller-Hauptmann in *Peppermint Peace*. Photo courtesy of Nourfilm.)

from various points in time—blending sexual guilt with Nazi crimes, Mr. Frieden and Nilla with under-the-piano wartime pleasures, and the victimization of Dr. Klug with that of Mr. Frieden. During the dream, Herr Expositus orders his female assistant to shove Mr. Frieden into an oven. When Marianne demands, "Where was He in the war, if He is all-knowing?" the assistant shushes her.

Once Mr. Frieden is gone, the threat of an apocalyptic war haunts Marianne. Herr Expositus's red-baiting sermons inflame her fears by conflating the communist threat with the anti-Christ.[9] The fake blind veteran (and faux victim) Herr Arira terrorizes her further by citing Mühlhiasl's predictions that "if women try to be like men . . . we'll have the worst war of all time on our hands."[10] During one of Marianne's nightmares, her beloved Mr. Frieden also takes on vividly menacing qualities. She associates him with the atomic bomb and with an injured and bandaged Asian child, presumably a reference to the victims of the horrific U.S. attack on Hiroshima, many of whom were women and children. In both her dreams and her conscious activities, Marianne tries to avert Armageddon by de-demonizing the Russians and regenerating the world community through her own Virgin-Mary-to-the-rescue persona: To Herr Expositus's dismay, she and her friend Elfriede decrucify a Christ figurine. A tinted Felliniesque oneiric sequence shows Marianne as Virgin Mary the popular performance artist, throwing knives at a radio—the same radio that is the real source of propaganda and cockroaches for the Worlicek household.[11] During the film's final scene, dispirited by the prospect of war and sick of not getting the truth, Marianne asks her father, "Where is Korea?" "Very far away. Don't worry," he replies and shows her Korea on an all-too-tiny globe. The film ends with a freeze-frame of Marianne's troubled, engaging look directly at the camera. Her gaze simultaneously evokes three different temporalities, positioning the audience within their continuum. These temporalities are: that of the immediate postwar era, wherein Marianne finds no communal space or language for *Vergangenheitsbewältigung;* the contemporaneous context of the early 1980s, in which cold-war antagonisms had escalated to ominous proportions; and, partly because of the girl's youth, a larger future, the shape and very existence of which are dependent on a deepened consciousness of the other two. As the credits roll, a peace-movement song plays in English, clearly alluding to the early 1980s debates about the deployment of Pershing II missiles in Germany: "Hello Mr. Frieden. Lay your weapons down . . . Lies and empty phrases . . . Peace is what they kill for . . . Freedom. Peace forever."

As this summary indicates, the film "talks back" to the psychoanalytic studies on authoritarianism developed by the Mitscherlichs, with their heavy investment in paternalism, masculinism, and the social gender hierarchy. By taking seriously the subjectivity of a small girl, *Peppermint Peace* militates against reading the child as a metaphoric representation of Germany's collective, irresponsible regression into an "infantile," "effeminate" identity.[12] For Marianne does not share the escapism and passivity of most of the adults around her; instead, she is more like her grandmother, an outspoken minor character who asks questions and rocks the boat.

Neither is Marianne sentimentalized or naïvely constructed as a "positive image" of feminine innocence and insight. To be sure, she *sees* a great deal. The child glimpses evidence of the Holocaust and the war's other horrors, retrospectively understands the disappearance of Dr. Klug, and, alone among members of her postwar community, expresses remorse when she reflects back on the "brickworks"—people's euphemism for the Theresienstadt concentration camp during the war; she also grapples with issues of volition and responsibility, applying the same standards of judgment to the destructive behavior of fighter pilots that her mother applies to her childish belligerence—in effect, deconstructing the double standard between culturally sanctioned and socially unacceptable acts of aggression. On the other hand, Marianne is also a social conformist and becomes a lightning rod for the contradictory signals that surround and confound her. For example, when her supposedly denazified father, a postwar teacher, tears out pictures of Hitler from the school primers and burns them, an astonished Marianne gasps, "Mein Führer!" and begs her father to let her keep "just one."[13] Later, she eagerly conforms with consumerist values, happily embracing the "chewing gum culture" and American commodities that betoken "peace."[14] And when Herr Arira absurdly asserts that women's masculine style of dress will usher in the end of the world, Marianne believes him, becoming the credulous student of postwar backlash discourse. Episodes such as these illustrate how Marianne is neither idealized as being immune to authoritarianism nor reduced to a symbol of underoedipalized Germanic regression. Caught up as she is in shifting historical currents, contradictory discourses, and intensely felt desires, her subjectivity both seems *hers* and becomes the basis for the film's social critique, its Brechtian alienation, and its brilliant deconstructive humor.

Indeed, the construction of Marianne's identity is also a filmic strategy, a highly revealing, expressionistically rendered optical point of view and acoustic *point d'écoute* (point of hearing) that defamiliarizes the film's social hierarchies and shifting socioideological markers. Distorting lenses and radical high and low camera angles—especially in the child's point-of-view shots—are used to stress the often-comic disparity between the girl's perspective and that of the adults. The adult characters' outlooks and behavior, according to Rosenbaum, mark them as *Sinnbilder* or *Sinnfiguren* (sensuous figures), representations which typify in Brechtian fashion the social structure of their times.[15] The cinematography aligns us as spectators not with them but with Marianne's position in the visual hierarchy, so that we too become decentered by the cinematography as by the com-

peting social discourses, and we thereby recognize the grotesque rational-
izations and hypocrisies of the grown-up world. Similarly, the film's shifts
in vocal volume—for instance, between repressed whispers and imperi-
ous shouts—audibilize power hierarchies. (The sequence depicting Marianne's forceful, telling redefinition of *Frieden* as "freedom" works well because its acoustic register defies the visual hierarchy signaled by the shot-
countershot with the father.) Further, the hyperbolic use of a wide-angle
lens to film the parents in the closing scene creates the feeling that the
parents inhabit a separate, quite distant space, alienated from Marianne's,
whose intense desire for world peace and freedom—for a genuinely postwar *world*—we grasp but they do not. The film's cinematography and
sound thus focalize, defamiliarize, and sharply criticize the hierarchies that
define political identities, implicating these structures in a warmongering
mentality that persists in postwar German culture.

Marianne's identity, moreover, is not only an aesthetic and political
strategy. The character also instantiates collective experiences of loss,
including both feminine experiences of privation and losses more specific to German culture. Ellyn Kaschak defines the former with eloquent
concision:

> As a result of the physical and psychological limits and restraints
> to which women are subjected in childhood and throughout life,
> an impending or actual sense of loss is contained within their psy-
> chological makeup. There is the loss of both self-control and self-
> definition. There is the potential and actual loss of one's own mean-
> ing and definition of what life is or can involve. Finally, there is the
> loss of the possible, the narrowing of choices and limits, missing the
> full range available in a particular time and society.[16]

Peppermint Peace confronts this sense of loss directly, through a narrative
and rhetoric that differ from the language of loss valorized by traditional
Freudian thought. Although both according to Freud and in the film, the
originary sense of loss is understood in terms of the child's relationship to
the mother, the film's mother-daughter dyad departs from Freudian and
Mitscherlichian theory.

In particular, Marianne's relationship to her mother and to the maternal
body sharply contrasts with the overly invested dyads etiologically implicated in studies of authoritarian men. Indeed, the mother-daughter rela-

tionship in *Peppermint Peace* is distant and portrayed with an utter lack of nostalgia. By looking to the model of Jocasta and Antigone, both Kaschak and Christiane Olivier theorize the kind of distance Marianne and Frau Worlicek experience. Kaschak's interpretation of the Jocasta-Antigone paradigm points out that, in Sophocles' play, "Jocasta is known to us only by her relationship to men. There is absolutely no indication of her relationship to her children other than to the one who became her husband. She seems to function only in relation to male power and sexuality as do her daughters."[17] Consequently, Antigone—emblematic of daughters in the "Antigone phase"—"turns away from and forgets her mother, dutiful to her father and brothers. She becomes a mother but cannot mother herself."[18] Olivier's theory, like the better-known work of Dorothy Dinnerstein, locates the source of mother-daughter and mother-son relational difficulties in the division of labor that makes child care the exclusive responsibility of the mother; that is, she evokes the *Kinder, Kirche, Küche* paradigm. The daughter, "undesired [by her mother as an oedipal object] in childhood, goes begging as an adult for the desire and approval of the man."[19] According to Olivier, this Jocasta-Antigone relationship forms a perverse complement to the overly invested mother-son dyad and gives rise to it, as the grown woman seeks in her relationship with her husband and son what she failed to receive from her mother. Yet her own daughter is, once more, a non-oedipal object to her, and the cycle continues.[20]

Marianne's tie to her mother is characterized by an affective poverty that meshes with these theories. Indeed, during the wartime segment of the film, when the mother is the only consistent presence in the little girl's life, the lack of a reciprocal gaze between them is striking. This distant relationship stands out further because of its contrast with Marianne's emotionally richer connection to her father and to Dr. Klug. The lack of maternal closeness is clearly exacerbated by Frau Worlicek's unquestioning compliance with the fascistic worldview and by her consequent suppression of her daughter's scopophilic and epistemophilic desires. The mother functions less as a mirror confirming an illusory identity than as a blinder, a censor, and a source of specular and acoustic negation. An example is a sledding sequence, which initially records Marianne's point of view in a low-angle close-up of her mother's face. When the mother gives Marianne's sled a push downhill, the handheld camera rapidly tracks back,

the one institution that survived the war intact, the church is represented as far more intent on propagating its unaltered patriarchal values than on assuming responsibility for morally guiding its followers in a confrontation with their nation's crimes.[24] Insofar as Herr Expositus implicitly continues doing what he has always done, the film suggests that the fascist patterns that now subtend the social structures have by and large remained unaltered from the time of the war. (In effect: "The Führer is dead. Long live the little Führers!")[25]

The film's critique of Herr Expositus develops concurrently along political, religious, and metacinematic lines, areas the film shows to be enmeshed. Three especially powerful sequences illustrate how this satiric critique takes shape. The first is a sequence that depicts boys playing a sadistic trick on Elfriede (they terrify her by calling out "Air raid!"), followed by Herr Worlicek's compassionate intervention and the priest's surveillance and judgment of their behavior. The priest is first introduced into the sequence and the film as a whole as a voice-off. "May the Lord be praised!" he says. While the phrase is a standard Bavarian greeting, in context it activates the theological implications of his momentarily disembodied voice, in effect pointing up a cinematic-religious intersection. The film then makes him visible to us. Sitting on a bicycle and accompanied by his German shepherd, he is decked out in a leather motorcycle cap, his priest's habit, and a long black leather coat reminiscent of the uniform of the SS (one quarter of whom were in fact Catholic),[26] and has a pair of binoculars—a spectacular embodiment of moral exhibitionism and fascistic hypocrisy. "I've been watching them all the time. At last you've intervened," he tells Herr Worlicek. Partially like Pastor Klein in von Trotta's *Marianne and Juliane*, Herr Expositus oversees without introspection, watches and judges but arrogates to himself a position that is above moral judgment. The priest's spectatorship emerges as a morally dubious, even sadistic activity which recalls the Catholic church's shameful wartime accommodation with fascism. The priest claims for himself a spectatorial field like that occupied by Jean Pierre Oudart's "Absent One," who has, as Kaja Silverman notes, "all the attributes of the mythically potent symbolic father: potency, knowledge, transcendental vision, self-sufficiency, and discursive power."[27] The film ridicules (the priest's assertion of) this kind of phallic power. Moreover, by using non-matching shot/reverse-shot in this sequence—editing that derails suture—Rosenbaum situates us to take a critical perspective not only on the position of authority claimed by the priest but also on our own relationship to cinematic discourse, spectacle, and social accountability.

A second illustration of Expositus's authoritarian governance of sight and knowledge and a further indictment of the antiegalitarian ideological mechanisms he embodies is afforded by a sequence in which Marianne and her parents go swimming. It begins with a shot of Marianne, transported by the intense pleasure of watching something offscreen. As the camera soon reveals, her look is directed toward Mr. Frieden and Nilla, who are playfully kissing on the shore.[28] Her father sees the girl's gaze with alarm, then sees Nilla and Mr. Frieden, whose kisses confirm his worst suspicions. Herr and Frau Worlicek now attempt to distract Marianne, the father by trying to interest her in observing flies and cormorants, the mother by offering her an apple and then by encouraging her to play with her beach ball. When Marianne does the latter, she spontaneously turns passing the ball into a game that includes Mr. Frieden and Nilla. To the accompaniment of the film's jazzy "Mr. Frieden" theme music, the sequence's marvelously rendered relay of gazes gives way to a relay of tosses and pleased looks among the five. Herr Worlicek, though maintaining his distance, exclaims to Mr. Frieden, jubilantly and in faulty English, "We are not more enemies!" The game thus breaks down barriers and hierarchies, momentarily equalizing and uniting the players, who are captured altogether in a single utopic shot. The moment, moreover, is enriched by the fairy-tale motifs, familiar from the Nausicaä episode of Homer's *Odyssey* and from the story of "The Frog King," that it conjures up: the setting by a shore or well, symbol of the unconscious; the girl's play with her ball, symbol both of utopic, global perfection and of her still-unrealized psychic potential; the throwing of the object, an evocation of the girl's sexual awakening.[29] But this moment and the sequence as a whole are brought to a quick halt with the appearance in the distance of Herr Expositus riding his bicycle. The antithesis of the life-affirming erotic, egalitarian communal energies unleashed in the sequence, Expositus embodies the dystopic forces that will, by the film's closing scene, engender a very different dynamic of globe and gaze when Marianne receives her fear-filled geography lesson on the war in Korea.

The third sequence that advances the film's critique of the "sacred" male gaze—now in terms that expose the social construction of gender hierarchies—is the unforgettable classroom scene in which the priest catechizes the children about lust and chewing gum, and which aptly follows the scene of utopic play. Using a print of Masaccio's *Expulsion* and a packet of the offending Wrigley's gum as visual aids, the priest recounts for his pupils a version of the fall wherein *Kaugummi* substitutes for the forbidden fruit. Expositus emphasizes both Eve's role as verbal temptress—the source of original loss—and God the Father's all-seeing, inescapable power to judge and punish.[30] The camera's quick zoom in to an illuminated symbol of the *oculus dei*, the famous eye in the triangle, parodies the ability of this supposedly transcendent male gaze to reach and subjugate its objects.[31] The zoom in both contrasts with the earlier use of the track and zoom out (deployed to convey limits placed on Marianne) and comments critically on classic cinema's alignment of the male subject with a naturalized invasive specularity. (In later sequences Herr Expositus in fact makes morally dubious use of this same image of God's eye as his peephole for a commanding view of the children in the tableau vivant. The symbol is also situated behind him when he delivers his red-baiting sermon from high up in his pulpit). Indeed, within the context of this film, the eye in the triangle emerges not only as a symbol of the triune God's power; it is also a sign of the interlock between the male gaze and *pyramidal* dominance hierarchies.[32] For her part, Marianne looks off into space at the start of the classroom sequence, chews gum, and fantasizes about Frieden and Nilla; she guiltily casts down her eyes during the priest's lapsarian narrative; and she is the one singled out as the silenced object for his illustration of God's surveillance.[33] In a telling gendering of speech, two boys align their voices with the priest's by reciting doctrinal accounts of God's power to see and His ability to penetrate the heart and mind. Thus the sequence evolves into a potent comic exposé of misogynistic religious indoctrination. By dramatizing how the female subject, more than the male, is taught to treat herself as an object to be overseen and overheard, the sequence also vividly subverts Freud's preposterous notion that the female subject's superego lacks the full force of the male's. For while the male children can partly protect themselves from judgment through identification with the words of the Father, the conscience of the female child is weighted down with a harsher burden—namely, the demand for her speechless obeisance, a demand justified by Eve's role in the drama of the Fall—an encumbrance under which she can muster fewer defenses.[34]

Concurrently, the sequence contradicts the Mitscherlichs and confirms Eli Sagan's view that "in a sexist culture, it is the superego that encourages sexism; and that in a fascist society, it is the superego that condones fascism."[35]

Indeed, Herr Expositus's classroom sermon on the gaze is implicitly identified with fascistic surveillance, terror, and violence, and succeeding sequences show its effects: the children's behavior grows stunted; their *Schaulust* becomes deflected and perverted; their playful interest in sexuality becomes poisoned with guilt; and their urge to obey is magnified by their fear. To be sure, Expositus never goes as far in governing the child's gaze as did one real priest from the Bavarian village of Bruckmühl—in 1946, that priest and a local teacher had children corporeally punished for watching Hollywood movies, films that had been approved by the U.S. Information Control Division.[36] But Expositus nonetheless succeeds all too well in generating neurotic inhibition and "spiritual" exhibitionism in the children, along with what the film makes us recognize as inappropriate guilt and fear. Moreover, at no point is the church shown to promote schoolroom or congregational efforts to address German culpability for fascist crimes and Jewish suffering. Quite the contrary. And just as over-the-shoulder shots and looks, sometimes used in combination, accent the dynamics of police-state surveillance in the film's portrayal of the Nazi years, these same shots and looks are reintroduced in a postwar socioreligious context. They are seen, for example, during Herr Expositus's cold-warrior sermon, which, in its contents as well, perpetuates mechanisms of psychological control similar to those of fascism.

Herr Expositus's terroristic classroom lesson, coupled as it is with Herr Worlicek's warning against using "their toilet," triggers the girl's preoccupation with syphilis, sainthood, and the stigmatic signs by which these are written in the flesh. Further, her sorrow over the loss of pleasure and self-possession that the priest creates finds expression in a series of theatrical performances, dramatic reminders that, as Juliana Schiesari observes, "[m]elancholia as a cultural category (or as a 'moral state,' as scholars of the condition like to think of it) . . . is essentially theatrical."[37] Marianne's creation of stigmata—a homeopathic gesture to ward off the syphilitic symptoms she fears—contributes to one such performative act. She poses before a mirror, dressed as the Virgin Mary for the priest's tableau, pointing a knife at her heart, stating in a voice-over, "My nose won't go rotten.

I'm going to be a saint." After pulling a picture of Christ from her heart-shaped purse, she kisses it, saying, "I'm your mother." Thus, like the *Mater Dolorosa* or Mournful Mother, she participates in and assumes "her son's" stigmata.[38]

By juxtaposing Marianne's playacting with some other children's depiction of Abraham's sacrifice of Isaac, the scene also emphasizes the ways in which certain religious and political ideals turn children into sacrificial victims, submitting them to the Father's will and encouraging young girls' aspirations to martyrdom. In the broader context of the film, the scene's implications accord with Tröger's recognition that "[r]eligions have built female victimization into a positive ideology of self-sacrifice as the highest virtue of womanhood, and fascism thrived on a secularized version of female sacrifice."[39] Because the power and pleasure of spectacular suffering that Marianne covets—the power of the bleeding wound—also partly dovetail with masochistic feminine roles inscribed in classic cinema, the film's critique extends to Hollywood cinema and its representations of female "lack."[40] Marianne, moreover, eventually forsakes her jam stigmata for "real" ones, by scratching the backs of her hands raw with burs during a hilarious sequence that depicts the children's "playing church" and treating a veteran's artificial arm as a sacred relic.[41] The children's naive play ritual, with its faux sacred phallus and aspiring "wounded" girl-saint, provides a marvelous satire not only of certain forms of "sacred" fetishistic scopophilia but also of the cinematic variety, with its related sexual underpinnings. Further, the satire targets the postwar positioning of the veterans of Hitler's unholy war, men whose masculinity had to be made good, to be miraculously redeemed, as it were.

While the paradigm of sainthood delimits Marianne's sphere of action and reflects her "maimed" relationship to desire, the girl nonetheless achieves creative transformations of this paradigm through her imaginative playacting and vivid fantasies. Marianne's identification with the Virgin Mary enables her to achieve parity with the young male friends who have bragged that they have the more important roles in the sacred drama. She also eventually seeks to alter the exemplary mother-son dyad of Mary and Christ—of mothers sacrificing their sons, be it to religious causes or to military ones—by decrucifying a Christ figurine and instructing it, "Don't say Thy will be done, Oh Lord!" The gesture is key. It suggests the paradigmatic obverse of countless accounts of male melancholia and mourning, based on the son's loss of his mother: Marianne imaginatively assumes the mother's point of view of loss, and responds not with ego debility or abjection of the son but with a direct protest against his and her capitulation to the almightiest of fathers. In fact, Marianne's actions imaginatively transform the privatized, abstracted maternal realm of *Kinder, Kirche, Küche*—neatly embodied in her *Marmelade Heilige* (jam-saint) identity—into public intervention, counter-spectacle, and activism, all taking the form of measures against patriarchal demands for self-sacrifice and suffering.[42] As the Virgin Mary with seven swords (traditional signs of her "seven sorrows"), the girl revises the *Mater Dolorosa* identity to become a knife-throwing circus artist. Instead of throwing knives around the usual blindfolded woman, she targets a radio mounted on a board. That is, she wields phallic power back against itself—against the disembodied voice that has been associated with propaganda, war, cockroaches, Herr Expositus, and mythic masculine potency. Finally, her shift in focus from her own "wounded" body, with its culturally manufactured stigmata, to the wielding of power in the name of healing links her with Dr. Klug, who healed her earlier "stigmata." Yet his absence—and the larger absence within German culture for which it is a metonym—are patriarchally inflicted losses and wounds she can only begin to address.

Indeed, for all the marvelous imagination her fantasies reveal, the film makes it clear that the past reality of the Holocaust and the present threat of nuclear annihilation are far more than an isolated young girl—or her private dreams of theatrical performance—can come to terms with; her desires need public, communal expression. Moreover, as the film insists, the means to the cure for the feelings of fear, guilt, loss, and sorrow that she instantiates are not symbolic embodiments of these in the figure of a guilty first mother (the fallen Eve or any other "primitive mother" imago), nor are they their "cancellation" through a fetish of feminine purity and ideal motherhood (Marianne's desexualized activist Virgin).[43] A symbolics and a system of social practices that are alternatives to those derived from religious orthodoxy are required—ones that do not fetishize or privatize either women or loss. Concomitantly, if cinema is to facilitate the process of digesting the past, an alternative optical politics to that embedded in mainstream filmic paradigms and Western scopic regimes must be created.

In sum, by thus reimagining and reconstructing Rosenbaum's childhood story, this film protests the oppressive, restrictive positioning of females within social and cinematic gender hierarchies. The film defines that positioning as antithetical to genuine peace, social regeneration, and accountability for history. The film's ending enjoins us, as members of the audience, to accede collectively to the introspection, work of memory, and subsequent antiwar activism that the girl's direct look at the camera asks for.

2

The Mother-Daughter Plot in History

Helma Sanders-Brahms's
Germany, Pale Mother

A reconstruction of events in Germany from the years 1939 to 1955, Helma Sanders-Brahms's *Germany, Pale Mother* (*Deutschland, bleiche Mutter*, 1979), like Marianne Rosenbaum's *Peppermint Peace*, is an antiwar film that bears an oblique relationship to history as it is commonly conceived and narrated in cinema. And also like *Peppermint Peace*, *Germany, Pale Mother* depicts the values of *Kinder, Kirche, Küche* in terms that challenge influential postwar theories about the relationships among oedipal dynamics, patriarchy, and authoritarianism. Yet as Sanders-Brahms's auto/biographical film reworks the past and reflects on the impact of historical events on her family and identity, it develops a very different oedipal narrative from that of *Peppermint Peace*. Sanders-Brahms's film centers on an intensely cathected mother-daughter dyad—a bond that contrasts sharply with the alienated "Antigone phase" represented in Rosenbaum's work. Partly because of its portrayal of this close filial relationship, *Germany, Pale Mother* has garnered far more attention than Rosenbaum's film—and far more controversy as well.[1] Indeed, paired with her reliance on the discourses of allegory and melodrama, Sanders-Brahms's concentration on the mother-daughter dyad has led critics to claim that *Germany, Pale Mother* evades German history rather than acknowledging accountability for it. In the eyes of some of her detractors, Sanders-Brahms does represent history, but history as a thing virtually apart from women's lives and responsibilities. As these critics see it, an essentialist, idealized, ahistorical perspective on feminine experience mars the film, much as ahistoricism purportedly undermines feminist psychoanalytic theories that valorize the pre-oedipal bond, theories which *Germany, Pale Mother* is said to endorse. For example, Angelika Bammer asserts: "In this film Sanders-Brahms seems to suggest that women are virtually outside history, as if history were literally '*his*-story' in which women had no part."[2] Eric Santner objects that the film identifies the mother as a "victim of history" rather than one of its "players"[3]—a bifurcation which, to be sure, disallows the possibility that she might be both. At the center of the controversy is a hermeneutic friction between older cultural and psychoanalytic models for coming to terms with the Nazi past and more recent, less universalist, feminist retheorizations of psychoanalysis and mourning.

My aims in this chapter are twofold. First, I will trace the roots of the tension between the discourses of feminism and those of *Trauerarbeit* (the "work of mourning") back to a psychoanalytic paradigm which I have already identified with the postwar era—the matrophobic, hierarchical oedipal model of identity formation that shapes Alexander and Margarete Mitscherlich's critique of postwar German culture in their often-cited study, *The Inability to Mourn*. In particular, I will consider the Mitscherlichs' theories as they have informed and directed the subsequent work of Eric Santner, one of *Germany, Pale Mother*'s detractors. Second, I will argue for a reading of Sander-Brahms's film—and, more broadly, for an understanding of women's identity formation and position in culture—based on Kaja Silverman's feminist re-vision of Freud's theory of the negative Oedipus complex. Silverman's feminist framework expressly eschews ahistoricism and essentialism in delineating the political implications of desire within the mother-daughter dyad.[4] Similarly, I maintain, *Germany, Pale Mother* does not simply conceptualize this dyad as if insulated from public events or from the symbolic order. Instead, the film's concern is to show how the daughter's libidinal investment in the mother works as the springboard for cultural critique and feminist authorial intervention.

Santner's approach to the problem of *Trauerarbeit,* although eloquently expressed and genuinely illuminating, illustrates important problems that arise when masculine elegiac experiences and nationalist typologies are overgeneralized into supposedly transhistorical collective phenomena. Drawing on the traditional Freudian ideas about melancholia and mourning that inform Alexander and Margarete Mitscherlich's work, Santner shares and extends the Mitscherlichs' conclusion that an inability to mourn and a pathological narcissism characterized the Germans of this era. Indeed, in Santner's view, the pathology not only extends back into the decades before the war, it also reaches ahead into ensuing decades, up to the present, apparently unchanged.[5] In effect, Santner regards the inability to mourn as an essential trait of "the German people"—just as Siegfried Kracauer so many years previously identified sociopsychic causalities of fascism with essentialized traits of Germans. By situating neither the Mitscherlichs' *theory* nor the human *subjects* of their study fully within the postwar context, Santner tends to dehistoricize their theory and the traits it seeks to explain. In his reading, the incapacity to mourn operates virtually as a reified entity, one that is for all intents and purposes independent from its human construction and from the postwar era's strong reinvestment in the social gender hierarchy. By treating the inability to mourn as something internal to the processes of German history—before, during, and decades after the war—he describes a closed loop.

To be sure, Santner goes beyond the Mitscherlich model to raise questions about how mourning and melancholia might be gendered. Yet his interrogation leads only to a very brief dispute with feminist views that privilege pre-oedipal mother-daughter bonds and place "female mourning within the closure of the Imaginary rather than at the site of its chastening."[6] What Santner underscores are similarities between male and female patterns of melancholy and mourning[7]—without investigating the consequences for the daughter of the fact that psychoanalytic paradigms of *both* mourning *and* melancholy are rooted in a devaluation of the mother/female—be she externalized and abjected, as supposedly happens in the case of mourning, or internalized and deemed the morally inferior part of the self, as has been theorized in the case of melancholy. Consequently, like the Mitscherlichs, who consistently choose to "take the case of the boy" as representative,[8] Santner underestimates the asymmetries in male and female identity formation. And like the Mitscherlichs, he accepts the discourse that metaphorically casts Hitler in the role of a mother-matrix who was merely masked as an authoritarian father figure. He asserts: "In Lacanian terms, the Jews were assigned the role of the ones who intrude into and disrupt the Imaginary, akin to evil fathers who brutally uproot the children from their native matrix and maroon them in the cold and abstract space of the Symbolic."[9] His analysis seeks to account neither for the conflation of Jewish manhood with femaleness that shaped the fascist discourse of abjection, nor for the fear of the pre-oedipal mother's power, a dread that likely bolstered fascist men's fanatic allegiance to paternal authority and enforced matrophobia in postwar theory.[10]

Santner's choice of the myth of Apollo and Daphne to illustrate a positive homeopathic elegiac paradigm illustrates the kind of oversight produced by assuming that masculinist models can be universal. As he recounts it, their story is one "in which the object of desire is transformed into the laurel tree from which the god then cuts and fashions a wreath, ... a legacy that will help him to master his loss."[11] Santner never raises questions about Daphne's loss—or Apollo's culpability—even though she is in one sense a "real" stranded object, metamorphosed through the agency of her father out of humanity and into nature or organic matrix. (In the myth, she prefers this fate to being raped.) Hence, even though the male god may master his loss and retain his autonomy, this paradigm of escape from melancholia, with its lack of compassion for the human woman, remains problematic.[12] As Juliana Schiesari puts it, "Mourning the [woman as] phallus does not mean—far from it—any empathy or complicity with other disempowered subjectivities!"[13]

In contrast to the work of Santner and the Mitscherlichs, Silverman's analysis of the negative Oedipus complex is of great value in illuminating the position of the mother in culture, in elegiac patterns, and in the daughter's bid for agency—the basis of intervention both on her own behalf and for others. As Marianne Hirsch has documented, the general cultural problem of mother-blame is a vexed one, even for feminists.[14] The difficulties increase in the case of *Germany, Pale Mother*. For if feminist analysis in general often reflects resentment over the mother's powerlessness and her refusal to claim power, the problem of representing the mother is rather thornier when her culpability includes her failure to resist the evils of fascism—the failing for which the daughter reproaches her mother in the film.[15] Silverman's model of oedipalization casts new light on these difficulties by exposing the fundamental cultural problem of the mother's devaluation that is the inheritance of the positive Oedipus complex. While Freud and his postwar followers saw this devaluing as necessary to the child's primary processes of mourning and individuation, it relegates the mother to a position of passivity and powerlessness. The devaluation of the mother has important implications for psychoanalytic approaches aimed at understanding the Germans' mourning of the past, insofar as that grieving is seen to replay the primal scenes of a child's identity formation.

Silverman theorizes the distinctive qualities of female identity formation in detail. Unlike Freud, but like Nancy Chodorow,[16] she eschews the view that the separation and autonomy attributed to the male identification process is normative. She argues that Freud's "'Mourning and Melancholia' provides a chillingly accurate account of a condition which may be pathological for the male subject, but which represents the norm for the female subject—that condition of melancholia which blights her relations with both herself and her culture."[17] Silverman draws on the work of Luce Irigaray to develop her argument, particularly the following assertion from *Speculum*: "In point of fact, if all the implications of Freud's discourse were followed through, after the little girl discovers her own castration and that of her mother—her 'object,' the narcissistic representation of all her instincts—she would have no recourse other than melancholia,"[18] a state in which the subject transforms object-loss into ego-loss. According to Silverman, when the subject is the daughter, and the lost object is the mother whom the young girl loves and with whom she identifies, the cure for the young girl's melancholia cannot be devaluation of the lost object, the procedure Freud identified as the cure for male melancholia. Instead, devaluation of the object "would seem to be exactly what *causes* female melancholia."[19]

Consequently, Silverman views the narcissism of the daughter and her love for her mother as potential sources of resistance to the patriarchal order, the phallus; the daughter's desire for the mother, unaccompanied by identification with the father, constitutes the negative Oedipus complex, and her identification with the mother entails perception of the mother as active.[20] Silverman further contends: "Feminism can't really manage without the negativity, which is an indispensable weapon not only against the name, meaning and law of the father, but against the female subject's unconscious investment in those things."[21] Silverman proceeds to argue for the "feminization" of the male as part of feminism's libidinal struggle against the phallus;[22] her position, I maintain, is congruent with Sanders-Brahms's antifascist film.[23]

Equally consistent with *Germany, Pale Mother* is Silverman's insistence upon the crucial role of the daughter's negative Oedipus complex as a site of resistance to dominant ideology. To be sure, the film has been criticized for the nature of its libidinal investment, for supposedly employing a "narrative structure—a daughter reflecting on her own telling of her mother's story—[that] is essentially circular, a closed, almost claustrophobic, circuit."[24] Yet reflection on the mother-daughter story and the healthy narcissism that seems to prompt it are precisely what enable the daughter's interventionist filmmaking: they open up a space and desire from which a strong critique of the postwar politics of home and family becomes possible. Without retrospection of this type, the film suggests, neither familial nor nationalistic patriarchal orders can be subverted, and the film vividly dramatizes the tessellation of these spheres.

It should be further noted that, in addition to enacting a negative oedipal narrative, *Germany, Pale Mother* has unmistakable resonances with the myth of Demeter and Persephone, a tale which stresses the mutual desire of the mother and daughter for sustained connection and their resistance to separation. This woman-centered myth, told in "The Hymn to Demeter," operates neither in circularity nor in linearity, but rather in *cyclical* time. For the myth encompasses both the patriarchal realities of separation and the matrifocal desire for feminine union and reunion. As Hirsch explains:

> The story of Demeter and Persephone does not simply reverse heterosexual plots of disconnection in favor of a model of female connection. More complicated affiliative patterns are revealed here. . . . Demeter's plot which progresses through *contradiction* offers an alternative to the limiting repetitions and deathly closures of Electra and Antigone.[25]

As we shall see, the film's affinities with this myth extend even to its express avoidance of those kinds of deathly closure.

Germany, Pale Mother is divided into three parts, all accompanied by Sanders-Brahms's voice-over. The first comprises the courtship and marriage of Lene (Eva Mattes) and Hans (Hans Jacobi), the parents of "Anna"/Helma, and the initial impact of the war, which brings about Hans's militarization/"masculinization." In sum, the first segment covers the time before Anna/Helma's birth. Caught up in each other, the parents emerge as ordinary, lower-middle-class Germans. They do not want the war, but as the voice-over emphasizes, they do nothing to prevent it or to aid its Jewish victims. Hans's refusal to become a Nazi party member results in his being one of the first men called up to fight. A Nazi friend offers false assurance that Hans, like the weeds, will survive— *"Unkraut vergeht nicht"* (Weeds don't perish). In a real sense, Hans's goodness, kindness, and gentleness are all casualties of the war.

The film's central section sets forth Anna/Helma's birth during an air raid and the blossoming of the mother-daughter dyad during the father's absence. After their apartment building is destroyed by bombs, Lene and Anna wander happily through urban and rural settings, their dyad somewhat disrupted only once, briefly, during an important few days that they spend with Hans at the deserted Berlin apartment of a wealthy uncle, an unsavory Prussian-bureaucrat type who works in the Air Ministry. Far from being presented as a victim of the war, Lene seems to emerge from it relatively unharmed, resilient even after being raped by an American serviceman at the end of the war.[26] Conversely, during the film's final segment, when, in the words of the voice-over, "the war moved inside," Lene's situation deteriorates dramatically. Hans is now dehumanized, callous to suffering, mean-spirited toward both Lene and Anna, and bitterly bent on success within the hierarchy of his workplace. Hungry for genuine intimacy, Lene struggles to resist Hans's authoritarianism, then lapses into illness, depression, and abuse of Anna. Anna's identification with and love for her mother lead to the daughter's further suffering and trauma when she witnesses, then forestalls, Lene's suicide attempt at the film's end.

This tripartite structure, as Barbara Kosta cogently argues, contains iconographic images that activate its religious connotations—especially images of Lene as the Madonna framed in close-up with her child in her arms. Yet, as Kosta also asserts, the film evokes the sacred symbolism of its triadic structure and the Christian maternal not to affirm the values of

5. An ironically liberatory moment: Lene's house destroyed, she becomes free in the midst of war. (Eva Mattes in *Germany, Pale Mother.* Photo courtesy of New Yorker Films and the Auraria Film Collection, Auraria Higher Education Center.)

Kinder and *Kirche* but to critique these ideals and the ways they were exploited during the historical period represented: "Like the Expressionist painters Max Beckmann and Otto Dix, and later the artist Francis Bacon, Sanders-Brahms polemically reproduces a religiously imbued form of representation and subverts it within its own framework. She shows how her parents' lives and hopes were shaped by ideals promoted for ideological reasons that were exploited in fascist Germany." [27]

One of the most important subversions within this filmic triptych is the iconographic shift created by the central focus on a mother-daughter dyad rather than on a Madonna and son—a move that sets off seismic waves in other discursive fields. Through its particular kind of centering on the mother-daughter dyad, the film not only subverts the mother-son focus of the Christian iconology exploited by the Nazis, it also resists the traditional oedipal paradigm and it destabilizes much secular and nationalist allegory, including the Brecht poem "Germany" that prefaces the film and gives rise to its title. Among these fields, my interest lies first in oedipal subversion—a process which the film both historicizes and uses to promote a self-reflexive cinematic commentary—and second in nationalist allegory and, by extension, issues of authorial voice and cultural self-representation.

It is above all the central segment of the triptych that develops the film's negative oedipal themes—including its oppositional relationship to authoritarian patriarchy and positive oedipalization. In this section, Lene is active and strong once freed of limiting domestic spaces, and her active role fits and expresses the child's perception of the mother prior to the devaluation of her produced by the positive Oedipus complex. Further, Lene speaks, sings, and narrates. We hear her voice throughout this portion of the film far more than in the first or last, and Lene's speaking part here reinforces the voice-over narrator's assertion, made near the beginning of the film, that Lene is Anna's first language teacher, teaching her her "mother tongue." In these ways and others, the film includes but transcends a pre-oedipal, pre-language conceptual framework, just as it resists other cinematic and theoretical paradigms that deny female verbal authority.

Moreover, in the film's middle section, Lene and Anna are *heimatlos*, vagabonds, "flying witches," according to Sanders-Brahms's voice-over, uprooted and nomadic in ways that starkly conflict with both Nazi and postwar ideals of the German people—especially of the "model" mother and child.[28] The film's aesthetic, which counterpoints chilling documentary footage, fairy-tale narration, and melodrama, is also at odds with the sentimental, idealist, essentializing realism of the Nazi aesthetic, with the religious overtones it evoked, and with the kind of audience subject position it constructed. In this way, the film opposes fascist values not only through its focus on the mother-daughter dyad but also through the oppositional aesthetics it uses to represent this bond.

While the central portion of *Germany, Pale Mother* affirms this feminine dyad, often showing mother and daughter close together in two-shots, the film simultaneously contextualizes their relationship to show a paradox, whereby the historical conditions that enable the special intensity of their bond also promote misogyny and an acculturation to racist, genocidal nationalism. The sequence in which Hans expresses his loyalty and love for Lene by refusing to take the soldiers' standard issue of prophylactics is illustrative in this regard. Mocking Hans, the men in his unit play a prank by spelling out L-I-E-B-E ("love") on his bunk with condoms. The joke reveals how German militarization promoted an anaesthesia of the heart, a disparaging of the love object, and a defeminization of the men to buttress their investment in military male-bonding and the law of Nazi patriarchy—both of which, as the film later demonstrates, clearly outlived the war.[29]

The sequence depicting Hans's leave with his family at the Berlin apartment reveals the growing intensification of his identification with the fascist order and Anna's budding opposition to him. During this time, for Anna, Hans is "only a troublesome rival," to cite Freud's description of the child's experience of the father at this developmental stage.[30] The voice-over asks, "What am I to do with a father?" and states, "I was jealous of him and he of me." In the Berlin apartment, Lene sings and dances with Anna, telling Hans, "The worse it gets, the more I sing. Not so much for the child as for me." Evocative of the Demeter-Persephone myth, with its validation of maternal emotion, her words affirm the importance of the mother's own real, if precarious, happiness within the film's mother-daughter dyad. Conversely, Hans's words and the mise-en-scène now align him fully with the military order and Nazi ideology. Feeling excluded, his ego hurt, he stands alone by an empty fireplace over which hangs a group portrait of Hitler, Goebbels, and Goering, a portrait with which the Prussian Uncle Bertrand has also been visually linked. Wagner's bust rests on the mantel. Hans proclaims to Lene, who is offscreen, that the men will fight to the death, and he echoes the Nazi rhetoric that his party-member friend Ulrich uses earlier in the film: "Victory or destruction, *that* is worthy of the German people." Offscreen to the right, Lene replies that she wants to live and that the rich relatives who own the apartment have fled Berlin because they already know the war is lost. Hans leaves, and the family reunion ends with little Anna triumphantly describing Hans as *"Weg! Weg!"* (Gone! Gone!)

During the last section of the film, set after the war, Anna's opposition to paternal authority becomes more articulate. Now, Anna's primary activity in her father's presence is to practice writing, her only work in which he takes any interest and an exercise whose importance the film, for different reasons, also stresses. The first sequence to introduce this pattern begins with a shot of Anna filling a sheet of lined writing paper with neatly formed *i*'s. At this point the voice-over states, "The war started inside while outside there was peace." "Write neatly," Hans commands Anna. "She must write neatly," he tells Lene, who counters by telling him to leave Anna in peace. Thus the scene depicts Hans's paternal surveillance of Anna's (virtually militaristic) inscription into the symbolic order—Anna's "taking dictation" from her drill-master father.

Throughout the sequence, Anna, Lene, and Hans each appear in separate frames, an arrangement reflecting not only the individuation but also the isolation and disconnectedness that this paternalistic inscription creates. Because this sequence comes immediately after one which reveals that neither Hans nor Ulrich is "denazified," its political implications are all the more pointed. In that sequence, Ulrich first sarcastically terms himself "denazified," then puts Anna up to calling Hans a "Waldheini"—a weirdo. Hans angrily beats her for calling him a rude name, and Ulrich does nothing to defend her. The camera lingers on her as she weeps and stands alone in the frame, save for the rubble in the background—a disposable daughter, her future denied. The men's indifference to her suffering conforms with their denial of their own feelings of defeat and sorrow. As Michael Schneider has argued—and as the film confirms—the ideal of manly toughness and the concomitant fear of "feminine" feeling that existed after the war were a perpetuation of the "manliness mania" propagated under National Socialism:

> "Clench your teeth and stick it out"—in accordance with this motto, the generation of the fathers had learned to stoically bear up under the pressure of military drilling, the monstrous misery and hardship of war, the omnipresence of death—not only on the military front, but on the home front as well. Even the deaths of those whom they held most dear were to be accepted without grieving. . . . Anyone who had, or who was permitted to have, so little compassion for himself was certainly unable to feel any compassion for others, for the victims of the system.[31]

This analysis of the postwar discourse of masculinity creates a telling contrast with the Mitscherlichs' postwar interpretation of authoritarianism as an expression of "effeminacy" and pre-oedipal arrest. Indeed, both Schneider and the sequence from *Germany, Pale Mother* help explain the misogynistic cultural climate that would *produce* the biases and blind spots in the Mitscherlich theory. The culture whose populace stereotyped emotion and mourning as negatively feminine and whose intellectuals identified the inability to mourn with effeminacy was caught up in a fundamentally debilitating confusion about social practices, psychological syndromes, and the genocide it had committed in the fatherland's name.

The second sequence to show Anna writing at her desk comes as Hans leaves to take Lene to the doctor to treat what seems to be a sudden facial paralysis. Lene's illness is in fact foreshadowed as early as the time in the Berlin apartment, when Lene tells Hans that what they have been through will show in their faces. It is there that we first see the facial twitch which later escalates into disfigurement. The implication here and elsewhere in the film is that Lene tries but fails to insulate herself from political events and involvement, seeking to repress and cover things over; her cold, unemotional response to her Jewish classmate Rahel Bernstein being taken away on *Kristallnacht*—she closes the shutters and drapes—prompts her sister Hanne's deserved criticism, "You can be so hard." In a similar gesture later on in the film, Lene covers the windows and turns her back on the world when her paralysis persists, and she covers the disfigured side of her face with a black veil, a further symbol of evasion and repression.[32] This telling cultural gesture of closing things off from view, especially of drawing the curtains, typifies the domestic world not only of *Germany, Pale Mother*, but also of *Peppermint Peace* and *Hunger Years*. Commenting on the significance of these self-insulating gestures, Sanders-Brahms explains that she "tried to accuse [her] parents of having shut the blinds, and of trying to get away from what was happening."[33] Lene's resulting hysterical paralysis, an analogue of her hardness of heart, provides the context for Anna's second writing scene.

Before Hans and Lene leave their apartment to get help for Lene,[34] Hans commands, "Don't move until we get back." Without moving, Anna looks at her reflection in the three-way mirror from across the room, then proceeds to write repeatedly, "Heini und Lene weinen" (Heini and Lene weep), completely filling a page. Anna's increasing isolation and alienation from her parents, coupled with her surveying her reflection in the mirror, fit Lacan's account of the mirror stage in some details. Yet Anna's visual self-recognition occurs not prior to entry into the symbolic order—that is, not in the Lacanian sequence—but as a self-identification that is always already conjoined with organized cultural representations. The inseparability of the pre-oedipal from both the negative and the positive oedipal stages thus becomes evident. Moreover, the names Hans and Lene are also the German counterparts to Dick and Jane in American primers,[35] a fact that makes Anna's substitution of "Heini" for "Hans" as the name that she couples with "Lene" serve as a small but significant point of cultural resistance, a subversion of narrative standards, and a displacement of the name of the father that recalls the "Waldheini" ("weirdo") name-calling scene. At least as importantly, Anna's sentence about weeping suggests the empathic child's awareness of her parents' need to mourn together—something we never see them do—and her own awareness of the failings in the restored heterosexual family contract that was deemed the foundation of culture, happiness, and freedom from fascism.

The last of the three writing scenes is also part of the final sequence of the film. The words that Anna writes are: "Onkel Asch und Tante Peter . . . vierzehn Kinder. Ihre kinder heissen Ingo und An[na]." (Uncle Ash and Aunt Peter . . . fourteen children. Their children are named Ingo and An[na].) Her writing now constructs a family paradigm, but destabilizes gender identities and associates the uncle with an image of death—fittingly, in view of her despicable Uncle Bertrand's amoral opportunism. The sentences reflect Anna's disturbance over the state of her own family. Indeed, in this same scene her parents fight again; the profoundly melancholic Lene renounces life, and Hans walks out. But since the sentences also suggest linguistic disruption and resistance to the traditional family, they can also be said to "prefigure" a facet of the director's *Kinoschreiben* (a translation of Agnès Varda's term *cinécriture*); that is, the construction of the film can be seen in retrospect as an outgrowth of the child's authorial subversion of the postwar patriarchal family romance.

There is a further way in which the film's last scene plays out the negative Oedipus complex and undermines the usual operations of the phallogocentric order. In images both powerful and painful, Lene locks herself in the bathroom and attempts suicide by turning on the gas from the water heater. Unable to see or hear Lene, Anna pounds on the door repeatedly, begging her mother to open the door, to come out, the camera lingering on the back of Anna's head in a close shot that strengthens viewer identification with her. Lene finally does come out, and the voice-over explains, "It took a long time for Lene to open the door. Sometimes I think she is still behind that door, and I'm standing in front of it, and she'll never come out, and I have to be grown up and alone. But she is still there. Lene is still there."

The scene operates in direct contrast to mainstream cinema's attempts to foster the illusion of the male viewing subject's wholeness by projecting his lack onto the female object. In fact, this scene creates a direct confrontation with the experience of the mother's being cut off from the self, the castration that, according to Silverman, precedes any perception of female genital lack. The scene fits exactly the scenario that Silverman identifies as intrinsic to cinema, if one rarely thematized so directly: "Cinema . . . revives the primordial desire for the object only to disappoint that desire, to reactivate the original trauma of its disappearance. Since the loss of the object always entails the loss of what was once part of the subject, it is—in the strictest sense of that word—a castration."[36] The parallel dyadic relationships between mother and daughter, cinematic image and viewer, are crucial to this film's impact, especially in its address to female viewers. The end of the illusion of the presence of the mother and the end of the illusion of the movie—*Germany, Pale Mother* as Lene and as film—intersect: both movie and mother are there and not there to the daughter who is/must be grown up and separate now—though not, in this case, necessarily alone. Put succinctly, the pain of the ending heightens the way cinema mimics the object's absence within the oedipal narrative.

While some scholars have chosen to emphasize the element of Lene's martyrdom in this scene, to see only melodramatic excess or iconographic suffering is to read the ending reductively. The voice-over's repeated insistence that "Lene is still there" and the poignancy of the lingering image of Lene are immediately followed by the filmmaker's dedication of the film "to Lene and to Anna," the latter being Sanders-Brahms's own daughter as well as the name she gives herself in the film. This three-generational community of women (a triangulation central to the negative Oedipus complex) suggests a way in which the film fortifies the female subject against her intensely felt loss without creating a demeaned and devalued Other or a demeaned and devalued self. In more than one sense, the filmmaker's speaking voice preserves her mother's life. Moreover, the film contains many images of the abject—Lene's vomit, Anna's excrement, the blood of birth, a corpse that Anna insists on seeing—as if to deny their status as utterly other, the means for determining the boundaries of the self. The film's presentation of Lene's abject misery in the end is countered by Anna's and the film's desire for the mother, to reproduce the mother and to refigure the relationship to her. Thus Lene is saved from the requirement that the mother assume the status of the abject in the child's identity formation. Like Demeter, Lene is part of a more intricate, less linear pattern of affiliation and female self-understanding.[37]

To rephrase Freud, it is also true that the child is mother to the woman—that is, the child at the end of the film is mother to the woman whose film we see, whose memories we share, and whose voice-over we hear from the first sequence on. The voice and images tell us both directly and indirectly what has become of Anna, the daughter, the (not unproblematized) filmmaker, her subversive desires and her proto-authorial subversions.

At this point, I want to turn to an analysis of the various forms of *Kinoschreiben* that shape and politicize the film from its outset, for these counterpoint both the illusion of a transparent cinematic fiction and the abstracting allegorization of the mother-son dyad called up by the Brecht poem which prefaces the film. The film's discursive subversions challenge established notions of what constitutes German history and how one, as a daughter, comes to terms with it.

Germany, Pale Mother's opening sequence uses images and Sanders-Brahms's voice-over to introduce the man and woman who will become the daughter's parents. The rippling reflection of a large swastika-emblazoned flag initially fills the screen; economically and reflexively, it defines the time and place. Then a rowboat containing the father-to-be and his Nazi friend glides through the flag's reflected image. The voice-over describes the men, and they discuss and call out to Lene, who is seen silently walking alone along the lakeside. She remains silent as she is harassed by Nazi officers on the path behind her and attacked by their German shepherd. The sequence ends with a close-up—the film's first—of Lene's face, as the voice-over meditates on Lene's silence and on her "mother tongue." The counterposing of the mature daughter's disembodied voice with the silent, bodily presence of the young Lene as mother-to-be effectively places these women in what Hollywood figures as desiring male and desired female positions, respectively. Conversely, the men occupy naturalized space as they watch and discuss Lene from their rowboat. As Silverman explains, in order to fortify the male subject, "Hollywood pits the disembodied male voice against the synchronized female voice,"[38] in an intermeshing of the psychic and cinematic apparatuses that this sequence effectively reverses and upends.

The threat to customary cinematic codes posed by the opening sequence merits further elaboration. As Silverman explains:

> To permit a female character to be seen without being heard would be to activate the hermeneutic and cultural codes which define woman as "enigma," inaccessible to definitive male interpretation. To allow her to be heard without being seen would be even more dangerous, since it would disrupt the specular regime upon which dominant cinema relies; it would put her beyond the reach of the male gaze (which stands in here for the cultural "camera") and release her voice from the signifying obligations which that gaze enforces.[39]

What the film proceeds to give us—again, contrary to classic cinema—is a deconstruction of the terms according to which the "enigmatic" Lene might ordinarily be defined, her enigma "solved." The sequence also disrupts the cinematic illusion and the essentialist perspective which that illusion subtends. Here and throughout the film, it is the daughter's voice-over, her intrusion as filmmaker/author, that is the film's most persistent anti-illusionist, anti-suturing device.[40]

In addition, the idea of Germany as motherland is evoked then deconstructed. As Bammer astutely explains:

> Sanders-Brahms acknowledges the inheritance of a cultural tradition in which woman has been made the carrier of ideological meaning even when politically her importance has been denied. . . . By shifting her attention to the concrete particulars of everyday experience, [Sanders-Brahms] begins to dismantle the allegorical structures. By revealing the specifics which the symbols at once refer to and, in so doing, hide from view, she exposes the symbols as ultimately hollow, meaningless in themselves.[41]

In other words, the film thus creates a dialogic interplay between the abstracting discourse of allegory and the discourse of domestic melodrama, with its emphasis on human connection within the private world of particular people. At the same time, the tensions between allegory and melodrama serve to suggest the tessellation of the public and private spheres. That is, the film not only deconstructs the allegorical equation of

Germany as mother in a move that parallels its dismantling of the mother as Madonna equation, it simultaneously stresses the contiguities and real similarities between state, religious, and familial patriarchal structures, both fascist ones and "postwar," "peaceful" democratic ones.[42]

It should be added that, in addition to praising its deconstruction of allegory, Bammer faults the film for its conception of Lene—for representing Lene as a woman who refuses to claim her autonomy and fails to teach her daughter to be strong.[43] Yet Sanders-Brahms's rejection of the "positive image" approach in favor of an ambiguous portrait is indispensable to her social critique and to the dramatic irony through which that critique is achieved. For example, Lene thinks nothing of looting the shop of a deported Jewish family in order to obtain embroidery thread—she is more concerned with embroidering a blouse to wear for Hans than with the Duckstein family's fate. Ironically, Lene's insensitivity and folly in thus imagining that her private world is sequestered from the monstrous events around her rebound on her: she wears the blouse when Hans returns on leave, only to be shocked and hurt as he, desensitized by war, roughly rips the blouse to undress her. Similarly, in the case of Rahel, whom she sees being taken away by thugs in the night, Lene callously refuses to respond to the violence, instead diverting herself by conversing with her sister about suitors. But Lene's dreams of domestic bliss ultimately give way to a "restored" postwar family that is anything but a haven. Richard McCormick focuses the ultimate irony in this way: Lene "believes politics (and 'history') can be evaded by retreating into the private sphere, an illusion that not only facilitates her complicity with the status quo, but also one that will eventually be her undoing."[44] No figure for easy audience identification, then, Lene is part of an ironic narrative that generates social critique through a more complex, unsettling positioning of the spectator than an unequivocally "positive" or "negative" image could have allowed.[45]

Like Sanders-Brahms's emphasis on everyday experience, her use of triple casting also works to subvert the nationalist allegory and counterpoints the film's realist elements as well. In addition to playing Lene, Eva Mattes is cast as a Polish peasant and a French partisan, both of whom Hans helps to execute—despite his recognition that the women are Lene look-alikes. (The first woman's death, filmed to evoke Goya's *Third of May, 1808,* is painful for him; when the second woman is executed, there is no reaction shot, the implication being that Hans, too, now suppresses any response.) These killings are both horrible in themselves and are ominous foretastes of Hans and Lene's postwar estrangement. Further, the linking of women's experiences across national boundaries through triple casting brings to mind Virginia Woolf's position in *Three Guineas* that a woman's claim to citizenship is with the whole world, not a particular country: "'For,' the outsider will say, 'in fact, as a woman, I have no country. As a woman I want no country. As a woman my country is the whole world.'"[46] In other words, the triple casting serves to throw into question the politics of nationalism per se. The "internationalizing" of Mattes's roles implicitly challenges the status quo that subordinated—and that still subordinates—women's identities and women's politics to a dubious ideological premise—the primacy of national identity.

Additionally, the film's reflections on allegory bring to mind the German Jewish poet Heinrich Heine and his critical perspectives on nationalist abstractions. Living in Paris as a political exile, Heine wrote "Nachtgedanken" ("Nightthoughts," 1843), a beautifully crafted elegiac meditation on the land and the mother he left behind. The poem's key contrast is between Germany as fatherland and the speaker's mother. The former is a "robust land" ("*kerngesundes Land*") and an "undying" ("*ewigen*") abstract entity, for which, as a thing in itself, the speaker of the poem feels no longing. His mother, conversely, is real, loving, aging, perishable—a woman for whom he longs just as he longs for others in Germany who suffer or who have died. Sanders-Brahms's evocation of Heine is a gesture that suggests their shared critiques of the fatherland as an abstraction that wrongfully demands human sacrifices. Sanders-Brahms's conceptualization of this problem locates it as extending beyond the years of the Third Reich.[47]

Not only does the film dismantle the allegorical conception of the mother/father/land, it also makes frequent use of anti-illusionist, reflexive techniques to undermine the essentialist conception of character that realism is said to imply. As already noted, the film begins with a close shot of a large swastika-emblazoned flag reflected in water, a reminder of our indirect access to profilmic and historical events. The dance scene in which we first see Hans and Lene together also begins with a flag—in this case, with a close-up of part of a large, insect-dotted Nazi flag. The camera moves back and up to reveal that the entire flag is infested. The scene then cuts to a shot of two unsavory-looking officers, one of whom bites into a long wurst. As in the works of Georg Grosz, the shot makes normal activities look disgusting. The flag forms the backdrop against which couples dance; the nonsynchronous piano music consists of deep, ominous chords.[48] The voice-over describes the courtship of Lene and Hans that begins here as "happy, perfectly normal, only it happened at this time, in this country." Brechtian audience distanciation results from the extreme disjunction between "normal, happy" on the one hand and what we see and the music we hear on the other.

The sequence that depicts events which immediately follow the parents' wedding continues to disrupt the illusionism of realist codes through its reflexivity and fairy-tale motif. Referring to their wedding, Lene tells Hans, "'It's like a film,' Frau Meierholt said." The couple sits in front of a three-way mirror, the triple reflection suggesting not only a Christian triptych but also a film strip, in a religio-cinematic conjunction reminiscent of *Peppermint Peace*. The voice-over states, "I cannot imagine your skin touching. I am between you. I never married. I unlearned that from you." During this same sequence, which directly follows Lene's closing the shutters and drapes on Rahel's victimization, the new bride pricks her finger on a needle that has been left in a window curtain, an act that focalizes key motifs in the film. In "Sleeping Beauty" a similar wound inaugurates what Bruno Bettelheim terms the sleep of puberty.[49] In *Germany, Pale Mother*, given the association of passive complicity that the window-covering motif and Lene's needlework both accrue, this fairy-tale element suggests the "sleep" or oblivion to the outside world that is induced by her exclusive devotion to romance and domesticity.

The daughter's film also reflects on the paucity of cultural models that can be used to illuminate the mother-daughter dyad or that envision this dyad as a psychological resource for speech or political action. For example, in the film's prologue, a daughter (Hanna Hiob) recites a poem written by her father (Bertolt Brecht), as the text of the poem, "Germany," is shown on the screen. Allegorizing Germany as a motherland despoiled by fascism, Brecht's lyric establishes a framework in which brother murders brother, to the mother's shame. Sanders-Brahms's film both interrogates the allegory and reconceptualizes the family drama in such a way as to indicate an inevitable slippage or failure in transmission of authorial power from Brecht's literary model to the film. Thus, while his poem and general aesthetics remain important, privileged resources for reworking the past, Brecht's example also emerges as an inadequate model for conceiving women's authorship and spectator positioning. Indeed, the secular allegory in Brecht's poem affords a critical contrast with the narrative trajectory of *Germany, Pale Mother* and takes on a relationship to the film that is partially analogous to that of the Christian iconology discussed by Kosta, as well as to the Mitscherlichian pre-oedipal dyad. That is, all three mother-son paradigms—the nationalist, the sacred, and the psychoanalytic—are prototypes *against* which the film defines itself. And in so doing, the film positions its spectators to reassess the value of these kinds of paradigms for illuminating the politics of home and "homeland," feminine agency, and national identity.

"The Robber Bridegroom," a Grimms' fairy tale that Lene tells her daughter during the central section of the film, emerges as another important yet unsatisfactory cultural antecedent. It is the story of a young woman betrothed to a man whom she goes to visit at his house in the woods. Upon arriving there, she is warned by birds and by an old woman that she is in a murderer's house. Following the old woman's advice, she hides and witnesses the robber—her betrothed—and his cohorts murder a girl by serving her poisoned wine. The men then cut off the murdered girl's finger in order to obtain a gold ring. The parallels to Lene and Anna's situation in Nazi Germany are unmistakable, for during Lene's narration, mother and daughter stop in an abandoned factory suggestive of a crematorium at the end of the war—a strong visual reminder that Germany itself is a house of death camps, a mass murderer's house. In the fairy tale, the young woman returns home, and when the robber bridegroom appears there in order to claim her as his bride, she tells the story of what she has seen, though claiming it was a dream; finally, however, she produces the finger from the body of the robber's victim, and the robber is taken away and punished. Like the young woman in the tale, Anna/Helma too becomes a narrator, her narrative being the whole film. And she too presents evidence of what has been cut off, cast away, or forgotten—precisely by Germans like her parents, who drew the blinds on the suffering and deaths of their Jewish neighbors and friends. In this way, the daughter takes responsibility not for those events and actions over which she had no control, but for the remembering of the past, for the narration of history. Yet while the fairy tale renders the mother absent, depicting instead the father-daughter and daughter-bridegroom relationships, the film itself re-

6. Lene tells her daughter, "Anna"/Helma, the climax of "The Robber Bridegroom," a
Grimms' fairy tale contextualized to implicate Nazi criminality. (Eva Mattes and Sonja Lauer
in *Germany, Pale Mother*. Photo courtesy of New Yorker Films and the Auraria Film Collection, Auraria Higher Education Center.)

trieves the mother and makes her a narrating agent. Lene's enunciative role
here is in fact paradoxical, for it both problematizes the silencing of mothers in canonical texts and emphasizes Lene's own quiet complicity in the
kinds of crime and suppression toward which the "Robber Bridegroom"
tale is made to point.[50] Yet also by having the murdered girl of the fairy
tale represent the victims of the Holocaust, the film reminds us of how
easily Nazism transposed hatred among a range of subjects deemed socially or culturally inferior.

Not unexpectedly, Hans gives voice to the authorial model included in
the film that is most alien to Sanders-Brahms's *Kinoschreiben*, as he performs a drunken recital of Faust's celebrated "Easter Morning" speech
during a scene of empty, joyless merry-making, near the film's end. An
Adenauer radio speech promoting European humanistic ideals in the
postwar era counterpoints the lines from Goethe's allegorical, autobio-

graphical play. As Anton Kaes points out, postwar Germans embraced the "humanity" of German Idealism which Goethe exemplified because it was experienced as a form of "apolitical" culture that supposedly transcended political parties and was not concerned with mundane socioeconomic conditions.[51] Goethian idealism, as expressed in Faust's "eternal striving" or in the Watchtower Society at the end of *Wilhelm Meister's Apprenticeship,* offered both an escape from the recent trauma of Nazism and simultaneously the comforting idea that one could participate in an all-encompassing "international" set of cultural abstractions such as the "organicism" of body and mind, the "noble soul," "intuition and aesthetic expression of the divine in nature," "the brotherhood of humankind," and so on. In the context of the film, however, the oppressive sexual politics of Goethe's work and romanticist values become glaring. Indeed, the striving individual Faustian man whose mission for self-fulfillment legitimizes the destruction of the lives of women—namely, Gretchen and her mother—and the repression of memories of their suffering can only serve as a negative reference by this point in Sanders-Brahms's story. The film makes equally clear the futility of turning to Goethe as a Lethe in which to drown sorrows and memories of catastrophic events—the indelible Nazi crimes against humanity, "that cynical mass homicide."[52] Thus the idea of a re-generated Germany, implied by the "Easter Morning" and Adenauer speeches, emerges in a context of scathing, double-edged irony.

As these examples reveal, the culture's major literary paradigms have little to say about the "reality" of the mother-daughter bond—and virtually nothing in terms that authorize their voices or integrate them into the public sphere of political agency and activism. The film dialogically appropriates such canonical literary texts, icons, and allegories for purposes of both revision and subversion. Because these privileged cultural models, like traditional psychoanalytic ones, subordinate and elide women's experiences within a hierarchical masculinism, the film involves the spectator in an active process of questioning to determine where emulation ends and critique begins. (Not surprisingly, a good deal of the critical debate about this film has focused precisely on such questions.)

In this way and others, *Germany, Pale Mother* brings its spectators to an awareness that reworking the past is a labor whose resources and contours for women differ dramatically from those for men. Compared with the example of Apollo and Daphne discussed at the outset of this chapter, the film's reinscription of history and loss involves quite dissimilar processes of recuperation and representation. Sanders-Brahms's endeavor to remember requires greater emphasis both on sustaining the connection between self and m/other—a bond which the triple casting of Mattes internationalizes—and on acknowledging crucial differences within each discursively constituted identity. Hence, the category "German woman" becomes less obscured by the established norm, "the German people." And hence, the idea that German women were either "victims" or "players" gives way to the more complex realization that they were, in unequal degrees and at different historical moments, both.

Moreover, just as the literary paradigms invoked by the film are subject to critique, so too are the cultural and psychoanalytic models scholars have called upon to illuminate the postwar experience. To refer back to an important example cited earlier, Michael Schneider selects Hamlet—that most privileged of all Western melancholics—as the patron saint of Sanders-Brahms's generation and quotes with approval Ernst Bloch's description of the Danish prince as a "disabled Orestes." If, like the Mitscherlichs, one imagines Hitler as a powerful primitive mother figure—a Clytemnestra, mother goddess, or "phallic" Gertrude—the evocations of Orestes and Hamlet take on resonance, and the postwar insistence on a restored gender hierarchy makes sense. But for women of Sanders-Brahms's generation who question the hierarchic, segregated gender roles embraced by both Mitscherlich and the postwar order, the matricidal Orestes cannot serve as a superior point of identification. For the mother-daughter plot to be successful, it must subvert these critical approaches. In the process, it must recognize that the phallocentric paradigms for understanding fascist history are historically bound and susceptible to radical change.

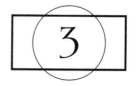

Self-Consuming Images

The Identity Politics
of Jutta Brückner's *Hunger Years*

In the universe of consumerism, there is an object more beautiful, more precious, more striking than any other—heavier with connotations than even the automobile; it is the body.[1] —Jean Baudrillard

A great number if not the majority of the citizens of democratic West Germany have been unable to identify themselves with anything beyond its economic system.[2]

—Alexander and Margarete Mitscherlich

I need the cinema in order to reconstruct my physical person. Women's physical persons have been destroyed by history. Thus, for us, we need the cinema in an urgent fashion.[3] —Jutta Brückner

Set in the formative years of the West German *Wirtschaftswunder*, Jutta Brückner's stark black-and-white film *Hunger Years in a Land of Plenty* (*Hungerjahre—in einem reichen Land*, 1979) precisely maps the complex cultural landscape of her youth: the nation's denial of the Nazi past, its division into East and West, the cold war, anticommunism, sexual repression, and bulimic consumerism (the term bulimia deriving from the Greek meaning ox hunger).[4] In particular, this fictionalized autobiography demonstrates the relationship between disordered consumption—whether of food, goods, or images—and postwar German political identities, a relationship that is symptomatically inscribed on the body of the film's protagonist. Split along the conceptual polarities of West/East, Right/Left, "free"/communist, abundance/dearth, present/past, public/private, and male/female, 1950s West German identity constructs depended on the social and psychological repression of the second term in each pair.[5] By focalizing the "hunger" of an emotionally disturbed adolescent girl, Brückner's film brilliantly examines and deconstructs these dualisms while exposing their cultural operations and consequences. The critical identity which the film explores is, on one level, Brückner's own, but undigested histories, private and public, emerge as interdependent; neither operates or can be understood in isolation from the other.

A key way in which this interconnection emerges in *Hunger Years* is in the film's articulation of its central autobiographical dilemma. The problem is, in a sense, a puzzle of self-invention, an adolescent girl's version of the riddle set forth in Joan Riviere's "Womanliness as Masquerade" and by Riviere's own life: What does it mean to be intellectual and female?[6] More precisely, for Ursula, Brückner's filmic surrogate, the questions in this coming-of-age story are: How does one become a politically self-aware woman in the aftermath of Germany's Nazi past? How can one command political effectivity and yet answer the contradictory demands of the 1950s for feminine prudery and for self-display? In the film the seemingly marginal story of a teenage girl's first encounter with this overwhelming constellation of challenges affords a key to understanding pivotal dynamics of the postwar culture. The ideal of femininity in the 1950s, which inflated the female body's iconic status as commodity to parodic proportions, made it the ultimate consumerist image. Yet, at the psychological level, this ideal fractured the female self, and at the historical level, it abetted a splitting off of the culture from the past it evaded through rampant consumerism.

Hunger Years is a return, then, not only to the repressed but also to the mechanisms of repression, the systems of substitution and commerce on which familial and state postwar power structures depended. The film depicts the apparatuses of exchange, bodily discipline, and control as they were enmeshed in the nexus of consumerism, consumption, and consummation—that is, as buying/spending, eating, and enacting a sexual identity.[7] Like Ulrike Ottinger's *Countdown* (1990), a documentary on the dismantling of the Wall, *Hunger Years* exposes consumerism as a substitute for and evasion of all kinds of vital but missed connections at a pivotal moment in history. In Ottinger's film, the transition to German unification is filled up, in terms of activity and awareness, with goods—buying food, clothes, souvenir pieces of the Wall, military hats and uniforms—activities which divert attention from the "walls" of poverty, xenophobia, homophobia, and sexism that remain. In the *Wirtschaftswunderwelt* being formed in *Hunger Years,* consumer goods, including food and sexual spectacle, impede personal, familial, social, and historical awareness and, in particular, the *Auseinandersetzung* (articulation), *Verarbeitung* (working through), and *Verdauung* (digestion) of the horrific Nazi legacy. And as *Hunger Years* reveals, in the postwar era, consumerism was not just a process of creating artificial needs rather than addressing natural ones, as it is theorized by the Frankfurt school; nor was it primarily a question of social climbing and differentiation, as it is in the Baudrillard model.[8] Brückner's memory reveals that it was also a *Verdauungsstörung*—a blockage of the process of coming to terms with the past, an obstruction in which reified representations of women played a crucial role. Commodity fetishism was the urge to accumulate goods in a futile effort to satisfy desires and eliminate feelings of deprivation unconnected with the products consumed. Consumerism was a lure away from addressing the social and cultural needs for remembrance, acknowledgment of affective ties with the Third Reich, and consequent guilt, shame, and mourning. It was, as well, a narcissistic diversion from the need for *Mitleiden* (compassion or sympathy) for the victims of the Holocaust. Commodifying the female body enforced the diversion and disavowal—especially for females. The reified feminine body constituted a special price paid for (evading) history. Thus *Hunger Years* not only corroborates the Mitscherlichs' findings on the *Wirtschaftswunder*'s amnesiac role in relation to Germany's fascist past, it also considerably exceeds them, for it radicalizes the implications of the Mitscherlichs' insight by elaborating the critical feminist and filmic ramifications of West German identification with its consumerist system.

Brückner's theories on the connection between women as film spectators and consumerism illuminate how these issues are treated in her film. According to Brückner, the fact that women's means of appropriating the visible world are constricted has made them especially susceptible to consumerist cinematic spectating. She points out that the most frequent cinemagoers during the heyday of the Hollywood "woman's film" were women.[9] Putting the situation into a broad cultural perspective, Brückner asserts: "because women couldn't conquer the outside world with their look the way men could, their look became voyeuristic, of necessity. So that, quite literally, for instance, they peeped through keyholes like Ursula watching her parents make love."[10] For women as cinemagoers, in Brückner's view, this situation means that

> women are particularly willing to submit themselves to this mechanism of identification which forms the basis of film—much more willing than men. The classic Hollywood film played on this [willingness] for a whole decade, by supplying women with films in which their daydreams came true—and the poverty of their situation revealed itself, because, for instance, their daydreams were never something radically different, but only . . . [b]eing married to an especially rich or loving husband, being especially beautiful and wearing especially wonderful clothes—never anything different! Always just "richer" or "better."[11]

To be sure, Brückner's use of "voyeurism" and her account of the woman's film differ from Mary Ann Doane's important theorizations in this area. Doane genders voyeurism male and associates it with a distanciated epistemological drive. She labels the kind of spectating activated by the woman's film nonvoyeuristic and identifies it with affect and spatial proximity.[12] Conversely, Brückner ascribes voyeurism to women and describes it as primarily a sociohistorical effect rather than in strictly psychoanalytic terms.[13] Brückner's perception seems to be that a female scopic drive, which is in large part epistemological and power-driven, becomes channeled through the woman's film into the kind of affective, over-identified, repetitive structures theorized by psychoanalysis. Her own aesthetics, both in theory and praxis, depend upon a well-conceived balance of identification and distanciation, affect and intellect. Her feminist politics clearly entail dilating the female gaze and the world it surveys. Moreover, despite their differences, Brückner's analysis of the Hollywood woman's melodrama accords with Doane's view that this genre served to reconcile women to the existing social order. In fact, both critics enable us to see an irony in America's belief that Hollywood cinema, along with other U.S. products, would promote German denazification during the postwar years, a time when American movies inundated West German theaters.[14] In direct reaction against certain Hollywood woman's films, *Hunger Years* shifts the identificatory capacity of women away from a neurotically repetitive, socially conformist commodity orientation and toward an alternative identification—"with the forgotten areas of their selves, with the repressed stories of their past," as Brückner explains.[15] Indeed, through *Hunger Years,* Brückner denounces as a form of violence the Hollywood woman's film's equation of femininity with aestheticization, and she redirects women's gazes toward moral and political engagement.[16]

Brückner's goals in this autobiographical film also match an objective that Doane has identified for all feminist cinema which retrieves history: "The task must be not that of remembering women, remembering real women, immediately accessible—but of producing remembering women. Women with memories and hence histories."[17] In *Hunger Years* that task is realized through the film's voice-over, spoken by Brückner, who looks back from the vantage point of a woman in her thirties. "I had tried to forget for years," she asserts at the film's beginning. "I could remember towns, houses, places, other people, but had managed to suppress myself out of my memories." The voice-over then details the hysterical symptoms that led her to make this film—a cinematic version of the "talking cure." The film, however, counters the Hollywood formula in which the patriarchal medical or legal apparatus induces and enforces a woman's recollection, as happens, for example, in Robert Siodmak's *The Dark Mirror* (1946). Similarly, the film quite forcefully contradicts Freud's assertion that for a woman of 30, "there are no paths open to further development."[18] The woman in *Hunger Years* speaks for herself—precisely as the path to further development.

Because the film is not well known here, and because much of its rhetorical power depends on its particulars—its intricate dialogical montage[19]—I will describe and discuss how *Hunger Years* unfolds in detail. Like *Germany, Pale Mother, Hunger Years* is narrated within a three-part structure. It covers the years 1953, 1955, and 1956, when the protagonist is 13, 15, and 16, respectively. Each of the film's three segments begins with a shot of a waterside restaurant, a setting that, according to Brückner, uses the water image to evoke the river Styx that borders Hades, separating life from death.[20] Combined with the tripartite structure, this Styx motif

brings to mind the descent into Hell of the pilgrim in Dante's *Inferno*—
another fictionalized autobiography, national critique, and work of remembrance in which the way down, paradoxically, becomes the way up.
Further, each film segment emphasizes claustrophobic interiors shot in
low-key lighting, the customary mise-en-scène of domestic melodrama
rendered in its most elementary, imprisoning, least accommodating form.

The first section of *Hunger Years* introduces the West German lower-
middle-class Scheuner family: Ursula (Britta Pohland), her ambitious, socially conformist mother, Gerda (Sylvia Ulrich), and her passive father,
Georg (Claus Jurichs), a man whose long-term socialist sympathies led
him to limited acts of resistance to Nazism during the war. The family
members' private dreams, isolation, and non-communication are conveyed through polyphonic interior monologues rendered in voice-over.
Dialogue between Ursula and her parents also reveals communicative disorders. Following a pattern typical of families with daughters who suffer
from eating disorders, Gerda neglects ego boundaries and ignores her
daughter's words, instead narcissistically projecting her own desires onto
Ursula.[21] For example, early in the film Ursula looks longingly out the
window of the family's new apartment and asks her mother, "Do you think
I'll find a new friend here?" Instead of responding, Gerda announces to
Georg that Ursula wants an accordion for Christmas, a wish Ursula never
expresses. Family exchanges, including those with the grandmothers, typically hinge on this kind of displacement of authentic needs and pleasures
by a discourse of consumable goods. In the first section and throughout
the film, scenes of eating and drinking, offering and taking food as compensation, substitution, apology, or evasion, abound. When Gerda secures
a job, it is to augment her consumer capacity in order to compensate herself for past deprivations: she stocks the family larder, and the family
proudly buys a used car.[22] Johannes Schmölling's mocking Brechtian-style
score provides ironic musical commentary on the new acquisition.

Editing juxtaposes public and private, visible and hidden forms of oppression, subverting the hierarchies that privilege the public and the visible. For example, in section one, editing dialogizes Ursula's quest for autonomy with East German workers' demonstrations for their rights, and
her psychological and intellectual famine with the workers' physical hunger. To that end, an early sequence graphically depicts Ursula's menar-
che—an event no one has told her to expect. Gerda masks Ursula's men-

struation from her father by pretending that Ursula ate too much, then places severe social restrictions on the girl to avoid any risk that she might get pregnant. Ursula revolts against the whole idea of periods and tries to resist her mother's confinement of her. At one point, she gazes at couples outside her window and announces her intent to take a bicycle tour of Europe. But Gerda abruptly shuts the window on her daughter's pleasurable spectating, rejects such trips outright, and decries the folly of girls who become unwed mothers. Counterposed with scenes dramatizing Ursula's hunger for experience, freedom, and knowledge is footage of the East Berlin uprising of June 17, 1953, a workers' revolt prompted by the bad state of the economy, unemployment, and food shortages. Newsreels expose brutal repression of the workers; two radio broadcasts, one from the East and one from Adenauer, construct conflicting discourses on the uprising. Hearing the events reported on the radio, Ursula demands, "Why don't they give the people freedom?" and, "What is freedom?" Her mother's self-absorbed response is, "When things are going well for us, and we don't have to be afraid," a reaction conditioned by her wartime memories. Gerda's timid misdefinition, in fact, recalls the *fear* of liberty typical of women with authoritarian leanings in the years prior to the Nazi rise to power.[23] And of course, Gerda's earlier identification of womanhood with illness and apprehension means that her sense of female identity is incompatible even with the inadequate idea of freedom she offers here. From the more progressive Georg, Ursula receives better instruction: he tells her that people play fast and loose with the word "freedom"—a term the West German government applies to the release from prison of a concentration camp *Kommandant*. These sequences and exchanges typify how the film deconstructs the discourses separating the "free" West from the East, public history from private experience, and current events from past atrocities. Brückner's aim is not to equate the terms of the various binarisms, but dialogically to expose and explore what has been suppressed to form each pair.

The complexities of repressive sexual politics are developed further when the father's leftist, antifascist positions are undercut by his marital infidelity—his conformity with the sexual double standard. When Ursula discovers her father's infidelity, she feels betrayed and angrily discards the sweet roll that he offers her as a token of apology; later, she retrieves and devours it in secret.[24] When Gerda notices that Ursula is troubled, she offers chocolate as a panacea. Ursula and Gerda, both estranged now from Georg, cling to each other, and in what Brückner calls "the most horrible moment" in the film,[25] the mother and daughter imagine sharing an exclusive, unchanging dyad into futurity, an arrested pre-oedipal bond much like the one that traps Gerda's celibate sister and, to a slightly lesser degree, Gerda herself, with their narcissistic mother. Section one ends with Gerda's attempt to win Georg back. Reluctantly following her mother's marital advice, Gerda has sex with Georg. Ursula peers through the keyhole to her parents' bedroom and witnesses the scene, chewing on some food as she watches. Then refusing the oedipal situation, the girl runs to the bathroom and flushes the toilet to drown out her father's noisy, orgasmic moaning.[26]

In the film's second section, dated 1955, 15-year-old Ursula's fantasies turn to heterosexual romance. Her daydreams are revealed at various moments in voice-over and are ironically paired with scenes of sexual harassment and with nondiegetic documentary footage of a Miss World beauty contest which shows an audience of gazing males judging contestants in swimsuits.[27] Just as the new family car serves as a symbol of prosperity in the beginning of section one, so the beauty contestants function as parallel signs of wealth at the beginning of section two. And just as discordant music mocks the car's symbolism, so a surreal, disembodied laugh-track, coupled with popular song lyrics about onanism, provides a distanciating, sardonic counterpoint to the pageant, exposing its degrading underside. Indeed, the female body's coding and function, like the car's, are revealed as public symbols of men's success and control and as a means of solipsistic escape from past traumas and deprivations.

The key organizing concepts of the 1955 section are lost youth and passive complicity with the status quo. Isolated and alienated, the girl yearns for popularity, admiration for her poetry, and a boy to love her. Gerda insists that Ursula stay away from boys, remain "innocent," and concentrate on her grades. Through voice-over, Gerda recollects the total lack of youthful independence in her own past, since she was forced to move directly from her mother's guardianship to that of her husband, and did not even experience the theater, cinema, or dancing until the age of 23. Her inability to question the conventional social arrangements that diminish and privatize female positions within patriarchy has resulted not only in her passing on the maternal legacy of loss to Ursula, but also in her earlier failure to oppose fascism. More starkly than Sanders-Brahms's *Germany, Pale Mother, Hunger Years* depicts a maternal legacy marked by unquestioning conformity with the status quo, both under Hitler and afterward.[28] The unsparing critique of the mother and maternal grandmother in *Hunger Years* dovetails with Claudia Koonz's analysis of socially conformist, apolitical women's roles in abetting fascism, perhaps more so than any other such critique in film. An old photograph of Gerda and her mother concludes this scene.

First Georg and later Ursula's teacher continue the pattern of self-absorbed reminiscence and sorrow over forfeited youth. Their recollections in each case are brought to a close by a series of historical photographs. The father's voice-over recounts in sadness and anger years of unemployment, war, and political disaffection. A poignant scene of the grown man alone, kicking a soccer ball, accompanies his narrative. It is during a physical education class that Ursula's teacher reflects on the past, recalling first the pleasure of participating in the BDM (the girl's side of the Hitler youth movement) and later the pain and extreme bitterness at leaders who deceived the young people and betrayed their youthful trust and idealism.

As in the film's first section, personal experience and public life, the past and the present, are shown to be interwoven. The scene with the teacher reveals that the history lessons never touch upon the atrocities committed under Hitler. The teacher's reminiscences, moreover, are contextualized in relation both to the ominous 1956 government plan to reintroduce compulsory military service and to the government ban on the communist party, steps reflecting a resurgent rightist extremism and implicitly connected to the repression of the past. In a characteristically deconstructive gesture, the film uses photographs and documentary footage from 1956 of police aggression and mass arrests in order to give the lie to the announcements we hear from Secretary Schröder that moderation will be used in enforcing the interdiction against communism.

The two sequences that conclude the film's second section starkly dramatize the fissures within and between the intellectual and sexual identities Ursula searches out. The first sequence shows Ursula's confrontation with Georg, during an outdoor luncheon, about his failure to resist the Nazis more forcefully. Pointing out that Georg's comrade lost part of his arm while an inmate at Dachau (a warden hacked it off with a spade),

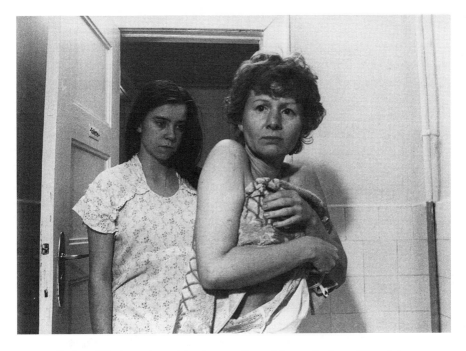

7. Gerda and Ursula, mother and daughter, are alienated from each other and from their own bodies. (Britta Pohland [Ursula, *left*] and Sylvia Ulrich [Gerda] in *Hunger Years*. Photo courtesy of Jutta Brückner Filmproduktion and Pahl-Film, Tübingen.)

Ursula demands to know why Georg has no proof of *his* antifascist stance. Similarly, Ursula criticizes her father's current lack of active opposition to rearmament and to the ban on communism. The final sequence, played out in a lush, natural, waterside setting, presents Ursula boasting to a young male companion about her (fictitious but much-desired) sexual independence. The film shows Ursula in medium shot, as the boy forces alcohol down her throat during an interminable take, the bottle's phallic shape becoming a symbol of rape. The sounds of raucous, disembodied male voices and dissonant music replace that of birds singing; the frame freezes, then fades to black. The pastoral setting and Ursula's earlier dreams of romance thus devolve into a brutal scene of violation and oblivion.

Eating disorders in young women often manifest themselves after an experience of sexual abuse or humiliation,[29] and in part three, Ursula's compulsive eating habits clearly emerge, becoming a source of further friction between mother and daughter. Rebellious but increasingly isolated, depressed, and self-destructive, Ursula resorts to laxatives and cigarettes to help lose weight. She also regresses to mutism. In one scene, sitting alone in a classroom where "1789," the date of the French Revolution, is written on the blackboard, she grooves a desktop with the point of her compass, then pierces her own wrist with the stylus. Later, in a haunting shot indicative of her need for rebirth, she lies in bed in a fetal position, sucking sweetened condensed milk from a tube. The voice-over—spoken by Brückner—encompasses the retrospective reflections of the thirty-something narrator as well as a whispering, destructive voice identified with the 16-year-old girl. The remembering persona explains, "I didn't feel at home anywhere," and describes her experience of herself as being in a state of perpetual flight from gazes and words, and as being superfluous, "like a machine racing around out of control." Documentary footage of nuclear explosions and their impact on test mannequins follows these ruminations. The images work both as oblique mirrors of Ursula's highly disturbed, apocalyptic emotional state and as reminders of the threat of nuclear war—an especially real danger for Germany, which was a probable first battleground in a war between the United States and the Soviet Union. By signifying both personal neurosis and the international insanity that passed for normalcy, the images of devastation indicate the intricate tessellation of the private and public spheres.[30]

The film then cuts to a scene at a public park. In the background of the shot is a fountain; in the foreground, Ursula lies prostrate, parallel to the picture plane, as a grandmotherly figure with a walker slowly passes "over" her in middle ground and stares at her disapprovingly. Parallel to Herzog's Kaspar Hauser, shown in a similar shot lying horizontal under the "weight" of the black-cloaked father figure who initiates him into the culture, Ursula is depicted as burdened by the weight of the maternal legacy. But while Kasper undergoes a terrible "fall" into language, Ursula experiences a regression into mutism—a highly gendered fall *out* of language and a fallout, the editing suggests, that is as inseparable from the global threat of nuclear fallout as it is from Germany's cataclysmic past.

The girl then sets the lap of her skirt on fire by playing with matches, an "accident" that betokens a confused mix of sexual desire and self-destructiveness. She runs to the fountain, where a black Algerian comes to her aid, douses the fire, and befriends her. A revolutionary, he tells her about the new face of war as it exists in his country and describes, with irony, how "the stupid colored Algerians are chasing the French, who have been so good to them, out of the country." Her Eurocentrism prevents her from immediately grasping his meaning; for her, war is World War II. Sensitive to her unhappiness, he offers her rare moments of emotional connection in a strikingly photographed lakeside setting made lushly surreal by the heightened sounds of birds. But pressuring her by claiming that girls of her age are already married mothers in his culture, he first tries to seduce her and then forces himself on her. Over her protests, he masturbates between her legs as she, ultimately resigned, stares off into space. After spending the night outdoors, Ursula and the Algerian go to the waterside restaurant which appears in the shots that partition the film. There, to Ursula's surprise and profound dismay, the man tells her he is leaving Germany to return to his own country.

For the spectator, whose desire for clear political, cultural, and moral intelligibility is frustrated, the sequence raises vexing questions of response: Is the film succumbing to racist stereotyping? Or is it trivializing a sexual assault by presenting the man so positively? Is one of these more problematic than the other? And why is Brückner taking this risk? Certain things seem clear, however: The Algerian represents a political sphere beyond or outside the cold-war binarisms that the film, to this point, highlights and deconstructs. Marjorie Garber's commentary on the third term—the term that transcends binarisms—is illuminating in this context:

> The so-called "Third World," which was always "there," but was invisible to Cold War myopia except as a potential sphere of influence against the encroachment of the "other" superpower, paradoxically contributed to the lessening of Cold War tensions by becoming more politically and economically visible—by (to use the once popular term) "emerging." The Cold War focus on one "other" was thus rendered both impractical and impossible.[31]

Implicit in the address of this "third" term by *Hunger Years* is a statement on feminism's need not only to deconstruct patriarchal, "First World" political and philosophical binarisms but, concomitantly, to conceive and create a space in between or outside the dualisms of male/female, West/East, white/black, right/left, "democratic"/"communist"—a space of crisis, struggle, and integration in which a complex, sometimes conflicting collection of "others" gains political and economic visibility. Put differently, if section one of the film reveals the necessity for transcendence of the dyadic unity of mother and daughter (without falling prey to feminine self-loathing), section three asserts the urgency for transcendence of the narcissistic patriarchal "economy of the same" that typified cold-war "First World" binarisms. The sequence also demonstrates the need for greater challenges to the sexism that has, historically, generated tensions, such as those experienced in Algeria, between the fight for women's rights and the struggle for national liberation.[32]

The film's concluding sequence returns to a focus on the imprisoning interior space of the home and psyche and reaffirms the need for revolution here, too. After her night out, Ursula faces Gerda, whose angry, punitive gaze epitomizes the mechanism of maternal control in patriarchy's service. Washing her hands of the girl, Gerda leaves for work, while Ursula, desperately alone, once more gazes out the window of the family apartment. In an exchange evocative of *Rear Window*, a woman with binoculars returns Ursula's look from the opposite window and in the process mirrors Ursula's voyeurism and domestic confinement. A variant on the panopticon described by Foucault, the situation presents the warden-spectators simultaneously as the prisoners of their jails. Brückner asserts that the moment is "at once real and surreal."[33]

After closing the window and curtains, Ursula resolves to "bake a cake." Consuming pills, sweets, and whisky, she engages in a voracious suicidal ritual, or so it seems. Then a photograph—a close-up—of Ursula's face appears, creating an edit that recalls and repeats a pattern from the "lost youth" segments in the film's central section. That is, the photograph offers the same kind of visual punctuation for the film as a whole that photographs did for the earlier sequences. The mother, in voice-over, asks why the daughter never said anything and insists that the daughter had everything, didn't she? As a flame eats across the photograph, Brückner's voice-over asserts, "Wer etwas ausrichten will, muss etwas hinrichten—sich selbst" (Whoever would achieve something must destroy something —oneself). As Brückner explained in an interview, Ursula "does not kill herself physically, but kills the images, the false representations that we carry inside ourselves and that choke us."[34] In other words, the "thing" repudiated and destroyed is the alienated image-object, the mode of being for the other, that has been confused with and substituted for an "authentic" identity. More reflexively, the incendiary gesture at film's end protests the consumerist dynamic that makes cinema a technology of image consumption for women in which alienation, in the sense of "sale" or "transfer of property to another" (as in the phrase "inalienable rights"), subtends representations of and for women. Further, the ending decries the vocabulary and syntax of the female face and body, the language that made the woman signify prosperity and fullness of being while denying both the needs of the woman who is freighted with this meaning and the reality of the horrific emptiness of being that Nazi criminality had produced.[35]

The implications and reflexive power of the film's ending become clearer still when we consider how it answers two related reflexive moments from part one—a mirror scene and the "primal scene." These scenes deserve special attention. The first entails a brilliantly conceived shot of Ursula practicing a feminine masquerade: Sitting in front of two mirrors, her body reflected in one on the right, her head framed by a smaller, higher one on the left, she hikes her skirt up, crosses her legs, pulls her socks down, and poses with a cigarette, contemplating her reflections. Her posing is interrupted when the doorbell rings, and the film cuts to a shot of Ursula's face juxtaposed with the comic mask of a pair of comic and tragic masks that hang by the front door of the apartment.

By demonstrating how Ursula "practices" femininity and works to become, in effect, a self-consuming artifact, the scene exposes what commodity fetishism conceals—the anxiety of artifice, the labor and the alienated laborer behind the manufactured "feminine" image, an image which is also fetishized according to the psychoanalytic paradigm, to gratify the male gaze. By depicting the adolescent girl's first efforts at self-surveillance, her divided consciousness, and her disassembled body, the shot also reveals her initiation into a splitting which, according to John Berger, inheres in classical feminine consciousness of self: "The surveyor of woman in herself is male: the surveyed female. Thus she turns into an object—and most particularly an object of vision: a sight."[36] Or, as Doane puts it, "the increasing appeal in the twentieth century to the woman's role as perfect consumer (of commodities as well as images) is indissociable from her positioning *as* a commodity and results in the blurring of the subject/object dichotomy."[37] Accordingly, Ursula constructs the reflections and yet mistakes the images for herself. In order to expose this perceptual blurring, the scene simultaneously figures self-production and consumption, masquerade and narcissism, self-alienation (or distance) and spatial proximity to the image. It both reveals woman's contradictory positioning under patriarchy and generates an engaged yet critical viewing point for its female audience. Female spectatorship within the filmic diegesis comments on nondiegetic spectatorship and heightens critical reflection on the culturally derived contradictions and fragmentation in Ursula's position.

Further, the decapitation that the mirror images create also signals the intrinsic violence of the male gaze that Ursula interiorizes, as well as the violence of the filmic close-up, a shot that the smaller mirror image effectively frames. Analyzing the relationships among the close-up, narcissism, and the commodification of women, Doane explains: "The face, more than any other body part, is *for* the other. . . . And this being-for-the-gaze-of-the-other is, of course, most adequate as a description of the female subject, locked within the mirror of narcissism."[38] Doane's conclusions about filmic uses of women's faces also illuminate the final image of *Hunger Years*—a still close-up in flames—in relation to consumerist dynamics: "It is not at all surprising that the generalized social exchange of women should manifest itself in the cinematic institution as a proliferation of close-ups of the woman."[39] The film's closing image refuses the terms symbolized by the earlier decapitation scene, in which "the goods" (that is, Ursula) are violently self-divided. In other words, the ending adumbrates a time in which "the goods get together," to borrow Luce Irigaray's phrase.[40]

The mirrored reflections that arrest Ursula's gaze also recall Freud's well-known reading of the Medusa's decapitated head as a symbol of the mother's castration. Looking at her body in alienated terms—as male spectator and as feminine masquerade—Ursula is in no position to see what Cixous calls the laugh of the Medusa, a perception that would find all of her body beautiful and recognize the idea of woman's castration/decapitation as utterly laughable. Instead, to use Riviere's words, Ursula sacrifices her own desire in the name of "the acceptance of 'castration,' the humility, the admiration of men" that defines "the conception of womanliness as mask."[41] To be sure, as noted before, Ursula's face is aligned with an apotropaic comic mask present in the mise-en-scène, a positioning that evokes the Lacanian view of sexual masquerade as comic.[42] (Ursula's posing, too, is partly humorous, as is her later peering through the keyhole when her parents have sex.) But the violence implicit in the mirror/decapitation scene creates suffering more aligned with the tragic mask that Ursula's face covers. It also recalls Riviere's view that feminine masquerade is psychically painful. Indeed, the scene fits the broader aesthetics of the film in being neither tragic nor comic but more precisely ironic and melodramatic.

Not surprisingly, the kind of self-alienation coupled with over-identification with the body shown in this double mirror scene has been implicated in studies of both female eating disorders and hysteria. As Noelle Caskey observes,

> It is the literal-mindedness of anorexia to take "the body" as a synonym for "the self," and to try to live in the world through a manipulation of "the body," particularly as it is reflected to the anorexic by the perceived wishes of others. Anorexia is the cultivation of a specific image *as an image*—it is a purely artificial creation and that is why it is admired.[43]

In contrast, the male subject's image—at least as created by mainstream cinema—has been theorized as a mirror of control, uniting body and identity as the basis of discursive authority.[44] What *Hunger Years* reveals is that, for the female, mistaking the body for identity is precisely the problem, an incapacitating dilemma that conventional cinema exacerbates.

Moreover, Ursula's disorderly eating, like that described by Caskey[45] and by popular author Kim Chernin,[46] is grounded in confusion about sexual identity and fear of sexual maturity. The daughter sees the mother as the embodiment of female maturity and associates her with limitation rather than with capability or competence. For Ursula, the mother is associated with complicity with fascism as well. At the same time, Ursula's refusal to take meals with her family on their terms suggests an unconscious political act of resistance. Her eating behavior calls to mind Chernin's assertion that "an eating disorder is a profoundly political act"[47] and, to a lesser extent, it recalls Valie Export's position on the politics of anorexia.[48] Export terms this disorder one of "the great feminine forms of rebellion," because it refuses the feminine body and patriarchal images of that body.[49] While Brückner literally incinerates patriarchal images of the female, she also asserts, "I need the cinema in order to reconstruct my physical person. Women's physical persons have been destroyed by history. Thus, for us, we need the cinema in an urgent fashion."[50] In the film, Gerda's intense antipathy toward her own body demonstrates that female somatophobia is also a patriarchal byproduct that must be refused.

As for Ursula's hysteria, her experience corresponds to Howard Wolowitz's description of the hysteric as someone caught up in a process that "leads further and further away from the self becoming the basis for gratification and experience into a sense of emptiness, experiential deficiency and a wish to regress back into the dependency of early childhood as a haven."[51] Ursula's behavior in the final segment of the film provides vivid images of this kind of retreat; one example is her curling up in a fetal position to suck sweetened milk from a tube. And like Josef Breuer's patient Anna O.,[52] whose hysterical symptoms included disruptive polylingualism, Ursula experiences speech disruption—in this case, mutism and, at one point, feeling more "at home" speaking French when she buys sugar. Analyzing Anna O.'s verbal symptoms, Dianne Hunter has argued that they "may reflect a refusal of the cultural identity inscribed in the order of (coherent) German discourse and an unconscious desire, become conscious in certain contemporary feminist writers, to explode linguistic convention."[53] Ursula's speech disorder signals an analogous refusal—an unconscious rejection of 1950s German identity and of the place of the feminine within it. Moreover, at the conscious level of cinematic utterance, Brückner's film remodels this earlier speech pathology into a strategy of disruption and intervention. Brückner's deconstructive method of including newsreels and photographs, her deliteralizing of the final image of *Hunger Years,* and her use of what Jacqueline Aubenas generally terms the film's "primitive" style[54] all exemplify such strategic disruption. Taking this process a step further, Brückner exposes symptomatically conflicted public discourses by foregrounding how East and West Germany generate politicized and highly contradictory media reports on strikes and civic unrest. Similarly, she underscores the public school's hypocritical doublespeak about the Holocaust. In a sense, then, the girl's hysterical symptoms are metamorphosed into the woman's feminist exposé. Brückner exposes duplicitous public discourses, revealing them to be sites of unresolved conflict, methods of containment, and, as it were, hysterical symptoms produced by repression and denial.[55]

The other reflexive scene already mentioned—a "primal" one from the

film's first section—presents Ursula eating and peering through the keyhole at her parents' intercourse. The scene evokes Freud's mythical originary moment in which hunger and sexuality are united, the root fantasy
of the maternal melodrama, as Linda Williams theorizes this genre.[56] It
recalls as well Metz's theory linking cinema spectatorship with the primal
scene and the founding moment of oedipal identity. Yet the complexly
historicized cultural dynamics within which *Hunger Years* situates this and
its other evocations of the primal scene create crucial differences from
Metz's theory and radicalize the scene's generic implications. Unlike the
purportedly universal cinematic process described by Metz, Brückner's
images of spectacle and spectating are contextualized to foreground hierarchized gender difference and (literal) cultural embeddedness. The parents' relationship is presented as typically troubled—not only by the wife's
sexual shame and the husband's infidelity, but also by the former's paralysis
of body and gaze[57] and by the latter's existence as what Gottfried Benn
termed an "inner emigrant," a man who is there but not there.[58] As an
"inner emigrant," Georg can simply use his wife sexually, despite his genuine capacity for passion and compassion, just as he could simply "go
along," in spite of his better, more socially responsible self, during the
Third Reich and World War II. (And a later scene makes it graphically
clear that Georg does, in fact, just use Gerda to gratify himself sexually,
while Gerda lies there, a silent, passive martyr. She is clearly Ursula's role
model for responding/not responding to the Algerian's sexual advances.)
The primal scene is also evoked through Ursula's repeated mindscreen images of her mother's naked body lying still in the grass, the shadow of a
man with a hat ominously cast across it. Kosta identifies this image as an
allusion to the murderer in Fritz Lang's *M.*[59] This is an apt association
indeed, given the scene's resonance with Brückner's assertion that women's
"physical persons have been destroyed by history."

According to Maria Ramas, the fantasy of the primal scene in which the
child views sex as sado-masochistic "quite simply . . . expresses erotically
the essential meaning of sexual difference in patriarchal culture."[60] Brückner, however, represents this scene and Ursula's reflexive keyhole view of
it not to inscribe the essential meaning of sexual difference but to focalize
the nexus of consumerism, consumption, and consummation within West
German postwar patriarchy. Gerda stands as the film's exemplar of that
pivotal tripartite dynamic. Acting on her mother's advice, she instrumen-

talizes sex, commodifies her body, and uses her physical person as a currency of exchange in order to buy back Georg's loyalty and affection. Sex is the consummation of a deal. At the same time, on the other side of the door, there is Ursula looking through the keyhole, trying to satisfy her own needs through eating, and reluctantly learning the sexual economy. The process is central to her socialization and self-alienation.

Moreover, unlike the spectator described in Metz's theory (who possesses the standard male voyeur's safe distance), Ursula's look through the keyhole signals a disconcerting proximity. This closeness is not presented as the expression of an *essentially* feminine relation to the visual; nor is it conceptualized simply as the result of an adolescent girl's insufficient oedipalization; and neither is it shown to be the consequence of what Thomas Elsaesser interprets as Ursula's desire to identify with her mother.[61] Quite the contrary, Ursula's nearness to what she witnesses, her spectatorial closeness, is depicted above all as the result of a "good girl's" incarceration.[62] Throughout the film, this sequestration is enforced by the patriarchally identified mother's demand that her daughter be someone with whom *she* can identify—a mirror of the kind that Gerda and her sister were required to be for their mother.[63] Ursula's proximity is thus a consequence of having a viable, vital, visually active place in the world otherwise denied her.

In a postwar order that narrows her space and her gaze, the daughter is thus forced to substitute voyeurism and self-surveillance for a look that directly desires and learns. Permitted only to become a woman at a keyhole, a window, or a mirror, she is reduced to apprehending life indirectly and naively. And what the mirror most often reflects back to her is her image reduced to the scope of the close-up—in film, a shot less tied than others to the spatiality and implicit agency of perspectival realism. Thus entombed inside a looking-glass trap, Ursula cannot satisfy her hunger to appropriate her own experience or her need for *Vergangenheitsbewälti- gung*—coming to terms with the past, with Germany's historical relations to "Others." Indeed, as the film reveals, like her spatial world, Ursula's relational world becomes regressively smaller, rather than expanding, as the teenager moves toward physical maturity and womanhood.[64]

Hunger Years as a whole is a profound work of grieving for the losses that coming of age as a woman entailed—not only for the daughter, but also for her mother, and for the opportunities to oppose fascist evil that her mother never seized. It is a work of mourning about the effects of a social gender hierarchy that, ironically, had been theorized as the antidote to authoritarianism and as the appropriate context for *Vergangenheitsbewältigung*. Brückner's film is a remarkable attempt simultaneously to historicize, expose, and transform the cultural terms of the female gaze on which it reflects. The film's incendiary ending aims radically to subvert the retrograde aesthetic, social, and economic functions of cinema and its positioning of women as self-consuming commodities. Brückner's cinematic auto/biography is thus an effort to liberate the film medium itself for the purpose of creating a new conceptual sphere, one that contributes to the construction of a transformative identity politics that serves related German and feminist needs.

Retrieving History

Margarethe von Trotta's

Marianne and Juliane

Trauern, das wird	[Among the various deeds,
zwischen vielerlei Tun	mourning becomes
ein einsames Geschäft.	a lonely business.] [1]

—Ingeborg Bachmann

The recognition that the private sphere, the life of the material body, and the processes of the psyche are political—in other words, that the *personal* is political—was an achievement of the feminist movement that grew out of and, in part, reacted against the student movement of the late 1960s and early 1970s.[2] One of the more important film accounts of these developments, Helke Sander's *The Subjective Factor* (1981), depicts the birth of the West German women's movement within the student movement as a history shaped by women's experiences of subordination. Indeed, while the student movement itself was initially energized by opposition to U.S. imperialism in Vietnam, politics inside this movement still allowed for the retrograde view that a woman's place is in the kitchen. German men's solidarity with oppressed and colonized groups rarely extended across gender lines; in this context, women discovered solidarity with each other. To its credit, the women's movement also developed an approach to women's devaluation that entailed not "either/or" but "both/and" interventionist strategies: in particular, feminists acted *both* to promote women's active, vocal roles in the public arenas that had historically been male preserves *and* to valorize spheres and activities traditionally stereotyped and commonly disparaged as feminine. That is, this response worked both against and within such conventional patriarchal binarisms as public/private or mind/body, and it has been a common thread uniting German, U.S., and other feminist movements. Focusing on the needs of feminist analytic writing but making a point with broader implications, Jonathan Culler further explains how the strategically productive disunity of this "both/and" strategy works:

> the example of deconstruction suggests the importance of working on two fronts at once, even though the result is a contradictory rather than unified movement. Analytic writings that attempt to neutralize the male/female opposition are extremely important, but, as Derrida says, "the hierarchy of the binary opposition always reconstitutes itself," and therefore a movement that asserts the primacy of the oppressed term is strategically indispensable.[3]

Similarly, defining a space, a politics, and an aesthetics that both addressed and confounded the familiar dualisms of self/other, public/private, and avant-garde/mainstream was crucial to the success of Margarethe von Trotta's *Marianne and Juliane* (*Die bleierne Zeit,* "The Leaden Time," 1981). A work of mourning and remembrance that encompasses the years 1945 to 1980, the film bears a German title with an interhistorical reference, simultaneously signifying the grayness of the 1950s and that of the 1970s, the latter a decade when movements for social transformation were met with frustration and disappointment. The film creates an intersubjective space, both between and within individuals, that is the space of memory and mourning, a traditionally feminine activity that the film valorizes as such. It generates a deconstructive politics that confronts both the double standards of and the hidden resemblances between the politics of the private sphere and the politics of the state. (Consequently, it demonstrates that historical accountability requires the reconnoitering of a moral terrain that, like charity, begins at home.) Further, it creates an aesthetics of ambiguity and undecidability that, while partaking of realism's identificatory potentials and melodrama's attention to suffering, is constructed so as to undermine the epistemological and moral certainty that realism and melodrama, as styles of "mass culture," are said to imply. At the same time, its elegiac aesthetics depend upon an affective engagement that becomes a kind of moral imperative.

The qualities that mark von Trotta's *Marianne and Juliane* as a feminist film, distinguishing it from much work by the male auteurs, can be further differentiated through comparison with two male-directed films that treat related topics: Rainer Werner Fassbinder's *The Marriage of Maria Braun* (1979) and Volker Schlöndorff and von Trotta's "collaborative" film, *The Lost Honor of Katharina Blum* (1975).[4] Like Fassbinder—for many, the central figure of the New German Cinema—von Trotta is concerned with the mutual illumination of past and present, with the intersection of public and private, and with the tension between remembering and forgetting. But where Fassbinder avoids an enunciating subject in order to promote a sense of objective historical realism, von Trotta foregrounds an actively remembering female protagonist, who embodies the processes of historical, gendered subjectivity. Whereas Maria Braun can be read allegorically as a figure for the German people, von Trotta's protagonist, the feminist journalist Juliane Klein, is no Germania figure. Instead, she is representative because she comes from a family whose classically oppressive patriarchal structures embody the familial ideals—and hence contradict the democratic principles—publicly endorsed by the postwar West German government. Unlike Fassbinder's specularized female protagonist, von Trotta's appealingly unglamorous Juliane is not naively unaware of the political dimensions of her public and private worlds. A composite fictional character based on Christiane Ensslin (the sister of Baader-Meinhof member Gudrun Ensslin) and on von Trotta herself,[5] Juliane becomes our point of identification for a potent, self-aware encounter with memory, loss, and accountability. Like Olga, the protagonist played by Hanna Schygulla in von Trotta's later film *Sheer Madness,* she is free of the flamboyant, fetishistic accouterments that make several of Fassbinder's heroines fascinatingly fascist and hence "safe" for the classic male spectator. Juliane's distinctness lies not in her "fascination" but in the awful intensity of her commitment to retrieving the truth.[6]

Von Trotta's approach in *Marianne and Juliane* also differs from the one that she and Schlöndorff used in *The Lost Honor of Katharina Blum.* A terrorist romance in an unmediated realist style, *The Lost Honor of Katharina Blum* includes none of the reflexive, deliberately ambiguous, deconstructive strategies that define *Marianne and Juliane*'s shape and deepen its vision. Katharina Blum's reason for getting entangled in terrorism resembles the motivation that Robin Morgan attributes to all women who become associated with terrorist men: because women are, in her view, essentially pacifists, the root of their attraction to "demon terrorists" is not ideology but love.[7] Even though Katharina's political awareness develops beyond anything contained in her initial position, Marianne Klein, Juliane's sister, emerges as a far more complex and ambiguous political figure than Katharina. Marianne is an articulate, action-oriented idealist who endorses violence and who is deeply affected by the Vietnam War, Third World issues, and her country's Nazi past. Our perspectives on her derive from a heterogeneously composed subjective flashback that cannot be reduced to a univocal judgment—and that, hence, cannot form the basis of a simple dismissal or a condoning veneration.

Not surprisingly, the lack of univocality within the film and its direct but complex mode of spectator address are factors that contributed to the film's volatile reception. At the time of the film's release, the vast majority of West German critics attempted to trivialize and dismiss it, with a rancor that recalls their hostility toward *Germany, Pale Mother*. Both receptions are indicative of the power of these films to strike a nerve—very literally, to hit home—with a directness and emotional force that find no clear counterpart in New German films by men, who simply do not attempt to represent the task of mourning with comparable emotional forthrightness. Ironically, Anglo-American promoters of the New German Cinema have often marginalized von Trotta's work in a way that parallels the student movement's subordination of women. Although in the United States von Trotta remains the best known of the contemporary German women filmmakers, studies of the New German Cinema typically treat her as ancillary to her husband, Volker Schlöndorff, with whom she collaborated until she realized that this arrangement—much like the conventional domestic one—placed her in a subordinate position.[8] Thomas Elsaesser, the author of the most detailed history of the New German Cinema to date, discusses von Trotta at greater length but still attempts to classify—and tame—her under the rubric of bourgeois humanist history—specifically that of the German Lutheran Church—even though her concern with the church, like that of Rosenbaum, is clearly subsumed in her feminist praxis.[9]

Partly because of its topical historical basis, *Marianne and Juliane* has received more attention than any other film by von Trotta. At the same time, there has been considerable debate about the success of this work, even as a feminist film. Due to the complex constellation of concerns that shape the film text and its international context of reception, some consideration of the terms of this debate is in order. The controversy stems partly from von Trotta's decision to structure the story from Juliane-Christiane's perspective and not to make the public figure Marianne-Gudrun the protagonist (a choice some saw as a capitulation to the antiterrorist hysteria of the time). In a subjective flashback or mindscreen, Juliane remembers and reflects on her investigation into the suspicious circumstances surrounding Marianne's death in Stammheim prison, where, according to the official story, Marianne hanged herself. Also central to Juliane's thoughts and memories are the sisters' strong connection and competition with each other from childhood through adulthood, their alienation from structures of the dominant culture, and their divergent pursuits of alternative political stances. The reminiscences playing on the screen of her mind span the years 1945–1980 and are bracketed by two episodes involving Jan, Marianne's repeatedly cast-off son—namely, Juliane's initial refusal to take reponsibility for him and her ultimate agreement to tell him what she knows of his mother's life.

The most hostile response to the film's concentration on Juliane comes from Charlotte Delorme. In an influential and error-riddled review for the German feminist journal *Frauen und Film,* Delorme attempts to discredit *Marianne and Juliane* as Christiane's and von Trotta's revenge on Gudrun and therefore as nonfeminist or antifeminist. To that end, Delorme argues that "the film script" states that Marianne-Gudrun leaves her husband for "a better lay." What Delorme fails to say is that this explanation comes from Werner, the husband Marianne left in order to pursue her political vision, and who is hardly presented as an impartial observer. Delorme also claims that Juliane's "willingness to suffer culminates in her own suicide attempts (by choking and by hanging)."[10] The claim is unequivocally false. Juliane performs experiments in an identificatory process aimed at understanding, bodily, what her sister endured when force-fed in prison and when hung from a noose in her cell, but neither effort is presented as a suicide attempt. Delorme also describes a "crummy scene at the end of the film, in which [Juliane] lets the child [Jan] tear up Marianne's picture for her."[11] In fact, although Jan does tear up the picture, he does so against Juliane's wishes. Delorme further claims that the end of the film establishes Juliane's monopoly on the truth about her sister, whereas in fact Juliane emphasizes that her knowledge of Marianne is incomplete. Most importantly, Delorme, like Elsaesser, totally disregards Juliane's quest to disprove that her sister's death was a suicide. While Delorme seeks to discredit the film for supposedly distorting the Ensslins' story, her attempt itself indulges in distortion. Jenifer K. Ward may be correct in suggesting that Delorme's response may in part have been motivated by von Trotta's apparent decision to increase the size of her audience by eschewing a feminist label for her films.[12] Clearly Delorme also wanted a more sympathetic, more differentiated portrait of the woman terrorist.

Marianne and Juliane has been further criticized for its formal strategies and, ironically enough, for supposedly maintaining a public-private split. In Ellen Seiter's view, the film's focus on Juliane-Christiane and its domestic melodrama detract from its feminist potential and evade broader historical issues. The faults Seiter finds with melodrama in her discussion of Sanders-Brahms's *Germany, Pale Mother* accord with those she sees in *Marianne and Juliane*: "Attempts to make a radical melodrama, one that offers a feminist or Marxist critique of the nuclear family, have been hampered by one of the genre's most enduring characteristics: an emphasis on suffering and the failure to understand that suffering in terms of collective rather than individual experience."[13] Moreover, both Elsaesser and Delorme consider von Trotta's reliance on doubling and parallelism politically controversial because it collapses distinctions between opposites. The result, for Elsaesser, is a film that leaves von Trotta open to charges of sympathizing with terrorists.[14] For Delorme, the result is a politically reactionary film that equates the right and the left, reduces Marianne's motivation to a rebellion against her authoritarian father, and establishes a good sister–bad sister contrast pair that vilifies the "radical" Marianne and vindicates the "moderate" Juliane.[15] Finally, E. Ann Kaplan qualifies her general enthusiasm for the film because it "leaves itself open to various, contradictory readings." She also believes that its realist codes are insufficiently critical and reflexive to work as feminist counter-cinema—particularly because, in her view, von Trotta establishes "Juliane as sole master of the discourse" at film's end.[16]

While it is true, as Seiter asserts, that von Trotta uses melodramatic codes to dramatize personal experience, the strategy is congruent with her feminist conviction that engaged spectatorship, private experience, and attention to suffering can themselves be politically meaningful—even crucial to a cinematic inscription of mourning. As I intend to demonstrate, certain reflexive segments of the film that foreground spectator positioning politicize spectatorship in compelling ways. At the same time, because melodramatic codes coexist with other discourses in her film (for example, documentary footage), spectators can both see the limits of melodrama and recognize the political as an integrated vision of the collective and the personal. As for the idea that a film centered on Marianne could have dealt more effectively with broad historical issues, this argument privileges Marianne's nonfeminist radical politics over both Juliane's investigative, historically engaged feminism and her *Trauerarbeit*. In my reading of the film, without vilifying Marianne, von Trotta both criticizes and deconstructs the radical political position Marianne represents.

Responding to Elsaesser and Delorme, I contend that von Trotta's deconstructive strategies function less to equate or to polarize opposites than they do to subvert the binary schemes underlying hierarchic and patriarchal discourse. The resulting ambiguity and the attempts to deal with it through interpretive reductionism—which is very much in evidence in both Elsaesser and Delorme—account in part for the contradictory readings the film has received. To be sure, ambiguity itself may be considered politically suspect. Yet, as Barbara Johnson observes, "It is so not only to the left, but also to the right. Nothing could be more comforting to the established order than the requirement that everything be assigned a clear meaning or stand."[17] Feminism's quarrels with the left and the right are thus potentially well-served by avoiding univocality.

Most importantly, the pervasive presence of ambiguity in the film is crucial to the film's distinct discourse on mourning and abjection. As traditionally theorized in psychoanalysis, mourning replays the early scenes of identity formation, the child's primary processes of grieving for and achieving individuation from the mother. It is thus concerned with exclusion and inclusion, with the separation of the subject from the abject, and by extension, with the defining borders of a society or culture. In her theory of abjection, Julia Kristeva explains that the abject is that which threatens the ego and challenges boundaries, both of the self and of the culture. Ambiguity, the blurring of divisions, typifies the heterogeneous space of the abject: It is "not lack of cleanliness or health that causes abjection but what disturbs identity, system, order. What does not respect borders, positions, rules. The *in between, the ambiguous, the composite*" (my emphasis).[18] Thus, to use a classic example relevant to the film, the conflicts brought into focus by Creon's refusal to grant burial rights and proper mourning to Polynices in Sophocles's *Antigone* center on abjection: on contested borders between genders (including those between the male Olympian and the female Chthonic deities), between the state and its enemies, and between civic and familial identities. As I have already argued, postwar psychoanalytic theory on mourning, focusing exclusively on the male subject, insisted on the need for a sharp severance from the abject maternal in order to avert sociopathology, degenerative melancholy, and the formation of authoritarian, "effeminate" sons. Feminist theories of mourning, in contrast, regard the persistence of the maternal imago in the child's psyche as a positive kernel, a resource for feminine agency and solidarity. Madelon Sprengnether, for example, sets forth an "elegiac" understanding of the ego for whom the pre-oedipal mother is "*both* origin *and* Other" (my emphasis), neither idealized nor erased, and whose presence becomes the basis for a "nonphallocentrically organized view of culture."[19] *Marianne and Juliane* aligns itself with these feminist theories, for it explores and affirms the multiple, composite, intersubjective nature of female identity as a basis for understanding regenerative elegiac experience—both women's and that of the culture as a whole.[20]

Viewed from still another, though closely related, perspective, the implications of ambiguity are also important to the shaping of audience address and narrative structure. Von Trotta's political and narrative strategies of ambiguity create a viable political position because they stress alternative stances toward violence and other forms of political action instead of affirming decisive choices and offering the spectator a secure position. The spectator sees the complexity of each political choice—and with an engagement that is created, in part, through the discourse of melodrama. Such engaged undecidability is intermeshed with an antiessentialist conception of character, a thriller plot whose moment of discovery yields strong doubt rather than conclusive proof, and a narrative built upon subjective flashbacks and repetitive, interreflective structures that promote engagement and identification while precluding both closure and a centralizing perspective. By highlighting the processes of retrieving history—through memory, the cinematic apparatus, and other media(tions)—von Trotta creates a film that is formally and thematically feminist and deconstructive. By representing and opening up for her audience an ambiguous, intersubjective space of mourning, she creates a paradigm of *Trauerarbeit* that stands as a radical alternative to matrophobic psychoanalytic theories on loss.

The protagonist of the film, Juliane Klein (played by Jutta Lampe), is a woman who places her desire to gain knowledge about her sister, Marianne (Barbara Sukowa), and herself over a long-standing relationship with her liberal and caring but uncomprehending companion, Wolfgang (Rüdiger Vogler). Juliane eventually chooses to take in her sister's tortured son, Jan, and agrees to tell him about his mother's life. Like von Trotta's *The Second Awakening of Christa Klages* and *Sheer Madness, Marianne and Juliane* uses an ambiguous flashback-framing structure. The opening and final scenes appear to take place in the film's present, perhaps on the same day. They bracket Juliane's memories, showing how she comes to terms with her sister's life, with her own past, and with issues of sororal and maternal bonding and differentiation. Flashbacks portray what she remembers. In particular, they trace the sisters' childhood and teenage experiences in a classically patriarchal, strict authoritarian household headed by a protestant minister during the 1950s, a time that repressed the Nazi era—hence, von Trotta has explained, the "leaden time" of the German title, *Die bleierne Zeit*.[21] Editing underscores parallels between self and other, past and present, private and public. Scenes emphasizing various media (documentary film footage, journalism, television, prison microphones and visitation windows) provide frequent reminders of how cultural apparatuses work to reveal and to repress experience.

From the outset, the film focuses on the process of reconstructing history. The first scene, which appears to be chronologically penultimate, is part of a larger frame.[22] In the opening shot, the camera gives a view from a divided window, then pulls back to contrast the bright light of the outdoors with the relative darkness of the interior in which Juliane moves. Accompanying the scene are the disquieting sounds of Juliane's pacing

8. Margarethe von Trotta (*left*), with Jutta Lampe (Juliane, *center*) and Barbara Sukowa (Marianne). (Photo courtesy of New Yorker Films.)

footsteps and, later, of atonal music. The disjunction between the initially stationary view out the window and the interiority of Juliane's movement and thought—she never once looks out—suggests not only the coexistence of outer and inner, conscious and unconscious "realities" but also, above all, Juliane's state of engaged indecision, a state or position in which the film comes to place the spectator as well. The divided window seems neither to suggest the transparent "window on the world" of an unreflexive realist style nor Juliane's subjective view. The impossibility of placing this scene exactly in the diegesis of the film distinguishes *Marianne and Juliane* from classic realist cinema, in which, as Peter Wollen explains, "everything shown belongs to the same world, and complex articulations within that world—such as flashbacks—are carefully signalled and located."[23]

   As the camera pans over rows of Juliane's dated files on crowded shelves, then follows her gaze to a black-and-white police photograph of Marianne, the focal point of Juliane's inquiries is indicated more clearly: it is, namely, to learn the truth about her sister. The distant expression seen in the photograph matches the subject's distance in space and time—Marianne is dead at this point, as the file, dated 1980, comes to make clear. Yet her absence is a palpable presence, a haunting lack that Juliane finds in herself and feels compelled to address.

From the photograph of Marianne in Juliane's study, the film cuts to a view out the back window of a moving car, evocative of a view on an unfolding past, thus reinforcing the mindscreen structure, as well as a feeling of change and instability. The person looking out the window is Jan, Marianne's son, who is about to be abandoned by his father, Werner, to an unwilling Juliane. It is, moreover, to the first three characters introduced in the film—Jan, Juliane, and Marianne (the last shown in a photograph)—that the narrative returns at film's end, completing its trajectory. In this last scene, Jan is in a rage against his mother; having been shuffled from home to home and burned in a hideous attack motivated by her politics, and having heard that she "threw bombs," he angrily tears her picture in half, consigning it to the trash. Juliane tells him, "You are wrong. Your mother was an extraordinary woman. Don't you believe me?" When he shakes his head, she offers to tell him all that she knows of Marianne's story—which, by her own admission, "is surely not all." Accompanied by the unsettling music repeated from the film's first scene, Jan twice harshly commands, "Begin!" (*"Fang an!"*), as the film points us back to its own beginning, to the story Juliane tells. A final freeze-frame close-up of Juliane's face and the reappearance of the film's title conclude the film.

Marianne and Juliane's self-referential frame heightens the disruptions of narrative linearity and the gaps and fissures that riddle the film. Just as the frame emphasizes the film as a construction, providing a crucial context for interpretation, so it also foregrounds the matched processes of Juliane's memory and the unfolding of the story. By freely and, it would seem, randomly incorporating smaller subjective flashbacks within the one signaled by the frame, the film conforms further to the rhythms of memory, its editing indicating—often subtly, at times more obviously—the complex connections that run through familial and social, private and public patriarchal economies. The frame signals, too, the fact that retrieving history and accepting the mother who has been denied are intertwined, certainly for Jan and, in another sense, for Juliane as well.

As the interior flashbacks to the mid-1950s reveal, Juliane's mindfulness of the past has a distinctly feminist coloration even during her teenage experiences, which show her concern with remembering repressed history and with the history of the repressed. As an adolescent wearing "black jeans" (and thus identifying with American modes of youthful rebellion),[24] Juliane rejects classroom study of Rilke's "Autumn Day," which she considers evasive kitsch, and argues instead for Brecht's "Ballad of the Jewish Whore," a poem about a German woman who is paraded in the streets with her head shaved as punishment for loving a Jewish man, or for Paul Celan's "Death Fugue," a poem about the concentration camps. Celan's refrain—"Your golden hair, Margarete, / Your ashen hair, Shulamith,"— implies the kind of sisterhood between apparent opposites that figures importantly in von Trotta's work.

This concern with women under Nazism reappears in stronger form when the adult Juliane, doing research for a feminist journal, is shown assembling a narrative to accompany photographs of mothers in the fatherland; the narrative she tapes explains that prolific mothers were awarded the Cross of Honor and that these women were both victimized and complicitous. The resultant attitude toward them is neither condoning nor compassionless. Their status constitutes one of the many ambiguities in the film. Juliane's work toward repealing an antiabortion act reflects her opposition to contemporary government regulation of women's bodies and highlights her awareness that motherhood and childhood are still regarded as the province of the patriarchal state, which currently cares more for the unborn than for the unwanted. These issues also have immediate importance for Juliane. Werner's suicide and Marianne's refusal to let motherhood interfere with her political work mean that Juliane, who also chooses not to mother, must perform the difficult task of finding adoptive parents for Werner and Marianne's child, who is now too old to be considered by most would-be parents. (Werner is, as Juliane's friend Sabine observes, an orphan who orphans his own son, while Marianne "gives up her child to save so-called humankind." Thus Sabine points to the contradiction inherent in both parents' choices).[25]

Juliane's most demanding research is her effort to disprove the state's claim that Marianne committed suicide and, concomitantly, to understand Marianne in the context both of the family's history and of German history broadly conceived. The film communicates the centrality of these concerns from the outset, its opening mise-en-scène defined by the police photograph of Marianne and by bookshelves crowded with the evidence Juliane has amassed. Discussing Gudrun Ensslin's death, von Trotta has explained in an interview that "[a]fter the death of Ulrike Meinhof and the death of the three Stammheim prisoners it was quickly asserted, despite contradictory evidence in the findings of the investigation, that it was a case of suicide. Questions were not even admitted." [26] Von Trotta's film strongly undermines this official version of events. In particular, it shows Juliane testing to see whether the electric-cord arrangement Marianne allegedly used in hanging herself would support a weighted model of the body. When the model quickly falls to the floor, the film's thriller plot comes to a climax. While Juliane's test casts strong doubt on the government's account of Marianne's death (without absolutely proving a cover-up for murder), the contradictions and ambiguities in the state's position and methods are nonetheless essential for Juliane as she attempts to deal with the past and to reconfigure her sororal relationship with Marianne. The conflicting evidence is also crucial for Jan, an innocent victim of anti-terrorist hysteria and a potential victim, as well, of his own ignorance of his mother. Indeed, Jan's act of tearing and discarding the photograph of his mother paradoxically reproduces her in her belief that, by choosing direct, violent action, "[y]ou can shed your past," a belief that she thought she proved. [27]

In a broader sense, too, Juliane's attempts to understand Marianne uncover ambiguity and contradiction rather than the kind of "simple truth" that enables a condemnatory withdrawal of affect or a falsely idealized retrospective view. For while Marianne's political allegiances move her to the margins of society, the film's imagery and flashbacks simultaneously affiliate her with traditions and problematics that are central to her culture. This affiliation is established from her first appearance, when Juliane goes to meet her at a museum, and Marianne contemptuously dismisses her sister's feminism and also claims that she has "no time to mourn" Werner's death. As Barbara Koenig Quart observes:

> The long row of grand statuary busts that lines Juliane's route to Marianne [is] like a florid wreckage of the grand German past, pa-

9. Marianne, who has "no time to mourn," becomes the subject of Juliane's profound work of *Trauerarbeit*. (Barbara Sukowa in *Marianne and Juliane*. Photo courtesy of New Yorker Films.)

triarchs on pillars, all jammed together, at the end of which we so dramatically first see Marianne's extraordinarily intense face, those figures seeming visibly to lead directly to her, she the product of them, like a wild avenging angel.[28]

The flashbacks place Marianne strongly within her liberal Lutheran family and the cultural traditions it maintains: as a teenager, she plays classical music on the cello, yearns to emulate Albert Schweitzer, and willingly gives Rilke his due when Juliane disparages him. Within the family, Marianne is her father's favorite, and at one point she sits on his lap to try to mollify him and soften his dictatorial stance toward Juliane. By cutting from the brick wall of Marianne's first prison to the wall bordering the yard where the young girls play, the film subtly connects state and traditional familial restrictions of freedom.

Yet traditional restrictions also mark the main image of Marianne with her male terrorist cohorts. When she and her two comrades pay their 3:00 A.M. visit to Juliane and Wolfgang's apartment and decide to drink coffee in the kitchen, it is Marianne who stands and both makes and serves the coffee, while the men sit and are served. Static long takes, reminiscent of *Jeanne Dielman,* reveal Marianne's activities in real time and thus underscore the typicality of these roles. Though Kaplan correctly notes the similarity in dress among Marianne and her comrades in this scene, she is incorrect in saying that "Marianne's gender is undifferentiated from that of her comrades, suggesting erasure of the feminine in terrorism."[29] On the contrary, the scene provides an ironic commentary on the notion that terrorist men willingly assume domestic responsibilities, a view Marianne expresses in the segment immediately preceding the 3:00 A.M. visit—that is, in the sequence dramatizing an exuberant letter she has written to Juliane from Beirut. Both the editing and the home-movie cinematography in this segment reinforce the irony.

Although Marianne believes, as do some critics, that she has jettisoned her girlhood identity and reversed positions with her sister to become the more rebellious of the two, she remains less radical than Juliane in several important ways. Her participation in an organization that perpetuates gender-based divisions of labor, her commitment to violent action, and her dissociation of the personal (parenthood) from the political (active concern for Third World children) all link her with the status quo under patriarchy. Terrorist organizations, like both the traditional left and the student movement of the 1960s and 1970s from which they grew, tended to disregard the importance of women's issues, and Marianne's ideological arguments with Juliane reflect this disregard. Conversely, Juliane's less spectacular, less simplified feminist commitments and engagements are coupled with an ability that von Trotta's Christa Klages had earlier acquired—the ability to wait. Such qualities sustain the tenacious resistance to patriarchal repression shown in her youth, simultaneously reminding us of the tenacity of feminism itself, which has endured despite some premature pronouncements of its kidnapping and demise.

The personal price Juliane pays for knowledge about her sister and about the circumstances of her death is, as has often been noted, extremely high. Kaplan asserts:

> Wanting to know exactly what Marianne went through, and suspecting murder, Juliane absorbs herself totally in reenacting Marianne's death. Ironically, she becomes as fanatical as was her sister as a terrorist. Through her obsession, she loses her (nearly ideal) lover, Wolfgang, on whom she had hitherto depended for a sort of fatherly love and protection and to support a rather fragile identity.[30]

One reason audiences feel this loss acutely is that the film actualizes codes of domestic melodrama, codes that promote engaged spectatorship and emphasize disproportions in power. As Seiter explains, the film's emphasis on emotion, suffering, and domestic spaces accords with melodramatic conventions.[31]

But von Trotta also examines melodramatic codes critically and thwarts expectations built on them. In cooking and caring for Juliane and giving her emotional support, Wolfgang exemplifies the strong, nurturing man who is an important type in certain domestic melodramas, similar to Ron Kirby in Douglas Sirk's *All that Heaven Allows*;[32] yet Wolfgang, while used to indict this convention, is partly indicted by it as well. That is, unlike Ron Kirby, Wolfgang proves not to be the answer to the protagonist's problems; and unlike the presumed audience of melodrama, he exhibits a perspective on suffering that is problematic in its detachment. When he appears, along with Marianne and Juliane, in a 1968 audience viewing *Far From Vietnam*, his reaction suggests an underidentification with the events on screen, for the film seems to have no subsequent impact on him. (In contrast, Marianne says, "I'll never agree that nothing can be done about that." Both she and her sister are visibly moved and presumably politicized by the experience.) Although, some years later, he is interested in attending public lectures by Peter Schneider, a radical leftist author who speaks for the student movement, Wolfgang has little understanding of or empathy with Juliane's political-personal need to discover the truth about Marianne, her need rightly to honor the dead. One of his attempts to engage Juliane in a "serious discussion" about Marianne is played out while he watches a soccer match on TV (here, he is an engaged spectator).[33] A later discussion culminates in his striking Juliane when she tells him that she would risk their relationship to learn the truth about her sister. Comfortable with the kind of *Gemütlichkeit* he creates, and with liberal gestures, he understands neither the importance of learning how Marianne died nor the basis of Juliane's need to know. And "in the end," von Trotta says of this film, "the theme [is] that there are only a few people who want to know the truth."[34]

While relative comfort with the status quo partly explains this general indifference to truth and the address of loss, another reason lies in the cultural apparatuses by which information is commodified and conveyed. In *Marianne and Juliane* these media systems are personified by the male journalist whom Juliane asks to publicize her evidence about the ambiguities surrounding her sister's hanging. Embodying the capitalist patriarchal order as well as "decade-think," he dismisses Juliane's information as "strictly seventies stuff." When she cites Marianne's concern about Third World issues as consistent with what is newsworthy, he remains unpersuaded. What is no longer new, he explains, gets consigned to the *"Misthaufen der Geschichte"* ("the dungheap of history"). Thus truth-value is reduced to what sells, and all that has currency is the absolutely current.

But another complication affects the construction and communication of historical truth. During a screening of Alain Resnais's 1955 documentary *Night and Fog* at Marianne and Juliane's school, their father, Pastor Klein, is shown standing beside the projector in two separate shots, controlling the cinematic apparatus and taking charge of the students' moral education. That he perceives his own position as unassailable is suggested by his surveillance of the spectators, over whom he is "keeping watch"—a phrase borrowed from *Night and Fog*—and whom he seems to watch more intently than he does the film. Klein aligns himself with Resnais in standing by the projector but distances himself from the film experience per se; we see little or no personal engagement on his part. The distance he maintains between public and private concerns is congruent with his domineering, authoritarian role in his own household, one backed by a barely contained threat of physical violence. In other words, though his educational intent is admirable, Klein embodies contradictions in the postwar patriarchy's dissociation of the personal and the political, contradictions made possible by a disproportionate distribution of power. This disproportionate distribution undermines the capacity of cultural apparatuses to transcend the violence they may condemn—as well as the patriarchy's ability to express appropriate affective responses to the suffering of the victims of aggression. (Ironically, it should be noted, the dissociation of the personal and the political persists in the reception of von Trotta's film. Elsaesser argues, "Personalizing conflicts as von Trotta does always entails a reduction of the political and social to psychological categories."[35] In this regard, he could hardly be more wrong.)

Further, the screening of *Night and Fog* suggests that coming to terms with the Nazi past is a different experience for women than it is for the men who control the dominant discourses involved in the process. In part, as the scene implies, gender-related differences in spectatorship account for disparities in male and female perceptions of filmed documents of the past. More subtly, in the scenes that bracket the screening, the sisters' references to Celan's "Death Fugue" and Brecht's "Jewish Whore" create a context for viewers' understanding of the gender-specific and dubious ways in which men's cultural products have defined women's guilt. *Night and Fog* shows victims of the Holocaust, whom the Nazi regime dehumanized and cast off as abject, in Kristeva's sense of the word; one scene included in *Marianne and Juliane* also shows women guards dressed in German uniforms being specially paraded, in effect, ritually displayed in a process that distinctly genders their guilt and problematically politicizes their gender.

The morally problematic treatment of women's guilt in Resnais's film is underscored by the adolescent sisters' presence in the audience, and their physical reaction to the screening is consonant with its definition of women's relationship to the past as bodily. In particular, Marianne vomits, as if expelling the "embodied" guilt the film implicated within her. (Not by chance, the next scene in *Marianne and Juliane* shows the imprisoned, emaciated Marianne on a hunger strike, trying to remember the poems the sisters shared as teenagers, as if emaciation and moral bearings intersected for her.) Through this segment of the film, then, von Trotta subtly exposes the biases shared by both fascist and antifascist patriarchal ideologies as they have defined and shaped women's guilt and moral development by repudiating women's bodies.

Von Trotta shows the dangers of repeating and perpetuating what one should oppose on the basis not only of content or ideology, as in the segment just discussed, but also of aesthetics. If one agrees with Mary Ann

Doane that the "simple gesture of directing a camera toward a woman has become equivalent to a terrorist act,"[36] then the risks von Trotta faced in making her film were insurmountable. In Delorme's view, the film's cinematography fails: "The camera is voyeuristic and spiteful," she avows.[37] I disagree. The film is antiterrorist in its treatment of those film staples sex and violence. It subordinates the terrorist theme, a natural for Hollywood suspense and mayhem, to Juliane's acts of remembrance. In focusing on the less spectacular story, von Trotta rejects the hierarchy of values that assigns more importance to Marianne's activism than to the kind of life Juliane has chosen.

Insofar as Juliane and the film's audience witness what might be called terrorism (a word the film avoids entirely), they witness its victims: the indelible images of the inmates of the Nazi death camps in *Night and Fog*; the images of children seared with napalm in the United States' undeclared war in Southeast Asia; Marianne, who is utterly isolated in prison and ultimately hanged; and Jan, who is burned horribly by anonymous agents.[38] Like most German films dealing with terrorism, this one deconstructs the difference between state-sponsored and antistate terrorist activities, not insisting on their identity but, rather, exposing the slippery ground of boundaries. Instead of attempting an airtight definition of terrorism, this film interrogates positions on violence, whether emotional or physical, familial or public, state-sanctioned or oppositional. Like Pudovkin's political melodrama *Mother*, the film connects figurations of collective and individual suffering, juxtaposing the two without necessarily equating them, as in the transition from images of Auschwitz to those of a red-eyed, drawn Marianne in prison. And like that film, it promotes audience identification and empathy.

Von Trotta's cinematography also condemns the violence that pervades the culture's invasive specularization of women's lives and bodies. When Juliane is shown being strip-searched at her first attempt to visit her sister, her objections to this treatment make clear that the state prison system perpetuates the negation of the private self. That is, her objections underscore how the state politicizes the personal. At the first prison where Marianne is incarcerated, her meetings with Juliane are always in the presence of male and female guards and observers, who violate the sisters' privacy and sometimes respond with sadistic pleasure when the two quarrel. This voyeuristic audience forms part of the surveillance apparatus that operates

10. Under the surveillance of prison guards, Juliane visits Marianne in prison. (Jutta Lampe [*left*] and Barbara Sukowa in *Marianne and Juliane*. Photo courtesy of New Yorker Films.)

outside the prison walls as well as within. It is an apparatus that, like the films within the film, makes *Marianne and Juliane*'s viewers conscious of their own spectatorial positions. Juliane responds to the surveillance by angrily confronting two men in a car who have been spying on her movements even after Marianne's arrest.

To be sure, being spied on is by no means an experience limited to women. The West German government's overreaction to terrorism laid the groundwork for the kind of sadistic voyeurism von Trotta represents, and as her film portrays it, this voyeurism is repugnantly reminiscent of Nazi surveillance, which had aimed to create a sense of its ubiquitous, inescapable presence in everyone's lives. Von Trotta's film demonstrates throughout, however, that the position of being a sight, governed by the patriarchal gaze, has also had culturally distinct, historically protracted meanings for women, and it makes the audience revel in such acts of resistance to the usual terms of that position as Juliane's protest against the men in the car, her wearing black jeans as a teenager in defiance of her school's and her father's dress codes, and her dancing alone at a school dance on a dare. Juliane and Marianne's exuberant, conspiratorial exchange of their white and black pullovers under the gazes of the dumbfounded prison guards is an equally memorable act of rebellion—and a sleight of hand that enables a forbidden note to be passed between them.

While the prison surveillance system is presented as a voyeuristic intrusion, the sisters' prison meetings paradoxically promote an intersubjectivity that lays the ground for Juliane's most interiorized self-reflection in relation to history—the self-reflection that evolves from processes of bonding and identity formation. Von Trotta provides an utterly haunting image of this bonding during the sisters' last prison visit—in a second, modernized institution (Stammheim), not long before Marianne's death: the sisters are divided from each other by a double-paned window, with Marianne's face appearing from the prisoner's side while Juliane's face is reflected in the glass on the visitor's side. For a moment, as Juliane shifts positions, their faces merge, evoking, with a difference, Bergman's fusion of the two women's faces in *Persona*. Kaplan suggests that the mirror imagery of this scene contributes to the film's development of patterns of pre-oedipal, female-female bonding, patterns reinforced in part by the film's criticism of Pastor Klein.[39] Indeed, the sisters' bonding emerges as a crucial part of Juliane's coming to terms with Marianne's life and her reconfiguration of her own past and identity.

The allusion to *Persona* is also critical to the film's concepts of mourning and sisterhood. Paul Coates's insights provide an especially instructive point of departure here. As he attests, *Marianne and Juliane* "includes both homage to and implicit critique of [*Persona*]."[40] Specifically, while Bergman's fusion of two half-faces creates "a single monstrous one with the sovereignty with which men have always manipulated the images of women," the melding of faces into a single composite one in *Marianne and Juliane* reflects an identification that "*mobilizes*" (Coates's italics).[41] Because both are composite, indeterminate images that blur the boundaries of the self, both can be seen as variations of what Kristeva calls the abject. But the former is a monstrous symbol of maternal malevolence, seen from the perspective of the artist as a young boy, while the latter is a reflection of the solidarity and multiplicity between and within women, whose necessary internalization of the maternal imago is reiterated in the daughter's identification and solidarity with other women—her sisters.[42] These contrasting images have important implications for the conceptualization of mourning. As Coates astutely explains, *Persona* might well have been subtitled "the inability to mourn," and in this regard it differs from von Trotta's film, which he rightly praises as a successful work of mourning. What Coates overlooks, however, is that *Marianne and Juliane* contradicts not only the terms of mourning established in *Persona* but also those of the Mitscherlichs' *The Inability to Mourn*. That is, even as von Trotta's film bears a special kinship to the 1967 German study and to the 1966 Swedish film, it pointedly refuses a conceptualization of mourning grounded in the conjoined fears of feminization and infantilization, fears that shape those earlier works. (In the Mitscherlichs' theory, these anxieties are reflected in the positioning of the so-called effeminate, underoedipalized, mother-dominated son as the classic proto-fascist; in Bergman's film, as Coates observes, the director expresses the dread that "the male artist's status may be reduced either through feminization, or through diminution to childhood.")[43] Very unlike these two works, *Marianne and Juliane* imagines the intersubjective space of women who are literally and metaphorically sisters as a potential space of culturally regenerative mourning, mobilization, and opposition to phallocentric concepts of culture. Missing the full scope of this reconceptualization, Coates points to the role that is played in *Marianne and Juliane* by "the father's willingness to confront his German daughters with a foreign view of the atrocities of war."[44] This formulation simultaneously evades and leaves in doubt the question of the father's own willingness to confront this foreign view. It overlooks his detachment from images of his nation's past, his overoedipalization, if you will. As we have seen, however, the film presents Pastor Klein's overseeing gaze in critical terms, contrasting it with the gaze of the sisters whom he instructs and whose chastening, enabling engagement with what they see on the screen finds its analogue in the later image of their melded faces. This image, too, shapes what is in effect the film's acknowledgment and contradiction not only of the Mitscherlichs' theory but also of classical psychoanalysis.

The film expands its imagery of mirroring and identification between the sisters in several ways. Their similar-sounding names illustrate this dilation, as does their closeness in age (and the internal rhyme of Jan and Juliane's names, of course, furthers the pattern). The sisters' exchange of sweaters in the prison scene and their shared memory of the identical undershirts they buttoned for each other as children, "even when we hated each other," are subtler, visual reinforcements of connection. So too is Marianne's dyeing her hair dark, creating in her underground disguise a stronger visual resemblance to Juliane. (Marianne also goes by the name Chris when in disguise, linking her with Christiane Ensslin, the woman on whose life Juliane's character is based.) A statement Werner makes to Juliane early on also supports the concept of bonding: "Marianne's ideas are in all of us, but we are either too rational or too afraid to act on them." In coming to the point where Marianne is no longer a threatening Other but is instead part of a composite, communal identity, Juliane incorporates some version of Werner's insight.

Not only does the film expand these images of intersubjectivity, it also uses them as the foundation of its resistance to and critique of the law of the father, manifest in the controlling apparatuses of church and state. For example, after the last prison visit, with its image of the women's merged faces, the sisters are not shown together again until Marianne is in her coffin, her face terribly and grotesquely distorted. The chilling scene is set in a nearly vacant cemetery chapel, where four armed guards with police dogs keep surveillance over Juliane, her parents, and Wolfgang. Hysterical with grief upon seeing her sister, Juliane is taken away in an ambulance, sobbing, "There will never be another face like that one," and, "I have to carry on, for her."[45] In the expressionistic nightmare sequence that follows, Juliane sees herself and her sister together as young children, facing their father in his pulpit as he towers over them in an extreme low-angle shot, looking down and gesticulating furiously. Behind him is a copy of the Grünewald painting of the Crucifixion; the small girls appear in their undershirts, the recurring childhood symbol of connection between them. Bathed in red light, the scene suggests the father's frenzied, heartless tyranny and the daughters' abject sense of guilt, but also a potent kernel of sororal solidarity and resistance.

As already noted, Juliane's close identification with Marianne mobilizes her. In the scene that comes after this dream sequence, she ascends the stairs of a large municipal building to consult the lawyer who had represented her sister. Her attempt to prove that Marianne was murdered begins here and ultimately becomes so consuming that it endows Juliane with the stature and ambiguity of a Sophoclean hero—a comparison invited by her relentless pursuit of truth, despite commonsense warnings from those around her, and by her search for answers that illuminate the intertwined identities of the individual and the state. In her allegiance to a dead sibling who has been deemed an enemy of the state, she resembles Antigone, with the significant difference that Juliane's allegiance is sororal. In her sacrifice of her own "marriage" to give honors to the dead, she also resembles Oedipus's daughter, who forfeits marriage to Haemon. And in taking up Marianne's cause when she is beyond the pale, Juliane resembles Ismene, who comes to revere the claims of sisterhood over those of patriarchal law. (In fact, von Trotta worked with Schlöndorff and Kluge on a segment of *Germany in Autumn* that draws strong parallels between Antigone and events surrounding the burials of the Red Army Faction members, and it was during this collaboration that she met Christiane Ensslin.) [46]

Juliane, moreover, embraces the abject—not only the dead "enemy" cast outside the "city's walls," but Marianne's repeatedly cast-off son. By doing so, Juliane also in some measure embraces the maternal, that ultimate image of multiplicity,[47] and a role she is at odds with at the beginning of the film. Her change of attitude is subtly foreshadowed in the second half of the film by her increased sense of intimacy with her own mother. The mother becomes more curious about her daughters as she grows more distant from her husband—"the Egoist," as she now calls him. The change is also presaged by Juliane's extended bonding with her sister, by her empathy for Marianne and for Jan's suffering, and by her continuing aloofness from Marianne's depersonalized politics. Since the opening scenes make the societal position of unwanted children an important issue, Juliane's ultimate acceptance of Jan and her efforts to aid him in accepting and knowing Marianne help to complete the trajectory of the film.[48] More broadly, her acceptance figures a bonding with all the film's images of abjection.

Finally, as for Jan himself, the film conceptualizes the process of mourning as one that requires his reconciliation with the "monstrous" mother (through the agency of her double, her surrogate) in order for a release from the vicious circles of fascist violence to be effected, the trap sprung, the curse overcome. In this film, the formula of the supposedly "dominant" mother and the "weak" or "absent" father that was seen by postwar psychosocial theorists as the recipe for authoritarian aberration, ultimately forms instead the only grounds for a genuine coming to terms with the family's and the nation's past. In other words, it is the unconventional, contingent, matrifocal family of Jan and Juliane that holds out—not the threat of the reproduction of a narcissistic regression, but the promise that the transformative and therapeutic powers created by Juliane's ability to mourn may bear fruit. (And though the classical patriarchal family does not emerge as a sufficient or precipitating cause of public terrorist violence, the film does identify it as an underlying one.)

If Jan is also a metaphor for his generation, or more broadly for post-war Germany,[49] then Juliane's care for and exemplary guidance of the boy would also seem a paradigm of women's larger potential roles in enabling the culture to remember, grieve, and evolve. The woman's isolation comments critically on the continued lack of shared communal contexts for mourning—indeed, on the culture's virtual abjection of mourning as weak and unmanly.[50] But the screening of her story as a history retold for Jan, for the film's audience, and for Juliane herself has the power to activate our desire to work toward the creation of an alternative, more emotionally developed public sphere, one that will be more responsive to women as complex subjects and more accepting of traditionally feminine ritual functions as they can enable the culture more productively to reconfigure its relationship to its problematic past. Toward this end, the film powerfully enjoins us to begin.

The Autoethnographic Aesthetic of Jeanine Meerapfel's *Malou*

> Habitudinization devours work, clothes, furniture, one's wife, and the fear of war. . . . The technique of art is to make objects "unfamiliar," to make forms difficult, to increase the difficulty and length of perception. —Victor Shklovsky[1]

Under the influence of the Russian formalists, mediated through Brecht, many German filmmakers and film theorists have regarded nondistanciated aesthetics as suspect. Seeking to avoid the emotional immersion that characterizes spectator positioning in fascist cinema on the one hand and mass-produced Hollywood movies—especially the "woman's film"—on the other, these filmmakers and theorists have developed and endorsed alternative strategies of audience address. Marianne Rosenbaum's *Peppermint Peace*, for example, uses a combination of tinted footage, radical camera angles, distorting lenses, and child's-eye perspectives to defamiliarize the fear of war, in accordance with Victor Shklovsky's account of artistic technique. The film offers one instance among numerous feminist uses of Russian formalism, in this case conjoined with deconstructive humor.[2] Yet Shklovsky's assumption that the reader, like himself, has a wife, tips us off to the alterations required for this sort of feminist appropriation. Not only does his assumption illustrate what Page duBois calls "the male narcissism of traditional scholarship"—a cultural context which depresses the status of women's speech and engenders the "scandal of women speaking"[3]—it also points toward the submerged story of the wife as *subject*, eaten alive by habitudinization, in a telling reversal of the *vagina dentata* myth.

Jeanine Meerapfel's autobiographical film *Malou* (1980), her first feature, stages the "scandal of women speaking" and the story of a woman devoured by habitudinization. *Malou* does so not by using the defamiliarizing techniques common to much New German Cinema, but instead by adopting an intimate, warm, lyrical, largely non-distanciated style. As a result, though the film is often mentioned along with other autobiographical feminist films of the early 1980s, it is nearly as often set off from them, as from New German Cinema generally.[4] Not surprisingly, *Malou*'s emotionally engaged acts of remembrance and its close-up look at the intersections and tensions between private lives and public history have been negatively stereotyped as feminine. For example, when the film was released, one reviewer pejoratively deemed it "ein Frauenfilm ganz und gar" (a woman's film through and through). The reviewer also took exception to what he termed its "strangely peripheral understanding of history."[5] The film's eccentricity, in this view, stems not just from its emotionalism, but also from its director's supposedly having *read* so little of the history of the time—a familiar phallogocentric privileging of written historical texts over discursively peripheral, often oral narratives of feminine experience. For her part, Meerapfel explains that her aesthetic choices are motivated by her fear that women are becoming *an*aesthetized, too distanced from themselves—in her words, "are becoming hard, picking up the worst from men in order to make it in their world . . . we lose a sensitivity to ourselves."[6] Her film's eccentricity is, moreover, tied to her rich, complex heritage as an Argentine-born, part French, part German-Jewish woman with a Catholic, working-class mother and cultured, haut bourgeois father. It stems as well from her contemporary experience of estrangement in Berlin—literally being outside the circle—during the present-tense time frame represented in the film. This chapter examines Meerapfel's autoethnographic aesthetic in its interrelated multicultural, gynocentric, and emotionally engaged dimensions. Simultaneously, the chapter suggests how *Malou*'s acts of remembrance productively dilate and breach certain norms of the New German Cinema.

In *Malou,* desire for proximity to the image is a diegetic and thematic element, as well as a defining aesthetic quality. Named after the mother it seeks to recollect, the film tells the story of Hannah (Grischa Huber), Meerapfel's tall, slim, dark-haired surrogate, and is organized around her flashback memories and fantasies of her dead mother, Malou (Ingrid Caven, in a highly gestural performance), a petite, blonde-haired, doll-like woman whose life spans the years 1905–1967. Malou is initially presented as a Strasbourg-based maid turned nightclub *chanteuse.* Her accounts of her own past vary: at one point she claims that she grew up in a circus tent and that her mother was a contortionist who died, along with Malou's father, doing a trapeze act; at another, Malou explains that she grew up with an aunt on a farm in Provence. Her adult life revolves around the men whom she attracts.

A devout French Catholic, Malou meets and marries Paul Kahn, a prosperous German-Jewish businessman (Ivan Desny), in 1932. She struggles to learn his language, converts to his religion, and lives with his wealthy, elegant, politically aware family in Sulzweier, Germany. When anti-Semitic violence erupts and hate propaganda dictates the headlines, Paul takes an activist role in protecting other German Jews; Malou interests herself only in Paul and the "family romance."[7] The Nazi takeover, however, soon forces the couple's flight to Amsterdam. There, Paul continues his activism and falls in love with a much younger Jewish refugee named Lotte (Marie Colbin) whom he helps. Malou, now pregnant and fearful of losing Paul on two fronts, begins drinking heavily. Hannah is born, and the Gestapo closes in on Paul. Malou and Paul are again forced to flee, and they set sail on an ocean liner for Buenos Aires. Paul, clearly tiring of Malou, expresses astonishment at her self-absorption and seeming obliviousness to the horrendous state of world affairs.

After their arrival in Argentina, Paul leaves Malou for Lotte. Eventually Paul and Lotte return to Europe, while Hannah and Malou, now called Maria Luisa, remain in exile in Argentina. Malou's life declines, her drinking worsens, and, to Hannah's dismay, she takes up with various "uncles." As Hannah reaches adolescence, her father refuses to send more money,

11. A woman ravaged by alcoholism, poverty, and despair, the exile Malou is the object of her daughter's quest for an elusive identity. (Ingrid Caven as Malou in *Malou*. Photo courtesy of the Auraria Film Collection, Auraria Higher Education Center.)

forcing Malou to give up her daughter, who moves to Europe at her father's insistence. Once grown, Hannah returns again to Buenos Aires to visit her mother, who has become considerably poorer and fatally ravaged by years of alcoholism and despair. Not long before Malou dies, she tells her dumbstruck daughter that Hannah must marry a man like Paul. Similar to that self-abnegating arch-heroine of maternal melodrama Stella Dallas in her acquiescence to patriarchal values, Malou proves to be like Stella too in her opposite wish to be "something else besides a mother"— that is, to experience womanly desire and pleasure. Thus, even on her deathbed, over which a small cross is hung, she grasps for a little sensuousness and vitality in her life and asks Hannah to apply polish to her fingernails—a last request which her daughter grants.

This portrait of Malou is related in a series of flashbacks through Hannah's mindscreens. It is motivated by Hannah's active quests to remember, mourn, and understand. As she explains in a letter to her husband, Martin Rothman (Helmet Griem), "I talk in your language, with your friends, in your country. Do you understand, Martin? I have everything, but I'm confused. . . . My mother gave up her language, her religion, her heritage, everything, for a man. I don't want that to happen to me. I'm afraid, and I am looking for . . . her and for myself." Hannah's present-day trips back to her dead mother's haunts and homes in France, Germany, the Netherlands, and Argentina are alternately literal and imaginative. She drives from Berlin to Strasbourg to visit the nightclub—now converted to a bistro—where Malou performed and first met Paul. Asked by a waitress there if Berlin is her home, Hannah replies with difficulty: "Yes . . . no . . . yes . . . I live there. My mother came from here, from Strasbourg, but I grew up in Argentina. But I'm really German." She also drives to Malou's grave site, which is set apart in the family cemetery both spatially and by its French art nouveau–inscribed marker; and she stops in a cathedral, where she starts to cross herself then stops in mid-gesture. Some of Hannah's "excursions," on the other hand, are fantasies, some presented with warm, soft, nostalgic lighting, while others reflect Hannah's actual memories of her mother in Argentina and exhibit a harsher lighting; all are edited into her contemporary life in suggestively dialogic ways.

In the present, Hannah teaches German to foreigners in Berlin and struggles to achieve what she calls "closeness without illusions" with her husband Martin. A tall, blond, conservatively dressed, professionally dedicated workaholic, Martin fails to understand or have much sympathy with Hannah's need to "rummage around in the past," as he terms it. "We won't solve our problems with that old stuff," he insists. To him, her attempts in effect to exhume her mother are a symptom of her emotional instability and, unlike his drive toward public accomplishment, seem a futile endeavor. In a parallel fashion, Martin fails to grasp the disparity between his advocacy role as an architect-spokesperson working to advance the interests of foreigners living in Germany and his silencing of his own "foreign" wife. Thus, when the couple attend a work-related reception and the topic of integration is being discussed, Martin assumes a nativist, husbandly prerogative and simply interrupts her effort at self-representation. A business associate then tells him that since Hannah is a foreigner, Martin can study the integration problem at close range. In rebellion, Hannah embarrasses Martin by questioning nativist-looking passersby about *their* foreignness.

For Hannah's part, as Meerapfel explains, "It's not her real mother, not the real Malou, my protagonist has to find, but what she has inherited from her. Hannah has Malou's fantasies: the vision of Prince Charming, of protection, of setting the focus of her life in something else."[8] Accordingly, in one sequence, Hannah is shown as a young girl looking at an illustrated book of *Sleeping Beauty* and at a miniature scene in a matchbook-sized glass box, and is then revealed in a look of outward regard, gazing at her mother, who is presented in a separate shot, lying upside down in bed after a sexual interlude with "Uncle Max." The sequence cuts back to young Hannah, her look sad, concerned, loving, and then cuts directly to a shot of Hannah in the present (1980), also lying upside down in the bed she shares with Martin. The editing thus reflexively accents the parallel between mother and adult daughter, both in effect critically "seen" through the eyes of Hannah's younger self. The editing contextualizes present-day Hannah's vacillations—between the sense that Malou is a negative model (what Marianne Hirsch terms a maternal model of "disidentification")[9] and the sense that she is an object of desire; between Hannah's fear that her husband will subsume her entirely as she assimilates to his country, language, and social sphere, and her desire for the same fantasy Malou wanted—for a life that conforms to conventional romance plots rooted in eighteenth- and nineteenth-century ideals of marriage, motherhood, and domesticity.

Indeed, through its depiction of Hannah and Martin's marriage, the film reveals this institution as a site of contested meanings, where emotionally charged, socially vital issues of sexual and cultural identity are played out. While some scenes in the film offer lyrical depictions of the couple's sexual tenderness and merging, others expose Hannah's ambivalence about such union or reveal her isolation, as when she masturbates, while Martin sleeps at her side. At times, Martin's Germanic dutifulness comes into conflict with Hannah's more self-indulgent amorous playfulness, with each spouse desiring mastery over the other. Martin's ambivalence about Hannah's Latin American–inflected style of dress, his condescension toward her occasionally faulty grammar, and especially his closed-off attitude toward her exploration of her family identity and past are symptomatic of larger problems. So, too, is her need for his indulgence, his excessive coddling, and his participation in her troubled play. While the film gives signals of progress in the couple's redefinition of the terms of this marriage, it aptly closes with a slow zoom out to an extreme long shot of Hannah and Martin circling after each other, repeatedly just missing sight of each other, atop a large rotunda—the building he aims to transform into a cultural center.[10] The film's *Malou* theme song is reintroduced with this closing image of circularity and search.

While *Malou* ends with an image of the grand, the exterior, the public, the collective, the architectural, an image of Berlin itself, and of the difficulties of two people forming a socially integrated "closeness without illusions" in this context, it begins on a very different scale. In the interior opening shot, behind the credits and to the accompaniment of the film's tango theme music (composed by Peer Raben and sung by Caven), the camera intimately pans memorabilia of Malou's life—photo albums, a book by Borges, odd pieces of silverware, personal letters, a scrapbook, a cigar box full of passports from various countries and another full of snapshots, a pair of white loafers. It comes to rest on an indistinct gray-and-white portrait of Malou as a young woman, in a dark picture frame.

In a sense these mute, metonymic objects behind the credits form Malou's unwritten, fragmentary autobiography. Produced out of material signs whose status as "quotations" matches Walter Benjamin's expanded concept of language,[11] it is a life text whose materiality also connotes the mother's mutability and mortality. The memorabilia signify a loss that motivates the film's narrative from its outset. At key intervals the film returns to these signs of the turning points in Malou's identity, including her menorah, honeymoon photos, and baby pictures of Hannah, as if to recover the cartography they imply and to give them a voice.

In her brilliant study on longing, Susan Stewart observes that "[t]he souvenir [of an adult's life] is intimately mapped against the life history of an individual; it tends to be found in connection with rites of passage (birth, initiation, marriage, and death) as the material sign of an abstract referent: transformation of status. Such souvenirs are rarely kept singly; instead they form a compendium which is an autobiography."[12] This account clearly accords with *Malou*. Yet the memorabilia in *Malou* betoken a life lived at a distance from those public spheres and lives traditionally deemed suitable subjects for literary autobiography or filmic auto/biography, such as that of Malou's husband, "Paul Kahn," might have been (and Oskar Schindler's was). Compendia of mementos, in particular, have been as close to an autobiographical form as most women's life stories in Western culture have come. Consequently, in the film, they comprise a highly appropriate way of embodying what Sidonie Smith terms a woman's "natural" nonstory within Western patriarchy: a narrative shaped "not around the public, heroic life but around the fluid, circumstantial, contingent responsiveness to others that, according to patriarchal ideology, characterizes the life of woman but not autobiography."[13] Further, insofar as each memento is the "material sign of an abstract referent: transformation of status," each betokens a change or adaptation to others that is simultaneously a loss, be it the loss that has occurred historically through the literal name change of women in marriage or that which has resulted from the displacements from nation to nation, language to language, and religion to religion that have attended Malou's particular marriage.

In other words, these objects form a fragmentary autobiographic "text," based on an alternative signifying economy and an alternative aesthetics: emanating from a "fluid," "contingent" life, they tell a story that normatively would have been masked and censored in *gender*-specific ways. Indeed, their very form suggests the sorts of loss and repression that have determined the nature of their existence.[14] Smith quite rightly emphasizes the woman autobiographer's need to retrieve precisely this kind of maternal *Urselbstbiographie* when she says it is imperative for the autobiographer not to lose sight of "that part of herself that identifies her as a daughter of her mother. Repressing the mother in her, she turns away from the locus of all that is domesticated and disempowered culturally and erases the trace of sexual difference and desire."[15] In the film, the memento is that trace recovered. And in the film, the memento forms part of a signifying economy that contrasts with men's phallogocentrism. The latter is made quite explicit on several occasions: when Martin informs Hannah that "integration" means that foreigners learn to speak German; when the rabbis instruct Malou that she must learn Hebrew if she is to be a good Jewish mother; and when Paul, evading Malou's plea that he return to her, tells her that the important thing is for her to learn to speak Spanish.

Fittingly, the memorabilia Hannah has inherited from Malou define the mise-en-scène of Hannah's first appearance, immediately after the credits when, her face framed by her dark tendrils and bangs and her eyes ringed with dark circles, Hannah sits surrounded and physically enclosed by these objects as she searches through them and ruminates about their meanings.[16] The attitude established here and developed throughout the film is clearly not one of repressing the mother, let alone one of killing her off to cure depression according to the Kristevan formulation;[17] rather, it is one of redefining and renewing the relationship to the maternal text both psychologically and aesthetically. The film creates this renewal through a dialogics of desire and an expressive use of film editing which reflect twin impulses on the daughter's part, one of which is toward a nostalgic, melancholic longing for a life story centered on the mythic "Prince Charming" (or self-destructive rebellion against him),[18] while the other is toward mourning and toward a longing for historical progress and change—again, in gender-specific terms.

According to Stewart, mementos typically combine nostalgic and historical dimensions. Souvenirs are both evidence of the "capacity of objects to serve as traces of authentic experience" and expressions of a nostalgic (hence insatiable) desire rooted in "inauthentic" rather than lived experiences; that is, they are rooted in ideology or fictions of experience that have had no existence except as narrative.[19] Similarly, the mementos in *Malou* engender narratives in Hannah's mindscreens that reach back in time and inwardly to private space. Like fetishes, they signify absence and offer compensation for it. But unlike the childhood and religious fetishes Marianne collects in *Peppermint Peace* and unlike the evidentiary records compiled by Juliane in *Marianne and Juliane,* the memorabilia in *Malou* occupy a space between the spheres of fetish and official documentation. They typify the film's self-conscious interest in issues both of autobiographical/historical authentication and of nostalgic, romantic desire, both in mourning and in melancholy, and the differences of gender within each.

Hence, Hannah wants to know about her mother's history, about her own life's story, and about the romantic fictions that shaped her mother's life and which mother bequeathed to daughter. And by means of these souvenirs and the "real" and imagined narrative journeys which they motivate, Hannah becomes a kind of tourist of her mother's past. In the process, she fluctuates between the need to create sharp boundaries between herself and her mother and her urge to allow those subjective borders to dissolve and even to become "contaminated" herself by the dissolution. Thus, in the Strasbourg bistro where her parents first met, she differentiates herself from Malou by contemptuously rebuffing a handsome man's approach by flicking cigarette ashes onto his lap. Contrarily, after leaving Martin's reception, she mimics Malou's self-destructive behavior and defies Martin by having a drunken one-night stand with a seedy man she picks up in a sleazy bar.

Yet Hannah herself and the maternal imago she carries within also authenticate her mother's existence, and the journey Hannah travels is as much a voyage toward *cultural* cathexis and rediscovery as it is a process of psychological differentiation.[20] The filmic interplay between her life text and that of her mother activates our awareness of change and its absence, of what Dominick LaCapra terms "working through" as opposed to "acting out."[21] But self-examination and the quest for the signature of the self—as daughter, citizen, subject, and auteur—also presuppose a quest for a mother who would be positioned otherwise—in the final words of the film's tango theme song—to have no more story/history (*"ne plus avoir d'histoire"*). Indeed, as the film reveals, insofar as nostalgia is "a sadness without an object,"[22] that absence and its causes may themselves be culturally and politically significant in an itinerary of self-discovery.

The process of re-collecting and sifting through the memories and memorabilia of Malou is from the outset associated with a darkened interior room of Hannah's home, a room visually tied to Hannah rather than to Martin or to the two as a couple. As the film conceptualizes it, the practice of re-collecting Malou's autobiographical artifacts within this space dovetails with Juliana Schiesari's concept of a "home economics of mourning." Employing an alternative symbolics of loss, this practice, according to Schiesari, is a daily undertaking, "a woman's work that brings everything back into the home." Crucially, it "accommodates the imagination to reality and not vice versa (as it would for the great [male] melancholic)."[23] That is, because this feminine labor is invested in the "reality principle," it differs from the culturally visible, discursively privileged phenomenon of male melancholia, which is etiologically implicated not only in creative male genius but also in compulsive, manic activity. (An example of the latter is the workaholism of Martin, who "just pushes everything aside," in Hannah's words, and who seems much more interested in the integrated Berlin he imagines than in the experiences of actual "Others" such as his wife.)

At the same time, the film represents Hannah's endeavor not in insular utopic terms, but as a complex, difficult, open-ended process that would ideally transcend its privatized confines. There is a need for a synthesis of Hannah's and Martin's spheres not unlike the desire for melding between those qualities symbolized by Ruth and Olga in von Trotta's *Sheer Madness*. Hannah's circling toward and away from Martin at film's end emblematizes the attempt to dialogize exteriority and interiority, public and private, feminine mourning and masculine public activism, as a necessary sequel to what is presented as a specifically feminine mourning process. Although both Freud and his successors have devalued the importance of the woman's work of mourning, the film dramatizes the ways in which the effects of mourning demand expression and incorporation into the public sphere. The architectural-integrationist metaphor at work both within the film and at its conclusion helps bring into focus the need for a new synthesis of public and private and a reconceptualization of the present as a disruptive meeting point of past and future.

The architectural-integrationist metaphor serves another, related purpose as well. It is the activist architect Martin, *Malou*'s opposite, who is conceptually and visually tied to the large building seen in extreme long shot at film's end. As a publicly oriented idealist dedicated to a more ethnically integrated future, Martin occupies a domain that encompasses exteriority, public achievement, and the authority of the collective. But as shown by the sequence in which he and Hannah attend the reception, both he and the public institutions for which he works elide *self*-representation and *self*-expression by those whose gender, class, ethnicity, nationality, and language mark them as other. In fact, in his failure to validate Hannah's need to re-examine Malou's life, he represents a point of view not unlike that of the film reviewer who felt that Meerapfel should have read more of the history of the period represented in her film in order to correct her peripheral perspective. As the film *Malou* reminds us, Hannah/Meerapfel's perspective would not have been so peripheral, and her need to mourn not so great, had German-Jewish identity not been denied its own self-representations, its visibility, and its public validation under the fascists.

Not only feminine mourning but also feminine nostalgia and melancholy in the film are distinct from the masculine melancholy of the European humanist tradition. A primary way in which *Malou* evokes its nostalgic mood is through imagery of interiority and the miniature. This imagery is emphasized not only in the film's opening visuals but also through song lyrics, dialogue, and Malou's placement within the mise-en-scène. For instance, Hannah speaks of Malou's dreams of "a family, a safe world, a tidy doll's house," and she imagines one of Malou's first sights upon entering her new husband's beautifully appointed family home as an upstairs scene in which girls play with a toy tea set. Here and elsewhere in the film, the fantasies that Hannah projects onto Malou evoke the dollhouse and the symbolic attributes culturally identified with it: the motifs of wealth and nostalgia; its *display* value (as opposed to *play* value); its status as private property and ornament to be consumed by the eye; the tensions it represents between the exterior and the interior space and time of the bourgeois subject; the tensions it signals between different modes of interiority, within the home and within the unconscious; its status as a domestic space that is both "sanctuary (fantasy) and prison."[24]

As this list intimates, the diminutive and the dollhouse are not only expressions of Malou's and Hannah's nostalgic longing, they also symbolize the ways in which Malou's life and aspirations typify those of the "non-autobiographical" female subject. For Malou's presence and visibility as a subject—not to mention her autonomy and power—are diminished, reduced, blurred, and "devoured" through an extended, normative cultural process of "habitudinization." The film makes us see this problem *up close*, feelingly, and by *that* means increases "the difficulty and length of perception." A telling case in point is the Kahns' wedding scene: after the ceremony, Malou is shown dwarfed by Paul's family and friends as she proceeds toward the backtracking camera down a gauntlet of wedding guests. Though she is the bride and the scene's focal point, she is visually overwhelmed by their kisses and embraces. The ambiguity and tension of this tightly framed scene are palpable. Hannah's evocation of her parents' wedding thus affords one example of how the film effectively problematizes the aesthetics of the miniature and creates a competing discourse that counters purely nostalgic desire. The sequence illustrates how *Malou* brings nostalgia and mourning into tension within an intimate aesthetics. And as the wedding sequence also reveals, what the film itself grieves is a legacy of loss: it laments women's diminished, constricted possibilities under patriarchy—even patriarchy at its most beneficent. It engages in an elegiac revery on those experiences lost to women confined within the prison of the dollhouse. Moreover, the film attempts to liberate female spectatorial longing from its confinement within the language of a certain kind of nostalgia, even as it attends to the real needs over which that nostalgia is limned.

Not only does *Malou* attempt to retrieve the mother, to imagine her subjectivity, it also focuses on the language through which the dynamics of female self-portraiture have been and might be represented. Expressly tying command of verbal language to fathers and husbands, the film offers a nonverbal countersystem of material signs that implicitly oppose phallogocentrism. In other words, the film's rhetoric resists what duBois terms the Marxian (or commodity) fetishization of the phallus as a sign that takes place in Lacan. An abstraction and reification of the male sex organ (the organ already commodified in Freud), this symbolic Lacanian phallus gives way, in *Malou,* to tactile, material, partial signs, "personal effects," whose connotative and denotative values speak of a life gendered female, deracinated, and consumed by poverty; a life for which such mementos ultimately constituted a large part of *having* at all. *Malou*'s autobiographic voices speak through a different signifying economy, and the difference encompasses not only the material but the acoustic and cinematic as well.[25]

The Latin dance music in films such as Detlev Sierck's last German work, *La Habañera* (1937), emerges as a locus of escapist foreign fantasy, an illusory place that allowed women audiences steam-valve release from Nazi German realities, defined by patriarchal control and so-called Aryan ascendency. In *Malou,* conversely, the tango is an autobiographical and autoethnographic sign. It simultaneously denotes a nostalgia that the film complicates and connotes a site of resistance to European hegemony, to a modernist European culture that belittles emotion, and to those New German Cinema practices defined by a Euro-American (or German-Hollywood) dialogue on melodrama.[26] It is, further, the sign of the complex bequest of the mother, who must repeatedly be summoned up and laid to rest for an autobiographic female self to be written or filmed or heard.

Malou's mood, according to Meerapfel, is deliberately, unapologetically emotional: "During filming in Madrid," she explains, "we heard an Argentinian singing tangos in a bar. It became clear to me that the sentimentality of the story in the film, this longing for the past, this melancholy mood, were feelings which I had learned or discovered in the tango."[27] The nostalgic mood Meerapfel conjures up through the film's tango theme song has a specific set of cultural resonances in addition to its evocation of the repressed maternal. From the tango's origins in Africa to its Brazilian appropriation and its later incorporation, during the 1930s, into the indigenous Argentine film genre, the tango melodrama, this musical form traverses a history inscribed by a complex cultural *métissage*.[28] Along with musicals and comedies, as Ana M. Lopez explains, the melodrama "became synonymous with the cinema in Latin America after the introduction of sound," and the hybrid Argentine tango melodrama became as well a form of resistance to Hollywood domination of the film industry. While this popular Argentine genre shares with mass-culture Hollywood melodrama expressive zooms, revelatory mise-en-scène, and an "emphasis on anaphoric events pointing to other implied, absent meanings or origins," its distinctive Roman Catholic inflection and themes—passion, sin, suffering, self-abnegation—and its incorporation of at least one or two musical performances invested with melodramatic pathos set it apart as distinctly Latin American.[29] Indeed, Lopez stresses the point that "the term [melodrama] has a different currency in Latin America than in the U.S. or Europe."[30] The identification of melodrama's *melos* as tango is one of several Latin conventions and inflections that can be seen in Meerapfel's *Malou*. These distinguish *Malou* both from other, less multicultural forms of melodrama in German cinema and from other evocations of Latin culture in that cinema. Further, *Malou*'s politically astute deployment of latinate melodramatic conventions also accords with recent views that the Argentine melodrama possesses progressive political potential.[31]

The Malou tango theme song—sung over the opening credits, first in German and then in French—provides a lyrical narrative of Malou's biography to counterpoint the visual autobiography of memorabilia. With its melodramatic lyrics (typical of the tango), the song immediately activates certain conventions of the tango melodrama. (For example, diminutive imagery within the lyrics intensifies the effect of the pathos of lost origins: Malou is "the little French woman," "a little lost child," whose "little foot would stumble over luck and love.")[32] Beyond this, the song's dissonances and Caven's delivery—her pauses and inflections—recall Kurt Weill and the tradition of cabaret songs going back to the 1920s in Germany, allowing a modicum of ironic distance. Reinforcing this association of the tango with Germany, but simultaneously complying with a convention from the Argentine tango melodrama itself, the character Malou also sings the theme song within the diegesis later in the film. The scene is the casino at Baden-Baden, where she and Paul go for a special weekend. Her performance is represented in a mindscreen fantasy that is attributed to Malou but that of course emanates, *mise-en-abîme*, from Hannah's own mindscreen. With Malou framed and reflected in elegant mirrors, her imagined rendition of the song marks a peak moment for her. Its context is the sweetest point, indeed the climax, of her fairy-tale marriage to Paul, when she wins repeatedly at the gambling table and seems like a princess dressed in gold and white. But appropriately, Malou's mindscreen is an anaphoric event defined by nostalgia for earlier times and places in *her* life, in particular her childhood home and her work as a nightclub *chanteuse* when she and Paul first met. Malou sings: "The little French woman in a strange land / She would like to fly homeward. But her wings have been burnt off. / So she wanders through the streets that are made up of memories."[33] Thus the moment of happiness for Malou is neither ever present nor deferred but perpetually retro-projected, referred backward nostalgically, in a deconstructive laying bare of the dynamics of longing that fractures the fairy tale at its climax. The ensuing scene furthers the effect. In keeping with melodrama's narrative and aesthetic rhythms, its juxtaposition of emotional peaks and depths, Malou is again displaced. For during Paul and Malou's absence, the Nazis have appropriated the Kahn family house and evicted the Kahns, who now must flee. The Nazis' presence at the margins of the scene in the casino at Baden-Baden has promised exactly this eventuality. In this way, the two scenes doubly deploy tango melodrama's rhetoric to hone the critique of the romance fairy tale: they point up both the absence at the fairy tale's center and the brutal fascist realities that refuse to remain at its margins.

Further, as in certain Latin American family melodramas, in *Malou* the locus of the nightclub forms the counterpoint to the physical and psychic space of the home. Lopez describes the two locales and their ramifications as follows:

> the home [is] a private sphere valorized and sanctified by Law, and the nightclub, a barely tolerated social space as liminal as the home is central. Only marginally acceptable, the nightclub is nevertheless the part of the patriarchal public sphere where the personal—and issues of female subjectivity, emotion, identity, and desire—finds its most complex articulation.[34]

The casino scene at Baden-Baden illustrates this complexity well, but the nightclub as liminal space of self-disclosure and expression becomes the site of Malou's most overt, emotionally charged revolt in a "scandalous" scene with her and Paul on the ocean liner to Argentina. Feeling betrayed in love by Paul, "at sea," and fractured by her multiple identities ("I no longer know if I'm French, German, Jewish or what," she laments), Malou flouts her husband's authority, drinks heavily, and flirts with strangers, embarrassing Paul by the attention she draws. When he tries to sober her by reminding her of the horrendous state of world affairs, she counters, "And me?"—then asks for another cognac. A German named Jaeger asks Paul, "Would you permit me to dance with your wife?" A tango plays, and Malou and the stranger dance. Malou then proceeds to dance wildly alone in the Bacchic ecstasy of lost selfhood, finally collapsing on the floor in despairing, intoxicated laughter.

Her defiance targets equally the world that has made her *heimatlos* and, symbolicallly, the *Heimat* itself as the space whose sanctity and propriety her speech and actions most offend. In other words, although Malou's rebellion bespeaks her longing for an inner sanctum, security, and a stable identity (the dollhouse), it also serves as evidence to the spectator of the need for a future that escapes that sanctum and sheds the skin of old romance. Paul's reminder to Malou of the catastrophic events that define their historical moment, paired with Malou's self-concerned response and performative excess, focuses the power dynamics that have segregated the private sphere from public discourse, making Malou blind both to those victims who have not escaped Nazism's horrors and to the diverse sources of her own oppression. Conversely, Malou's "and me" response to Paul highlights *his* imperviousness to the discrepancy between his public heroism and his private improbity—his betrayal of her. The film's melodramatic orchestration of the nightclub and the tango thus generates a culturally specific nostalgia and a deconstruction of nostalgia. It generates as well a critique of patriarchy's hierarchic segregation of the public from the private, the masculine from the feminine, the world of social agency from the dollhouse.

In the sequence that follows the ocean-liner sequence, introduced by a dissolve from Malou to Hannah dancing in the present, the cultural status of the tango itself is discussed within the filmic diegesis. The sequence expressly establishes the film's oppositional relation to Eurocentrism. The context is a gathering of Latin Americans at one of their residences in Berlin. As Hannah dances, she complains to a woman friend that her father, with his "European ears" and "his gooseberry sauce and Spätzle culture," dismissed the tango as "Indian music," primitive, popular, low-brow stuff. The scene segues into the kitchen, at the entrance to which hangs a Chilean flag.[35] As Hannah enters, she enlarges her critique to encompass class, a social hierarchy she delineates in polyglot culinary terms. Speaking first in German, then in French, then in Spanish, she refers to the leeks her mother used to cook as "the asparagus of the poor." The sequence deftly knits the tango into a critical discourse on the parallel hierarchized relationships that obtain between masculine and feminine, Europe and the Third World, *Kultur* on the one hand and the *culture* and *cuisine de misère* on the other. The metonymic centripetal force that the tango gathers here anchors the film's multifaceted aesthetics of resistance.

In the context of West German postwar discourse on patriarchy, this oppositional aesthetics takes on still further significance. Alexander Mitscherlich's *Society without the Father* is permeated by a nostalgia for traditional European patriarchal values, norms, educational experiences, and labor practices. Although in this work Mitscherlich points to the "recognition of equal rights for women in the eyes of the law," he mentions it as one factor that, along with the development of technology, science, and mass culture, contributed to the fragmentation of civilization, the weakening of authority structures based on the paternal image, and the enormous sense of inner loss suffered by individual men.[36] Mitscherlich's melancholic lament for the erosion of the Old World paternalistic way of life is thus rendered in a very different mode from *Malou*'s music. In Mitscherlich's work, of course, there are no maternal elegies.[37] His is a lament for the absence, the lack, that his work's title describes—a loss that is both in the world and in the male ego; Meerapfel's work is, in a sense, a quest to identify and weed out the inheritance that made her believe in precisely *that* kind of illusion of masculine power and protection, to transcend the phallocratic faith she inherited from her mother.

Finally, in the same present-tense sequence that shows the gathering of friends, the tango also engenders reflection on Hannah's particular identity and on concepts of selfhood that take no single ancestral *Heimat* as their point of reference. For even as Hannah criticizes her father's Eurocentrism, she laments her own inability to tango, to "authenticate" herself as fully Argentine. Here and elsewhere, she emerges not only as a fluid, multiple, contradicted subject, according to Teresa de Lauretis's formulation,[38] but also as a divided, ambivalent subject whose "worldwide homesickness" radically transcends that ascribed to films of Meerapfel's directorial counterpart, Wim Wenders.

Thus, although *Malou* does not create multiple perspectives and aesthetic distance by incorporating diverse media or genres as some other New German Cinema productions do, it does highlight multiplicity within—within Hannah the daughter, within Malou her mother, and within the film's variegated melodramatic mode. And while its nostalgia and reliance on illusionist formulas might make it seem aesthetically or politically retrograde—a product of mass culture—the film is more accurately seen as an intimate, aesthetically imaginative engagement with our nostalgia for romance plots, Old World patriarchal fairy tales, and the shape they once *seemed* to bestow on life before a plurality of cultural, ethnic, class, and gender differences became a highly conscious part of the realist terrain.[39] In effect, the film revises old plots and styles, and seeks alternatives, reaching for new relations between narrative and epistemology—between plots and truths, between women's remembered life stories and the meaningful, multi-ethnic, socially engaged feminist subject positions they might still create.

Although the film desires closure and cure, it posits no ultimate mastery of the past, nor any "cure" for Hannah's desire, despite her literally closing the memorabilia-filled case of her mother's things near film's end and announcing her intent to move in, to claim this space with Martin as home. Hannah's efforts to sort out inappropriate plots and identities from her "true" or "ideal" self may invest viewers in the protagonist's story, but the film's terminus is not an epiphany or discovery of homogenized self-identity. In fact, the film recalls Carolyn Heilbrun's assertion that "[w]hen the hope for closure is abandoned, when there is an end to fantasy, adventure for women will begin. Endings—the kind Austen tacked onto her novels—are for romance or for daydreams, but not for life."[40] The film also resembles von Trotta's *Marianne and Juliane* in its insistence on the provisional nature of story, the impossibility of telling the "whole story," capturing the "real life." *Malou* further resembles that film because it highlights an emphatically female desire to remember both personal and public history, a female desire to seize the implications of history's differential

mapping of women's lives.[41] Beyond von Trotta's film, though, *Malou* bespeaks a multiculturalism that makes it as much "New World" cinema as
"New German."

And herein lies the film's distinct but generally overlooked contribution
to cinematic history. For when we think of the New German Cinema, we
are more likely to recall the "worldwide homesickness" attributed to Wenders, the appropriation and politicization of Sirk's Hollywood melodramas
that define much of Fassbinder, or the fascination with Latin American
locales and "authentic types" in Herzog than we are to focus on any German women's films, let alone on Meerapfel's *Malou*; yet Meerapfel's marginal position within the New German Cinema offers a vantage point that
is the more revelatory for its marginality. As already noted, the multiple
cultural and geographic spaces inhabited by women in *Malou* give rise to
a sense of displacement that is considerably less metaphoric than that
evinced in Wenders's films. Indeed, the Wenders who claimed that "my
fantasy is just going to break if I have to imagine a dialogue in somebody's
home," and that identity and awareness mean "not having a home," "not
being at home," elides contradictions in the meanings of identity, home,
and homelessness that are at the center of Meerapfel's film.[42] The Fassbinder who rewrote Douglas Sirk's *All That Heaven Allows* as the interracial
love story *Ali: Fear Eats the Soul* foregrounded Sirk's progressive dimensions and demonstrated that a hybridized German Hollywood melodrama, coupling thought and feeling, is a viable model of cultural critique.
But when we juxtapose Sirk/Sierck's Eurocentric use of Latin American
elements in *La Habañera* with the more genuinely multicultural deployment of Argentine tango melodrama in *Malou*, we again recognize significant differences in their cinematic coding of alterity and concurrent differences in how German film genealogy might be conceived. Herzog's
romanticist nostalgia for cultural authenticity, his layering of European
opera over Third World narratives, and his focus on homosocial rite-of-
passage contests, though perhaps too much maligned, never take into account women's place of difference or the specific addresses to women
within Latin American or German culture, issues that *Malou* explores.

In this same general context, perhaps most telling of all is the relationship of *Malou* to the discourse of and around feminine rhetorical figures
of German nationhood, such as Maria Braun, the culpably amnesiac
Wirstschaftswunder Germania of *The Marriage of Maria Braun*. The mar-

riage of Malou, in contrast, is a kind of ultimate paradigm of the assimilation and adaptation—to country, culture, religion, and language—that
Western civilization has expected and demanded of women historically.
Mary Wollstonecraft famously quotes and lambasts a passage from Rous-
seau's *Émile* that typifies the tenor of these demands:

> *Every daughter ought to be of the same religion as her mother, and every
> wife to be of the same religion as her husband: for though such religion
> should be false, that docility which induces the mother and daughter to
> submit to the order of nature, takes away, in the sight of God, the crimi-
> nality of the error.* [emphasis is Wollstonecraft's] [43]

Malou documents the price of such requirements for assimilation and adaptation. It repeatedly reminds us of these costs through juxtapositions of
Malou, Madonna icons, crucifixes, and the menorah. Further, *Malou* is a
film about the art of assimilation and adaptation at two interrelated levels—that of subjectivity and that of aesthetics—both of which, as we have
seen, are represented in terms of a complexly multicultural heteroglossia.

Lastly, *Malou* illustrates how an engaged aesthetics can shape self-
representation for women, who have not been able to take their own subjectivities as a given in life or art, but whose subjectivities remain important even—and especially—in the context of German fascism and its
complex aftermath. If, as Andreas Huyssen suggests, "[w]arding something off, protecting against something out there seems . . . to be a basic gesture of the modernist aesthetic, from Flaubert to Roland Barthes
and other poststructuralists," [44] then reclaiming something, bringing it in
closer to the self, in all its complexity and difference, can be said to constitute a position of dissent from modernism's masculinist values. Discov-
ering within a medium of intimate illusionism a "sensitivity to ourselves"
and a "closeness without illusions" is the aim that *Malou*'s autoethnographic aesthetic embraces.

Epilogue

By the late 1980s Thomas Elsaesser was able to point to West Germany as having proportionately more women filmmakers than any other film-producing nation.[1] This ratio—in large measure a result of impressive efforts by the Women's Film Workers Union (*Verband der Filmarbeiterinnen*)—remains noteworthy, as does the high quality of the films themselves. These films have found an important place in courses on women and film in universities in the United States, as evidenced by the attention accorded them in such standard texts as Lucy Fischer's *Shot/Countershot*, Ann Kaplan's *Women and Film*, and Patricia Erens's *Issues in Feminist Film Criticism*.[2] Moreover, both *Marianne and Juliane* and *Germany, Pale Mother* have been singled out as the most powerful, honest, and effective German films to take up the question of *Vergangenheitsbewältigung*.[3] Nonetheless, one of the genuinely perplexing questions surrounding German women's cinema concerns the reasons for the existence of a striking disproportion: How can we account for the sharper resistance that women filmmakers' works have generally encountered—and still encounter—relative to productions by German male auteurs? At least as important is a second question: Why have the extraordinary historical films by German women been subject to disproportionately greater neglect than the men's, despite the women's more forthright approach to critical issues of cultural prejudice and xenophobia in general and to fascism and mourning in particular?[4]

To this point, my own study has tackled issues of reception at the level of individual films. My arguments about negative reception have targeted critics' misrepresentations of the film texts and misinterpretations of their strategies of audience address. Here, I want to speculate more generally and somewhat more polemically about the problem of reception by focusing on the two questions just raised.

On a general level, the critical reaction to West German feminist film auto/biographies corresponds to the problematic responses encountered by contemporary British and American women auto/biographers who *write* about family members, especially mothers, and who incorporate diaries, letters, and other forms of personal discourse into narrative. This parallel suggests a transnational pattern that includes and transcends the German context. Linda Wagner-Martin explains the hazards that women authors of autobiographies face in this way: "If the act of writing is a way of giving a name and identity to a person, then to bestow that gift on one's mother seems appropriate. Yet because writing about loved ones has been called sentimental, the fact that a writer writes about her mother or other family members can undermine the reception of the best writing."[5] Accusations of sentimentality, of playing too obviously on the viewer's emotions, have similarly undermined the reception of key West German women's films, even though the films are far more emotionally differentiated than the label "sentimental" can possibly suggest.

Moreover, as Wagner-Martin documents, in the United States, men's autobiographies tend both to receive more prominent coverage than women's do and to elicit considerably more laudatory responses, even when the men's and women's texts deploy similar techniques, such as the postmodern practice of blurring the boundaries between factual and imaginary prose forms, or between biography and autobiography. The resulting indeterminate genre may become an asset in a man's writing but is less likely to be perceived as such in a woman's. To illustrate this difference, Wagner-Martin cites a review which praises a male autobiographer who "'learned at his father's knee that it is pointless to stick to facts when fantasy is so much more rewarding,'" then cites a contrasting review that unsympathetically categorizes a woman's experimental auto/biography as sociology.[6]

A roughly analogous pattern emerges in Anton Kaes's contrasting views on Fassbinder's and Sanders-Brahms's fictionalized appropriations of their mothers. In his discussion of the autobiographical dimensions of Fassbinder's films, Kaes first explains that although the director drew on his youth in the Adenauer era, he had little interest in "'the way it really was,' but

rather wondered how the thoughts, feelings, and actions of his contem-
poraries could be explained historically."[7] Kaes notes the exceptional nature of Fassbinder's role in his 26-minute contribution to *Germany in Autumn*—in no other film does the director play himself—and Kaes also
describes how, in that film, "Fassbinder gives us a document of shameless
self-revelation, a psychogram of his anxieties and aggressions. He inter-
cuts the apartment scenes with an inquisitorial (scripted) interview with
his own mother, who has appeared in many of his films"—although only
here as strictly herself.[8] Kaes notes and unequivocally affirms the productively troubling sequence—the juxtaposition of Fassbinder's condemna-
tion of his mother's authoritarian yearnings with his own authoritarian,
almost sadistic treatment both of her and of his gay lover.

But while Kaes approves of Fassbinder's creation of these hazy margins
between documentary and fictional filmmaking, he is far more equivocal
about Sanders-Brahms's blurring of similar boundaries in *Germany, Pale
Mother*. Kaes registers unease about her editing of 1945 documentary footage into the reconstructed historical fiction in order to create the illusion
of dialogue between Lene and a forlorn boy amid the ruins of 1945 Berlin,[9]
even though the contrast between the two kinds of footage is readily dis-
cernible in the film. Further, Kaes objects to the inclusion of the rape scene
since, according to Sanders-Brahms, Lene herself was not raped but rather
feared that she might be. Here, Kaes emphasizes that "an essential attrib-
ute of autobiography is its claim to truth and authenticity," but claims
that "this did not prevent Sanders-Brahms from fictionally reshaping
her life and that of her parents, condensing their lives and imparting to
them a higher level of generality. . . ."[10] While Kaes does not simply condemn Sanders-Brahms, clearly he feels more comfortable with Fassbinder's negatively critical scripting and deployment of his mother as a representation of her generation (and gender?) than with Sanders-Brahms's
deviation from strict biographical fact to reveal a more general pattern of
the wartime oppression of women.

One of the elements that distinguishes the German context from that
of Anglo-American literary reception is the often unacknowledged, oxy-
moronic assumption, typical of some leftist thought, that the German
process of mourning itself should be an unemotional or dispassionate
confrontation. Indeed, the bias against personal emotion *of any kind* in
certain leftist discourses and historiographical practices has been well-

documented,[11] and the overvaluation of distancing strategies in New German Cinema and concomitant undervaluation of both feminist films and feminist issues have been two consequences of this slant. Rejection of emotional and highly personal family content in auto/biographical films, of course, also reflects the culture's urge to perpetuate the segregation of experience into public and private spheres, thereby allowing power dynamics to operate in private that are deemed intolerable and retrograde in public.

A more subtle but perhaps more significant key to the films' problematic reception lies in the patriarchally implicated rhetorics and discourses that we as critics have inherited and that we continue, unreflectively, to employ in our assessments of film. A recent volume of *October* dedicated to Helke Sander's *Liberators Take Liberties* (*BeFreier und Befreite*, 1992) is illustrative in this regard. It opens with an introductory essay titled "After the Fall: Women in the House of the Hangmen."[12] The text of the essay is lucid and insightful and offers generally fair-minded criticisms of Sander's film's title and its opening commentary. Yet the title of the essay itself—a reference to the fall of Berlin in 1945—unavoidably evokes Eve and the biblical Fall, subtly but surely creating a subtext of culpability and punishment that implicates women on a mythologizing level.[13] With their title, then, the authors ironically contribute to the homogeneous history of gender they clearly seek to avoid.[14]

No less important than these vestiges of retrograde religious typologies are the highly enmeshed rhetorics of national identity and of the creative male genius or inspired melancholic man, a type whose dubious morose double is the focus of the Mitscherlichs' study. As I have argued, from the Mitscherlichs onward an ahistorical humanist discourse on melancholia has molded the dialogue about coming to terms with the Nazi past. It is not surprising, then, that patterns in the reception of New German Cinema also mirror that powerful and problematic tradition in several of its particulars. Indeed, the tendency to honor male melancholic genius while neglecting female "depression" as "non-universal" and at the same time too normative or trivial to be worthy of interest finds its counterpart in German film criticism and historiography.

To wit, preeminent film scholars and critics largely forgive the transgressions of the one auteur who, more than Wenders, is synonymous with New German Cinema—namely, Rainer W. Fassbinder (although Fassbinder is certainly not without his detractors). Negotiating the troubled terrain of German identity with brash panache, flaunting his unsettling relationship with his mother and theatricalizing his sexuality, identity, and political *aperçus*, Fassbinder was/is the melancholic New German film genius *par excellence*. Forgiven *more* because he was a genius—and a prolific one—he continues to be pardoned more as well because he presented himself as the "ugly German," and in that way mastered even the discourse of blame. Manic, shameless, hypercritical, rebellious, possessing a "keener eye for truth than other people who are not melancholic,"[15] his dispairing, creative directorial persona closely fits Freud's prototype of the culturally validated melancholic male. True to type, Fassbinder's narcissism did not impede his higher intellectual and moral discriminations but instead sharpened them, or so the reaction to his films would indicate. And most unmistakably, in *Germany in Autumn*, a filmic labor of mourning, he is there replaying the melancholic narcissist, opposite his insufficiently repentent mother. While he may be the double or twin of the weak melancholic man who cannot mourn, the creative melancholic genius who makes brilliant films about the "collective lack" he is said to embody commands our admiration and attention. And, I believe, Fassbinder should and will continue to deserve our study.

But on the other hand, according to the same tradition, women's depression, sorrow, and grieving are all unworthy of special attention. Normative, banal, routine occurrences, they are nonstories—not the stuff of great art, remarkable cinema, or noteworthy auto/biography. And hence some of the neglect and even hostility toward feminist films that assume otherwise. Canonical "Western" narratives on melancholia invest interest in a female if she *causes* melancholia—the famous instance being the filial pathology which Gertrude's "insufficient" mourning for Hamlet's father induces. "Woman" also accrues interest if she *is* Melancholia—as an abstraction, a trope, or a visual emblem, Dürer's representation of melancholy being the most famous example. However, if the abstraction is deconstructively embodied in a female character whose own particular debilitating "depression" is precisely the point—an example is the post-1945 Lene in *Germany, Pale Mother*—then the particulars may be seen as trivial and excessive, while the potential of the abstraction to signify for the collective (i.e., Germany) may retain its cultural currency and interest. And as for female mourning on its own behalf, it is culturally tied to "excess" and "sentimentality," the embarrassing stuff of low-brow tearjerkers. Or worse, it is infantalized as mere "whining."

A related point obtains in the positioning of "female" rhetorical tropes within patriarchal discourses on fascism. In *Divine Decadence,* a remarkable study of fascism and female spectacle in literary and film treatments of the Sally Bowles figure, Linda Mizejewski writes:

> Fascism itself emerges as a variety of questions and tensions testing how the "nightmare" of the ultimate Fatherland can be understood and disavowed within other patriarchal cultural moments. In such a story of fathers and sons, fascism as the ultimate patriarchal fantasy must be exposed as secretly female, and thus not identical with male authority.[16]

I have argued that it is not only popular Hollywood films such as *Cabaret* that participate in this rhetoric of disavowal, it is also the postwar discourse on authoritarianism. Alexander Mitscherlich's equation of the "mass leader" with a "mother-goddess lavish with her milk" spectacularly does, and in the process vests authority in the patriarchal superego. (This, despite the fact that for two thousand years the highest authorities of Church and State had validated anti-Semitism.) West German feminist auto/biographical films generally refuse to indulge these fantasies, and hence, I suspect, some of their difficulty in reception. Fassbinder's conflations of wartime and postwar spectacles with female figures (played most memorably by Hanna Schygulla), though appreciably more complex and politically differentiated than the Sally Bowles texts, clearly sit more comfortably with notions that gender fascism as feminine.

But here our trail seems to double back on itself. For, it has been argued, another discursive practice figures not fascism or Hitler as female but the German nation itself, depicted in the guise of a "hapless victim" of those same (now presumably masculine?) fascist forces. More particularly, Eric Rentschler contends that several of the most celebrated works from the New German Cinema, including films by Fassbinder and Sanders-Brahms, allegorize German history as a woman. The effect, according to Rentschler, is a shameless misrepresentation of the nation as a martyr or victim, innocent of its chilling crimes against humanity. This kind of revisionist filmic strategy "represents the nation as a violated or vulnerable female body, a stand-in and medium for a hapless Germany," and, at least

in Rentschler's view, makes this cinema complicit with the right-wing dis-
avowals and distorted views on German victimhood that gave rise to the
Historikerstreit.[17]

While Elsaesser would exempt Fassbinder from Rentschler's assessment—and I, *Germany, Pale Mother*—insofar as the New German Cinema is indeed shaped by such distortionist allegories of national innocence, their presence is not entirely surprising. For they form the obverse
of and complement to metaphorizations of guilt for fascism as female—
Hitler as the evil primitive mother of effeminate sons (the "real men aren't
fascists" theory). Thus the Eve/Mary, whore/virgin dichotomy has its
counterpart in feminine national emblems. Best known is the case of Fassbinder's Eva Braun/Maria Braun binarism, in which the discourses of
Christian typology and nationalist emblematics are ironically conflated.

The relevance to film reception of the rhetorical gendering of Germany
becomes clearer still when we recall that Rentschler offers his provocative
insight within the context of an arresting discussion of Alexander Kluge's
Brutality in Stone (*Brutalität in Stein*, 1960), a film which Rentschler identifies as "Young German Film's earliest sign of life," and one which itself
foregrounds the allegorical gendering of Germany.[18] Specifically, in the
film a male voice-over reports Hitler's plan to redesign Berlin and rename
it Germania. Some of the few images of human faces and bodies to appear
in the film accompany this report: shots of Hitler pompously posing as
architect and shots of a group of women arranged as allegorical figures,
positioned liminally between architectural and human status. Yet while
Brutality in Stone is, as Rentschler argues, a deconstructive documentary,
the film does not deconstruct the nationalistic practice of allegorizing
women per se, despite Kluge's emphasis on the absurdity of Hitler's pre-
tentions and on that of the female images used in apposition to them.
Brutality in Stone, the initial step toward what would become New German Cinema, thus also marks the inauguration of that cinema's problematic allegorical discourse on the female as city and nation.[19]

Insofar as Rentschler's characterization of New German Cinema here is
accurate, it provokes many questions; what, for instance, were the social
conditions that, even in the 1970s and 1980s, positioned women as culturally resonant representations of martyrdom, victimhood, and suffering?
During the immediate postwar era, in order to shore up national identity,
the West German government passed so-called protective legislation that

was based on what Heide Fehrenbach terms "a generalized desire—among men and women—to remake autonomous and productive women and children into wayward or vulnerable victims, who needed the protection of revitalized German men"[20]—a state of affairs whose consequences are vividly dramatized in *Germany, Pale Mother*. Another question raised by Rentschler's characterization of New German Cinema is why, during the heyday of the West German feminist movement, did a variant on this triangulation of national identity, women's status, and the rhetorics of victimhood reemerge? Or was it the case that women as such were largely irrelevant to the discourse of national identity that took shape in the 1970s and early 1980s? If, as Michael Geyer and Miriam Hansen claim, the search for a new language of collective identity had led not forward but back to the recovery of older, more universalist expressions of Germanness,[21] did these expressions, embraced in the 1970s, inevitably elide differences of gender, despite the presence of the women's movement? And if not, then what is it specifically that enables Rentschler to take it for granted that the recourse to a symbolics of women's suffering can simply be deployed by auteurs to deflect or divert attention from the "real" suffering of the Holocaust?[22] And to speak more polemically and contemporaneously, what motivates Anglo-American Germanists who, rather than speak of injustice, invoke a right wing–inflected discourse about "victimhood," not so subtly to discredit feminist politics? Similarly, what is at stake for the German left as it persists in its unwillingness to take feminist issues seriously? What enables this failure toward feminism to function as a supposed guarantor of the left's sincerity about its guilt for the genocide of the Holocaust?

Noting the ubiquity of female figures of national identity and of the metaphorizations of national homelands as violated female bodies, especially in the discourse of war, the editors of *Nationalisms and Sexualities* assert, "If Britannia and Germania can be gendered feminine, this iconography operates despite or rather *because* of the actual experiences of their female populations"—that is, it operates because women's subsumption into the national body politic has been more symbolic than real.[23] In my view, the auto/biographical films by women, grouped collectively, reveal a countercinematic pattern powerfully resistant to the one that displaces women with the nationalist trope of woman—and that displaces feminism with the politics of nation *tout court*. *Malou*, for example, shows a racked and ravaged female body, but not of a Germania figure. Instead, Malou is a multinational subject, a distinct if not atypical wife and mother, and an apt illustration that women's "claims to nationhood [are] frequently dependent upon marriage to a male citizen."[24] Indeed, she enacts the consequences of women's liminal positioning as markers of "the limits of national difference between men."[25] Moreover, she gives concrete form to Meerapfel's knowledge that women's issues need not fall under the umbrella of a nationalistic politics *in order to be genuinely political.* Similarly resistant to the nationalist metaphorization and allegorization of woman, *Hunger Years* reveals how the commodified female body became part of the West German arsenal of amnesia during the cold-war era, a role that inevitably and destructively confused issues of guilt, shame, and innocence. And *Peppermint Peace* focuses on the wounded hands of a small girl, atypical in her sensitivity, concern, and remorse, as it develops a critique of the Eva/Maria polarity. How ironic and even disingenuous, then, that *Germany, Pale Mother,* the film that has been most susceptible to a misreading as an unproblematized nationalist allegory and hence as a throwback to German universalist discourses of identity, is also the film that is most used to represent a monolithic "woman's point of view" in film courses and film discourses on German cinema.

While the culturally overdetermined confusions about representations of the oppression of women have created serious problems of reception for feminist filmmakers, it should be emphasized that women's auto/biographical cinema itself definitively does not attempt to correlate what is incommensurate. Simply put, it does not participate in historiography à la Ernst Nolte. It never pretends or insinuates that there was a Nazi policy of femicide or matricide or institutionalized misogyny capable of causing suffering even remotely proportionate to the unspeakable agonies and loss produced by the Nazi politics of genocide.[26] The films themselves in no way obviate recognition of the incommensurability and uniqueness of the Holocaust. Nor do they allow our awareness of that cataclysmic event to occlude our consciousness of the existence of lesser but equally real injustices. Instead, by subverting hierarchic ideas about what constitutes a suitable subject and approach for historical or political filmmaking, the films reveal the oppressive dynamics that structured the casual emotional violence which permeated the "normative" functionings of *Kinder, Kirche, Küche* within the German postwar bourgeois family.[27] That is, the films

deconstruct the difference between what Ernst Fraenkel and later Adelheid von Saldern term the "prerogative state" (*Massnahmenstaat*), which
was dominated by Nazi criminality during the Third Reich, and the "normative state" (*Normenstaat*), including the "postwar" politics of family,
with its extreme hierarchizing of gender functions and its latent threat of
domestic mayhem.[28] Indeed, this cinema implodes the romanticized view
of domesticity. And its feminist historiography, I maintain, is important
not only for feminists, but for us all.

According to Geyer and Hansen, "The problem is no longer 'never to
forget': it is how to remember"—that is, how to represent the Holocaust.[29]
If we follow the insights of women's auto/biographical cinema, at the
heart of the "how" is a problematic of incorporating rhetorics and rituals
of remembrance into the public sphere that offer genuine alternatives to
older humanist paradigms and universalist ideals. The distinctive discourses and emotional paradigms which women's auto/biographical films
develop have yet to be fully translated into parallel discoveries of alternative film reception practices. New interpretations and contextualizations
of cultural images and narratives are needed to replace the current ones,
which are too often tethered to the retrograde and highly tessellated patriarchal rhetorics of nation, creative genius, and faith. Older modes of
reception must give way to heuristic methods that are liberated from un-
reflective obedience to dehistoricizing and mythologizing nationalist discourses. Only then can the "symbolic capital" that these films represent
yield its full cultural promise.[30]

The stakes in the process are high, most obviously, but not exclusively,
for women. By redressing the balance that has left women and children
overlooked and misrepresented in the discourse of mourning and melancholia, German women's auto/biographical cinema speaks to a wide range
of feminist concerns. By considering how women's voices and desires, no
less than the actual processes of mourning, have been occluded from the
public sphere, these films also offer an important alternative perspective
on a question posed by Dominick LaCapra: "[D]oes modern society have
suitable public rituals that would help one to come to terms with melancholia and engage in possibly regenerative processes of mourning . . . ?"[31]
LaCapra's implicit answer, like that of the films, is: not yet. But as the
films uniquely demonstrate, the reasons behind this lack cannot be seized
through the eloquent androcentrism that dominates current discourse on

mourning. Nor can they be grasped if the question remains cut off from considerations of the need for public and private arenas that eliminate gendered divisions of access and acceptance, arenas in which contempt for women and for the emotional processes with which they are associated have no place. While the women's films are neither univocal in their stances nor fully accomplished in terms of their goals, they nonetheless open the way to alternative social and cinematic visions and ritual functions. Given the wider audience and more differentiated understanding that they deserve, they have the power to generate spectatorial longing for a future in which women and men collectively become active agents of opposition to patriarchal fascism, be that fascism an overt nationalist politics, a relatively more subtle politics of race and class, or a structure that insidiously shapes the politics of family and home. The films, in short, can help assure that the women's work of mourning becomes reimagined as the positively accredited labor of an inclusive, pluralistic, nonphallocratic culture.

Notes

INTRODUCTION

1. These terms refer to the drive to know and the eroticized desire to see, instincts or drives that Freud theorizes in relationship to the male child. See Freud, "Three Essays on the Theory of Sexuality," 191–192, 194.
2. See Jameson, "Cognitive Mapping."
3. See Mitscherlich, *Society without the Father* (e.g., 300–303); and Mitscherlich and Mitscherlich, *The Inability to Mourn* (e.g., 36).
4. For relevant discussions of cold-war politics in the United States, see especially Corber, *In the Name of National Security*, and Rogin, *Ronald Reagan, the Movie, and Other Episodes in Political Demonology*, 236–271.
5. See Huyssen, "The Politics of Identification," 97.
6. Elsaesser, "Primary Identification and the Historical Subject," 546–548. This position is partly modified in Elsaesser's *New German Cinema*, 245. His attempt to historicize psychic processes through his concept of the "social imaginary" is deservedly controversial. See, for example, Patrice Petro's critique of Elsaesser in *Joyless Streets*, 14–17.
7. Jay, "Once More an Inability to Mourn?," 75.
8. Schiesari, *The Gendering of Melancholia*, 18.
9. Ibid., 12–13, 18. Schiesari further notes that a hierarchy of difference even marks the distinction between male *melancholia* and female *depression* (89).
10. Ibid., 17.
11. Ibid., 56.
12. Mitscherlich and Mitscherlich, *The Inability to Mourn*, 36–37.
13. See especially Mitscherlich, *Society without the Father*, 284.
14. On the issue of children's continuing lack of representation in discourses of the 1970s, see Sander, "Nimmt man dir das Schwert," especially 37.
15. For an important discussion of related patterns in Weimar Germany, see McCormick, "Private Anxieties/Public Projections." For a discussion of maternal scapegoating in postwar Hollywood film (specifically in Hitchcock's *Notorious* [1946]), see Modleski, *The Women Who Knew Too Much*, 64, 131,n.6.

16. Mitscherlich, *Society without the Father*, 284.

17. Freud, "Group Psychology and the Analysis of the Ego," 123.

18. Freud, "Mourning and Melancholia," 247.

19. Schiesari, *The Gendering of Melancholia*, 9–10. Schiesari corroborates her insight through a brilliant reading of the Renaissance text of *Hamlet*, whose eponymous protagonist is the most privileged of all melancholics in Western culture and the only named subject of melancholy in Freud's essay (see 10–11, 233–264).

20. Mitscherlich and Mitscherlich, *The Inability to Mourn*, 36. Also see Santner, *Stranded Objects*, 5–6. Similar to the Mitscherlichs, Santner views the cathexis between Hitler and the Germans as a form of primary narcissism, as the desire for a "return to the purity of self-identity," with a de-abjectified maternal imago. Conversely, feminists such as Dorothy Dinnerstein argue that patriarchal despotism is founded on the son's fear of maternal power and what that fear produces—his need to effect a radical separation from her, his subjugation of women, and his radical embrace of the seemingly less capricious authority of the father. See Dinnerstein, *The Mermaid and the Minotaur*. When we recall that the early leadership of the Nazi party was made up of single homeless men who generally despised attachment to women, organized themselves in elitist hierarchies, and worshipped the stern-willed, indomitable male leader, Dinnerstein's theory is compelling indeed.

21. Schneider, "Fathers and Sons, Retrospectively."

22. Ibid., 30–31.

23. Schneider's too easy sliding from "father" to "parents" and from "sons" to "sons and daughters" gives him away as tokenistically interested in female subjectivity. While Schneider does discuss some women authors, this analysis is undertheorized. For an alternative assessment of *Vaterliteratur*, see Figge, "Fathers, Daughters, and the Nazi Past."

24. Schneider, "Fathers and Sons, Retrospectively," 50.

25. Ibid., 3.

26. Similarly, when Schneider explains that the sons identified with Hamlet and consoled themselves with James Dean, his argument remains tangled in the net of androcentric narcissism (36), for the Danish prince and the rebel without a cause are high culture/pop culture cousins, hampered by the usual culprits, their wayward mothers. See Schiesari on Hamlet in *The Gendering of Melancholia*, 240–241 and 263–264, and Silverman on *Rebel Without a Cause* in *The Subject of Semiotics*, 139–140.

27. An example from U.S. history and cinema can help illustrate this point. The convergent derealization of the suffering female and suffering other in the language of self-reproduction and loss is well demonstrated by Brian de Palma's

film *Casualties of War.* As Pat Aufderheide observes in "Good Soldiers," "In *Casualties of War,* American atrocities lead back to American casualties. The farm girl's suffering—filmed in a style that makes it, horrifyingly, a pornography of pity—is the vehicle leading us to the film's central tragedy: the collapse of a moral framework for the men who kill her. The spectacular agony of her death is intended to stir not the audience's righteous anger at the grunts . . . but empathy for the ordinary fighting men who have been turned into beasts by their tour of duty" (88). Aufderheide makes a strong case that Hollywood Vietnam "grunt films" in general have narcissistically derealized and allegorized the Vietnamese in the name of representing an American psychomachia and for the exclusive purpose of grieving U.S. losses. The technique of derealization in de Palma's film relies on the abstraction of woman.

28. In this context, it is noteworthy that the Mitscherlichs skirt the issue of the male narcissist's fear of sexual difference, an even more inaugural difference than that of race or nation. This is no small oversight, given their focus on ego structures dependent on the devaluation of others.

29. See Haraway, *Simians, Cyborgs, and Women,* 19.

30. Ibid., 17–18. Haraway does not mention Mitscherlich per se, but her critique of the ways in which the principle of domination was made to "penetrate" the tools of science, granted the role of a fetish, provides an indispensable context for evaluating Mitscherlich—and any other work that assumes science to be outside ideology. It should also be noted that the authoritarian personality studies were neither univocal nor uniformly sexist. In *The Authoritarian Personality,* for example, Else Frenkel-Brunswik links America's weaker-than-German fathers to America's reduced susceptibility to a fascist ideology. See Adorno et al., *The Authoritarian Personality,* 370. Conversely, Mitscherlich views the United States as a land that had witnessed the "shocking collapse of paternal authority," and as a land where "Father never knew best" (*Society without the Father,* 147).

31. Haraway, *Simians, Cyborgs, and Women,* 18.

32. Mitscherlich, *Society without the Father,* 269–270. Mitscherlich's demonized public mother-goddess recalls the false Maria from *Metropolis* and seems equally a male fantasy's creation.

33. His brief discussion of women's need to transcend maternal identity is limited to a consideration of the desire for status, consumer goods, and leisure (*Society without the Father,* 56–57). Completely overlooked are women's needs for political involvement and accountability, knowledge of the world, and creative self-expression. Also disregarded is the historical dynamic that first made the bourgeois woman's *not* working outside the home a mark of status for her husband. (Confinement of women to a private sphere was related to the emer-

gence of the bourgeois public sphere.) On the postwar discourse that charged women with corrupt materialistic self-interest, see Fehrenbach, *Cinema in Democratizing Germany*, 103 and 105.

34. On feminist social science, see Haraway, *Simians, Cyborgs, and Women*, 19; on ancient matrifocal social organization as an opposite to fascism, see Eisler, *The Chalice and the Blade*, especially 21–28; on the nonhierarchic aesthetics of von Trotta and other German women filmmakers, see Knight, *Women and the New German Cinema*, 144–146. Also relevant to the debate about authoritarianism are Dinnerstein's criticisms of Norman O. Brown in *The Mermaid and the Minotaur*, 182–184 and Haraway's critique of Brown in *Simians, Cyborgs, and Women*, 9–10.

35. See Wrangham and Peterson, *Demonic Males*.

36. Ibid., 205.

37. Ibid., 221.

38. I do not want to give the impression that Mitscherlich is concerned with women's rights for their own sake. His focus lies exclusively on the homosocial order—or what he terms the "unisexual" nature of contemporary political struggles. He asserts that at present, "the whole problem of the father-son relationship as well as the rivalry between sons themselves, have assumed great, perhaps primary, importance" (*Society without the Father*, 301). The rhetorics of "feminization" in his text identify actual women as marginal.

39. Mitscherlich, *Society without the Father*, 145–146. Huyssen's analysis of modernism's gendering of both mass culture and technology as feminine is relevant here; see *After the Great Divide*, 44–81. Also see Schiesari's discussion of gender nostalgia (*The Gendering of Melancholia*, 31–32).

40. For an analysis of the constitutional and judicial measures taken in West Germany to reinstate and fortify patriarchal authority in the family and government, see, for example, Kosta, *Recasting Autobiography*, 169–170. Kosta explains: "The conservatism of government policy toward the family extended into the legislative branch, acutely polarizing gender roles. In acts such as Amendment 1356 of the nation's constitution (Bürgerliches Gesetzbuch, BGB), women were reminded of their primary obligation to the private sphere. . . . Such laws betray a desperate desire to reinstate the father, who traditionally functions as a symbolic embodiment of the state." Also see Kolinsky, *Women in West Germany*, 43ff.

41. For a critique of Schelsky's family politics, see Moeller, *Protecting Motherhood*, 117–120, 191. Cf. Mitscherlich, *Society without the Father*, 302.

42. The most positive response is that of Robert and Carol Reimer. They argue that "Sanders-Brahms's *Germany, Pale Mother* offers viewers perhaps the fullest experience of any of the Nazi-retro films" (*Nazi-Retro Films*, 203). Conversely,

the film's various detractors believe it disavows a certain political responsibility for fascism. I will address these issues in chapter 2.

43. Kawin, *Mindscreen*.

44. For example, she asserts that, "like [the film's protagonist], I was rebellious, a non-compliant schoolgirl" (interview, New Yorker Films press packet). A similar directorial autobiographical component can be detected in Agnieszka Holland's retelling of Solomon Perel's life in *Europa, Europa*. For a discussion of the blurred boundaries between biography and autobiography, see Wagner-Martin, *Telling Women's Lives*, especially 74–77.

45. Elsaesser, *New German Cinema*, 233.

46. See von Trotta, *Die bleierne Zeit*, 79.

47. For an analysis of the ways fiction functions within autobiography as a means to captivate the spectator, especially in order to overcome spectatorial resistance to difficult truths, see Roger F. Cook's insightful "Melodrama or Cinematic Folktale?"

48. See Kosta, *Recasting Autobiography*, 162. For additional perspectives on the complex fictionalizing processes within filmic life stories, see Linville, "*Europa, Europa*: A Test Case."

49. Rosenbaum, "'Frieden' hat für uns Deutsche einen amerikanischen Geschmack," 28.

50. My application of the label "feminist" is not limited by the directors' stated positions on feminism, any more than my reading of their films is circumscribed by their stated intentions and interpretations. Helma Sanders-Brahms, for one, does not affiliate herself with feminism as she defines it. Her explications of her films, moreover, lend credence to Barthes's view that the author should be invited as a guest to the table of interpretation. See Helma Sanders-Brahms, "Helma Sanders-Brahms: A Conversation," especially 36–39. Similarly, von Trotta has resisted the feminist label—a label that can be the kiss of death for a film that seeks to be commercially viable. For an astute discussion of von Trotta's "choice" of mainstream audience support over vocal solidarity with other feminist filmmakers, see Ward, "Enacting the Different Voice," 54.

51. Miller, "Representing Others," 15 and 3. This cold-war rhetoric is, of course, also anti-authoritarian rhetoric according to the lights of the times.

52. See Friedman, "Women's Autobiographical Selves," 42–43. Christine de Pizan's groundbreaking *Book of the City of Ladies* (1405) is one early example.

53. Miller, "Representing Others," 3.

54. Ibid., 9. This observation is strikingly relevant as well for Agnieszka Holland's *Europa, Europa*, a film based on Solomon Perel's memoirs, and for Louis Begley's remarkable novel *Wartime Lies* (New York: Ivy Books, 1991).

55. Bunch stated, "There is no private domain of a person's life that is not political

and there is no political issue that is not ultimately personal. The old barriers have fallen" (as quoted in Bordo, *Unbearable Weight,* 17).

56. See Gilligan, *In a Different Voice,* and Gilligan et al., *Mapping the Moral Domain,* especially 3–19.

57. Kosta, *Recasting Autobiography,* 19, 33.

58. Ibid., 156.

59. And as Mark Crispin Miller has demonstrated (in "Deride and Conquer"), self-reflexivity can be the tool of cynical commercialism. Though it is a crucial component of feminist aesthetics, there is nothing *inherently* progressive about it.

60. Knight, *Women and the New German Cinema,* 65.

61. Certainly, as Knight notes, "women's cinema in West Germany has been based to a considerable degree on autobiographical material" (*Women and the New German Cinema,* 65). The phenomenon of the New German auteur as *star,* on the other hand, has been largely limited to male directors. For further discussion, see Timothy Corrigan's analysis of Alexander Kluge in *A Cinema Without Walls,* 115–122, and Elsaesser on Fassbinder in "Historicizing the Subject," 31–33.

62. Concomitantly, for a feminist filmmaker to conceptualize history in terms of the distinctive individual who guides and directs it is tantamount to reproducing history à la Hollywood.

63. Flitterman-Lewis, *To Desire Differently,* 21–22.

CHAPTER ONE

1. These comic qualities re-emerge in two later, better-known auto/biographical films that address the fascist past: Michael Verhoeven's *The Nasty Girl* (1990) and Agnieszka Holland's *Europa, Europa* (1991). For an assessment of the former, see Linda Mizejewski's excellent commentary in *Divine Decadence* (237–239). For an analysis of the latter, see Linville, "Agnieszka Holland's *Europa, Europa.*" For a discussion of the reception of *Peppermint Peace,* Rosenbaum's first film, see Rosenbaum, "'Frieden' hat für uns Deutsche einen amerikanischen Geschmack." Rosenbaum emphasizes women's positive responses to her film and explains that by 1984 she had traveled a great deal with the film and spoken with more than 10,000 people about it. The film won five prestigious awards and, up to the present, has continued to be shown on German television.

2. For an extended analysis and critique of these movements, see McCormick, *The Politics of the Self.*

3. The woman-dominated "nuclear freeze" movement in the United States of this period—a movement which most Republicans opposed—also merits men-

tion. (Outrageously, in political discourse of the 1990s, that antinuclear position continues to be reduced to a form of "risk-aversion" typical of women.) For suggestive perspectives on the continuing relevance of the values espoused by one of the more important German pro-peace filmmakers, see McCormick, "Cinematic Form, History, and Gender."

4. Tröger, "German Women's Memories of World War II," 299.

5. The Bavarian Catholic church even came under scrutiny by U.S. officials, so threatening to American goals for democratization did its activities appear. See Fehrenbach, *Cinema in Democratizing Germany*, 121ff. Also see Fehrenbach for perspectives on the incapacities, sometimes feigned, of German veterans, and their attempts to reclaim sexual dominance (95–99).

6. For West Germans as for audiences in the United States, both Peter and Jane Fonda were actors whose antiwar politics were encoded into their representation on screen.

7. Weinberger, *Nazi Germany and Its Aftermath in Women Directors' Autobiographical Films of the Late 1970s*, 126.

8. Joint Chiefs of Staff (JCS) directive 1067, based on the assumption that German history proved Germans to be intrinsically militaristic and antiliberal, forbade fraternization between the occupation forces and German nationals in order to prevent the spread of the so-called German contagion. As Fehrenbach documents, "Shamelessly engaging in tourist-variety national stereotyping, the official instructional film for U.S. soldiers, *Your Job in Germany*, counseled wariness and extreme caution when confronting the natives, 'no matter how charming and clean and blond and music-loving they seem, no matter how prettily and innocently they execute peasant dances in the village square.' It even 'specifically warn[ed] soldiers to ignore children, all steeped in Nazi propaganda'" (*Cinema in Democratizing Germany*, 53–54). Thus Mr. Frieden defies the rules by fraternizing not only with Nilla but also with the children.

9. For a relevant discussion of the differing positions the Catholic and Protestant churches were to take on the issue of West German rearmament, see Malhlmann, "Kirche und Wiederbewaffnung," and Moeller, *Protecting Motherhood*, 104–105. Herr Expositus resembles those Catholic politicians who saw not only the "Commie" but also the "Ami," or American, as a danger to the family.

10. Mühlhiasl (Mathias Lang from Apoig [1758–1825]). Weinberger explains: "An integral part of the prophecies of Mühlhiasl are male-chauvinist scare tactics, implying that women who try to be like men would be to blame for the biggest war ever. From Mühlhiasl's days on in the spiritist circles in Bavaria . . . , this prediction has served as a perfect instrument to keep women in their traditional role" (*Nazi Germany and Its Aftermath*, 109–110). By having Herr Arira endorse these views, the film, in hindsight, seems to anticipate and refute erroneous post-*Historikerstreit* conflations of two very different phenomena: the

German war veterans' claims to victim status and feminist critiques of the patriarchal oppression of women under the Nazi and postwar regimes. For a discussion of the *Historikerstreit*, or Historians's Debate, in relation to issues of feminist film, see, for example, the special issue of the journal *October* devoted to Helke Sander's *Liberators Take Liberties* (co-edited by Stuart Liebman and Annette Michelson).

11. For a valuable discussion of the influence of not only Italian culture but also Czech filmmaking on Rosenbaum, see Weinberger, "Marianne Rosenbaum and the Aesthetics of *Angst*."

12. To be sure, as Steinborn and Hilmes observe, Marianne commands a more sophisticated vocabulary than a young child is likely to have possessed. Rosenbaum's rationale for giving relatively advanced verbal skills to this representation of her younger self is that she now has the words to match the feelings she experienced then; she therefore sees no discrepancy in her film (Rosenbaum, "'Frieden,'" 28).

13. Her father's embarrassment over the preschooler's inappropriate loyalty generates humor. So too does his contradictory role as a paternal authority asserting himself by negating reverence for such authority. At another level, the girl's reaction to the burnt portraits points up the self-deception of the father's iconoclasm. The father cannot sever his relationship to the Reich simply by destroying the visible evidence that the Reich itself fetishized. Ironically, the belief that he can do so perpetuates the Reich's fetishization of the visible, and it obliquely recalls Nazi book burnings as well.

14. The phrase "chewing gum culture" is Rosenbaum's. See Rosenbaum, "'Frieden,'" 28.

15. Ibid., 30.

16. Kaschak, *Engendered Lives*, 182.

17. Ibid., 76. Because Ismene is dutiful to Creon and Antigone to her father and brothers, the sisters seem opposites. Yet neither identifies with Jocasta, nor she with them.

18. Ibid.

19. Olivier, *Jocasta's Children*, 50. Both Olivier and Dinnerstein see the antidote to matrophobia as an alternative child-rearing arrangement to the present one of maternal dominion in early childhood and paternal dominion thereafter. Founded on an early parenting partnership with shared responsibility, theirs is a model that grants both parents equity in both the private and public spheres. Dinnerstein argues that this familial arrangement could help make patriarchal despotism and the equation of the feminine with the regressive obsolete. Also see Tania Modleski on Dinnerstein and on Klaus Theweleit's *Male Fantasies*, in *Feminism Without Women*, 67–69.

20. See Olivier, *Jocasta's Children*, 96–97, for further discussion.

21. A contrast with Wenders is revealing. In *Wings of Desire*, as Modleski notes, the camera "moves in the same kind of prying manner (frequently from high above, craning down to a particularized view) that Hitchcock would often use—only Hitchcock would manage to suggest the moral dubiousness of such voyeurism" (*Feminism Without Women*, 106). Further, as Kathe Geist has shown, Wenders creates an idealized, fetishized view of childhood that, unlike Rosenbaum's, suppresses the child's historical subjectivity. See Geist, "Mothers and Children in the Films of Wim Wenders."

22. The situation demonstrates the problematic nature of Mitscherlich's contention that "no social arrangement can ever adequately take the place of the intimacy of the mother-child relationship; the child can acquire basic trust with its mother and with no one else" (*Society without the Father*, 282).

23. To be sure, like Rosenbaum, Alexander Mitscherlich is critical of the methods of indoctrinating children that are used by the Catholic church (*Society without the Father*, 91). But unlike Rosenbaum, he fails to realize that the problem with the church is structural and that solving it is not simply a matter of injecting the church hierarchy with more "enlightened" educational attitudes.

24. Helma Sanders-Brahms's *Germany, Pale Mother* generates a similar indictment of the church by portraying Lene's unsavory Uncle Bertrand as a high-ranking official in the air force ministry under the Nazis and then, after the war, as an administrator with a comparable position in the church.

25. For a brief discussion of related perspectives on fascism in the work of André Glucksman and Michel Foucault, see Weinberger, "Aesthetics of *Angst*," 238–239.

26. See Koonz, *Mothers in the Fatherland*, 268–269. Koonz also provides an extended analysis of the similarities between Hitler's messianism and Catholicism. An additional resource on the subject is Alison Owings's interviews with Catholic women in *Frauen*.

27. Silverman, *The Acoustic Mirror*, 204.

28. Weinberger compares the presentation of Marianne in this sequence with compositions familiar from "paintings by Romantic artists (especially Caspar David Friedrich). The viewer does not only see the action from the girl's point-of-view, but she is presented through the act of looking. Although removed from the action Marianne becomes the subject with the authority of the look. The action is transmitted to the viewer by her perception: The feelings and sensations she observes are foreign to her. The movie viewer's direct identification with observed action is blocked by the alienated viewer within the picture. . . . The visual set-up with a figure whose back is towards the viewer is used repeatedly by the filmmaker. It is a constant for this film's alienated perceptions" (*Nazi Germany*, 149–150).

29. For a discussion of "The Frog King," see Bettelheim, *The Uses of Enchantment*,

286–291. For a further discussion of fairy-tale motifs in *Peppermint Frieden*, see Linville, "Fairy Tales and Reflexivity in Marianne Rosenbaum's *Peppermint Peace*."

30. The priest's main concern, as Richard W. McCormick notes, "is obviously the sexual freedom manifested by the single German woman [Nilla]," ("Fascism, Film, and Gender," 19). For a highly elucidating analysis of the attacks on women's sexual freedom during this era, see Fehrenbach, *Cinema in Democratizing Germany*, 98–117. Quoting the Protestant High Consistory in Stuttgart as evidence, Fehrenbach asserts, "If the rhetoric of gender in the immediate postwar period was to be believed, then, the National Socialist war of aggression was a mere prelude to a more devastating national catastrophe brought on by the betrayal of German women" (99).

31. A similar symbol, with a pyramid in place of the triangle, appears on the U.S. dollar bill.

32. See Rosenbaum's critique of pyramidal power structures, which she contrasts with the nonhierarchic, decentralized roundness of the world (quoted in Weinberger, *Nazi Germany*, 110), and her comments on the relationship between hierarchy, corporeality, and economics ("'Frieden,'" 30). Also see Weinberger's discussion of the terrorism of church and state as these are conjoined in Herr Expositus's sermon to his congregation (*Nazi Germany*, 118).

33. This surveillance becomes internalized just as male judgment of female beauty does. John Berger asserts, "The surveyor of woman in herself is male: the surveyed female. Thus she turns herself into an object—and most particularly an object of vision: a sight" (*Ways of Seeing*, 47).

34. *Hunger Years* and *Marianne and Juliane* also affirm the idea that the female subject is made to internalize a harsher standard of accountability. Valuable critiques of Freud's erroneous views on the underdevelopment of the superego in women can be found in Silverman, *The Acoustic Mirror*, 157, and Schiesari, *The Gendering of Melancholia*, 60.

35. Sagan, *Freud, Women, and Morality*, 63.

36. For an extended discussion of the Bruckmühl incident, see Fehrenbach, *Cinema in Democratizing Germany*, 78.

37. Schiesari, *The Gendering of Melancholia*, 236.

38. See Warner, *Alone of All Her Sex*, 218.

39. Tröger, "German Women's Memories," 299.

40. I refer to Laura Mulvey's well-known and influential essay, "Visual Pleasure and Narrative Cinema."

41. Marianne also has a private stash of fetishes, including both chewing gum and religious emblems. Rosenbaum's skill at satirizing simultaneously the church, America's ideas on democratizing Germany, and fetishism is finely honed.

42. In so doing, as Weinberger points out, Marianne becomes a Virgin Mary who

"defies the image of the passive, suffering Mary invented by the Catholic Church. Mary's seven sorrows (or dolors) of the Catholic dogma, represented in religious images as knives thrust into Mary's heart, become in Marianne's imagination 'seven swords' with which she counters wrongdoing" (*Nazi Germany*, 120). In fact, Marianne's stance can be likened to Hildegard of Bingen's resistance to the Christian idealization of suffering. See Schiesari, *The Gendering of Melancholia*, 159.

43. Marianne whispers a prayer to Mary to ward off war: "Stop Him, Holy Mary, stop God from letting people do what they want, like in the last war, or like in paradise." She then shouts to God, "If they drop the atom bomb, your church will be destroyed too!" The film thus brings its critique of the symbolic cluster Eve/Mary, war/peace, guilt/redemption into focus.

CHAPTER TWO

1. For summaries of the film's critical reception at the time of its release in Germany, see Bammer, "Through a Daughter's Eyes," 94; Kaes, *From Hitler to Heimat*, 250; and Fischetti, *Das Neue Kino*, 121–124, especially her discussion of Olav Münzberg's article, "'Schaudern vor der *bleichen Mutter*.' Eine sozialpsychologische Analyse der Kritiken zum Film von Helma Sanders-Brahms," (*Medium* 7 [July 1980]: 34–37). As Fischetti explains, Münzberg analyzes the almost universally and aggressively negative response to the film as a sign that it created a too unprotected, too personal autobiographical act of *Vergangenheitsbewältigung* for those of Sanders-Brahms's generation to be able to endure. Hence the critics' efforts to deny or trivialize the film. Contradicting Münzberg, Renate Möhrmann argues that it was the film's unprecedented treatment of motherhood that caused male critics to be repelled by it. See Möhrmann, "'Germany, Pale Mother': On the Mother Figures in New German Women's Film."

2. Bammer, "Through a Daughter's Eyes," 101.

3. Santner, *Stranded Objects*, 155.

4. Silverman, *The Acoustic Mirror*, 123–140.

5. The Mitscherlichs' foreword to the 1975 American edition of their work reflects qualified optimism about change: "Still," they affirm, "there is no ignoring the fact that some radical effort to confront the issues of guilt arising from the events of the 'Third Reich' has taken place" (*The Inability to Mourn*, xx). At the same time, as Ken Burns's documentary on the American Civil War (*The Civil War*, 1990) reminds us, a nation's coming to terms with the horrific chapters in its history is inevitably a protracted process.

6. Santner, *Stranded Objects*, 170.

7. Ibid., 170–171.

8. See Mitscherlich and Mitscherlich, *The Inability to Mourn*, 33–43, 198.

9. Santner, *Stranded Objects*, 5.

10. See Mosse, *Nationalism and Sexuality*, 143, and Modleski, *Feminism Without Women*, 68.

11. Santner, *Stranded Objects*, 22–23.

12. Arguably the loss mourned by Apollo is better understood as a forfeiture not of the object of his desire, but of the phallus for which the laurel tree stands. Daphne means laurel or bay in Greek; the elision of female subjectivity is linguistically enforced.

13. Schiesari, *The Gendering of Melancholia*, 263.

14. Hirsch, *The Mother/Daughter Plot*, 169. Hirsch's invaluable text inspired the title of this chapter.

15. "You say you didn't want it [i.e., the Third Reich], but you did nothing to stop it," says the daughter in voice-over.

16. See Chodorow, *The Reproduction of Mothering*, especially 7 and 188.

17. Silverman, *The Acoustic Mirror*, 155.

18. Ibid., as quoted.

19. Ibid., 158.

20. Ibid., 151.

21. Ibid., 125.

22. Ibid., 154.

23. Silverman's position also opposes much 1950s Hollywood film discourse on the family of the kind epitomized by Hitchcock's *The Man Who Knew Too Much* (1956). For a relevant discussion of that film, see Corber, *In the Name of National Security*, 111–153. The matrophobic elements reflected by the film's conceptualization of the mother-son dyad dovetail with the Mitscherlichs' emphasis on "effeminate," mother-dependent male personality traits in the case histories they present to illustrate the principle that "[t]he weaker our ego, the more unquestioningly it has to accept the distortion of reality offered by collective opinion and determined by our own inner development" (36–37, 41). Neither the film nor this postwar theory considers the prospect that eliminating the familial roots of dysfunction would require subverting patriarchy per se. Yet the solution to the problems the Mitscherlichs detail cannot derive from a system that fortifies the son's ego at women's expense and that thereby precludes, because it has no model for, healthy feminization.

24. Bammer, "Through a Daughter's Eyes," 102.

25. See Hirsch, *The Mother/Daughter Plot*, especially 5–6 and 34–36.

26. Not all women emerged from this experience so easily. The mass rape of German women by Allied, especially Soviet, troops at the end of World War II is the subject of a controversial documentary by Helke Sander, *BeFreier und Befreite (Liberators Take Liberties*, 1992). See Sander, "There Should Be No Scis-

sors in Your Mind"; and *October* 72 (1995), a special issue dedicated to discussion of the film and co-edited by Liebman and Michelson.

27. Kosta, *Recasting Autobiography*, 123.

28. At the same time, the film avoids a simplistic glorification of the mother-daughter dyad as experienced from the child's point of view. Richard McCormick explains: "[As the voice-over] mentions this fantasy of flying [witches], the scene shifts, and documentary footage is inserted: aerial footage shot from a plane flying over the bombed-out buildings of Berlin. Here the documentary footage provides the corrective to the idealized fantasies of the child, showing what it would actually have meant to fly over the houses of Berlin, many of which had no roofs" ("Fascism, Film, and Gender," 11).

29. Even the film's first scene shows Lene's harrassment by Nazi soldiers and Hans and Ulrich's passive acceptance of it. In that scene, Hans makes no protest, let alone any attempt to intervene to defend Lene from the soldiers. Instead of speaking up for her, he and Ulrich praise her silence.

30. Freud, "Female Sexuality," 226.

31. Schneider, "Fathers and Sons, Retrospectively," 30–31.

32. Her behavior conforms with Freud's notion that what is repeated is that which has been previously repressed—an earlier means of psychically negotiating one's world.

33. Sanders-Brahms, "Helma Sanders-Brahms: A Conversation," 37. Santner reads this cluster of images oppositely from me. He contends that the film fails to link Lene's symptomatic facial paralysis back to her lack of compassion for the victims of Germany's genocidal crimes: "Rather than providing an opening through which the second generation might catch a glimpse of a lost chance for resistance and solidarity with the Jewish victims, [Lene's] symptom closes the blinds once more on this other suffering—on the suffering of the other—and becomes a sign pure and simple of a woman's suffering under a particularly oppressive form of patriarchy" (156).

34. The man who diagnoses Lene's condition says she must have her teeth extracted to halt the spread of the paralysis, and with Hans's consent but over Lene's protests, the doctor pulls all her teeth—a pointless procedure that we witness in grueling detail. The ordeal underscores how utterly the social gender hierarchy strips Lene of her autonomy during the postwar years. The episode also recalls an earlier scene in which Uncle Bertrand sanctimoniously commands a famished, homeless Lene to eat slowly—"chew one chew for every tooth in your mouth"—as if he were admonishing a child.

35. My thanks to Eberhard Griem for pointing this fact out to me.

36. Silverman, *The Acoustic Mirror*, 9.

37. Hirsch's analysis of that myth is particularly relevant here; see *The Mother/Daughter Plot*, especially 35–36.

38. Silverman, *The Acoustic Mirror*, 39.

39. Ibid., 164.

40. In another sense, the film's use of female voice-over resonates with Silverman's view that "the maternal voice is . . . what first ruptures plenitude and introduces difference," and is also, in cinematic terms, the "first voice-over and voice-off—as the generator of sounds that proceed from beyond the child's range of vision, or that precede its ability to see" (*The Acoustic Mirror*, 86). Anna/ Helma's voice, then, suggests an acoustic mother/daughter synthesis.

41. Bammer, "Though a Daughter's Eyes," 96.

42. Some readings have pushed the film's allegorical dimensions too far, divining an unproblematized representation of a divided Germany in Lene's half-covered face throughout the last portion of the film (Kaplan, "The Search for the Mother/Land in Sanders-Brahms's *Germany, Pale Mother*," 302), or seeing the aerial footage edited together with Lene's rape as a figure either for the allies' "rape" of Germany (Seiter, "Women's History, Women's Melodrama," 580) or for Germany's "rape" by Hitler (Hyams, "Is the Apolitical Woman at Peace?," 46). Totalizing analogies between Lene and Germany reduce the film's dialogic complexity and can stem, ironically, from a reductive sense of the range of politically viable cinematic tropes. In seeking to weed out retrograde, masculinist discourse in films with feminist aims, critics sometimes end up articulating a smaller and smaller range of possibilities for feminist intervention rather than seeing how retrograde modes, such as allegory and melodrama, when recontextualized or deconstructed, can be made to serve new ends. For a superb analysis of Sanders-Brahms's subversive use of melodrama, see McCormick, *Politics of the Self*, 193–198. McCormick emphasizes the way Brechtian distanciation technique counterpoints melodrama and spectator immersion in narrative.

43. Bammer, "Through a Daughter's Eyes," 103–105.

44. McCormick, "Fascism, Film, and Gender," 12.

45. Of course, the *Kinoschreiben* constitutes Lene's identity not only ambiguously but also heterogeneously and heteronomously—as a product of subjective memory, in the context of a heteroglossia of discourses, including fairy-tale narrative and documentary footage, in illusionistic space placed in anti-illusionist contexts, and in terms of social class. It avoids a positive image approach, and thereby resists a bourgeois morality, a status quo politics, and the attendant realist aesthetics.

46. Woolf, *Three Guineas*, 109.

47. See Kaplan, "The Search for the Mother/Land," 290–291, and Kaes, *From Hitler to Heimat*, 147, for alternative readings of Heine's poem and its relationship to *Germany, Pale Mother*.

48. Jürgen Kneiper's music throughout the film deserves more commentary than I

can give it here, especially for its contribution to the film's finely differentiated elegiac aesthetics. As Sanders-Brahms explains, Kneiper's music adds a third level to the film, and its intelligence arises out of a remarkable capacity for feeling. See Sanders-Brahms, *Deutschland, bleiche Mutter,* 120.

49. See Bettelheim, *The Uses of Enchantment,* 225–236.

50. Moreover, in contrast to the female erotic spectacle that, according to Laura Mulvey, defines the usual terms by which women's presence intrudes on narrative forward progress (*Visual and Other Pleasures,* 19–20), the "Robber Bridegroom" story within the film's story creates disruption through a woman's enunciation—that is, through a woman's narration *en abime.*

51. Kaes, *From Hitler to Heimat,* 13.

52. Goethe, *Faust,* vol. I, l. 1055, p. 34.

CHAPTER THREE

1. Baudrillard, *La Société de consummation,* as quoted in Turim, "Gentlemen Consume Blondes," 106.

2. Mitscherlich and Mitscherlich, *The Inability to Mourn,* 27.

3. Jutta Brückner, "Entretien de Sceaux," 44.

4. To be sure, it was not only in West Germany but also throughout much of the West in general that a consumer dynamic became definitive in the 1950s, once the consumerism that had been delayed by the Depression and World War II was no longer impeded. This period saw the incidence of anorexia among daughters of middle-class families sharply increase (Caskey, "Interpreting Anorexia Nervosa," 177). Interestingly, Freud early on identified "the nutritional neurosis parallel to melancholia" as "the famous *anorexia nervosa* of young girls" ("Extracts from the Fliess Papers," 200). For a discussion of Freud's findings, see Schiesari, *The Gendering of Melancholia,* 55.

5. For a relevant discussion of the later feminization of the GDR and masculinization of the FRG during unification, see Morrison, "The Feminization of the German Democratic Republic in Political Cartoons 1989–1990." For an analysis of patriarchal binarisms, see Hélène Cixous and Catherine Clément's influential *The Newly Born Woman.* Stressing the underlying opposition of man/woman within patriarchal binary thought, Cixous terms such thought "a universal battlefield," stating, "Each time, a war is let loose. Death is always at work" (64).

6. Joan Riviere, "Womanliness as a Masquerade." Also see Möhrmann, "Jutta Brückner."

7. This nexus comes across effectively in the French verb *consommer* and its noun, *le consummation,* which apply to commodities, to marriage, and to meals. (The word "sumptuary," signifying "dress and food expenditures," is related.) For

relevant discussions of the reciprocal relationship between eating disorders (specifically gorging) and consumerism, see Mintz, "Self-Destructive Behavior in Anorexia and Bulimia"; and Bordo, *Unbearable Weight,* 201.

8. For a valuable summary of these theories, see Kellner, *Jean Baudrillard,* 14.

9. Brückner, interview with Patricia Harbord, 57–58.

10. Ibid., 56.

11. Ibid., 57.

12. See Doane, "The Spectatrix," and also her *Desire to Desire,* 12–13.

13. Brückner asserts, "In the course of time, over the centuries, women have delegated their epistemophilic gaze ['*Forscherblick*'] to men. In those instances in which women still have vestiges of the '*Forscherblick,*' it has become either restricted to a microcosm (in this sense it has indeed become more 'differentiated') or it has in fact grown into a voyeur-gaze. The real voyeur, I think, is the woman, not the man. She had no other recourse" (interview with Renate Fischetti, 200–201). For a relevant discussion of female voyeurism and fetishism with a difference, see Williams, "'Something Else Besides a Mother,'" especially 154–158, where she asserts the need for "examining the contradictions that animate women's very active and fragmented ways of seeing" (157).

14. John Sandford observes, "It was an axiom of the American 're-education' programme that if Germany were flooded with the products of American culture, the Germans would, by some mysterious process of osmosis, be transformed into shining exemplars of Truth, Justice, and The American Way. Hollywood was delighted: here was a vast market, potentially the biggest in Europe, that had been closed to them throughout the war years. A great backlog of films that had already paid their way elsewhere could now be rereleased at prices that would undercut any competition. The Germans, not unnaturally, were pleased too, and flocked to see the films they had been denied access to by the Nazis" (*The New German Cinema,* 9). Also see Fehrenbach, *Cinema in Democratizing Germany,* 51–77.

15. Brückner, interview with Harbord, 57. Despite this generalized address to the female spectator, and despite the strong critical response and numerous awards *Hunger Years* received in Europe, it has only recently begun to garner the kind of attention it deserves from film scholars in the United States. Gabriele Weinberger speculates about the causes as follows: "Many reasons could be named for [the film's] rather reserved—although generally positive—reception [in the United States], among them probably the film's expressionistic aesthetic, its negative portrayal of motherhood, its special kind of sexual explicitness, ending in a suicide attempt and the interspersed violent visual clusters of German political memory which have neither denotational nor connotational meaning for the American audience" (*Nazi Germany and its Aftermath in Women Directors' Autobiographical Films of the Late 1970s,* 166).

16. While Fassbinder's *Marriage of Maria Braun* deals with the same era and with some of the same economic and political issues as *Hunger Years,* his cinema in general is characterized by a pronounced aestheticization of women, of violence against women, and of women's suffering, all of which militate against a positive feminist reading of his work. For further discussion, see Elsaesser, "*Berlin Alexanderplatz:* Franz Biberkopf/S/Exchanges," 40.

17. Doane, *Femmes Fatales,* 93.

18. Freud "Femininity" *S.E.* 22: 135.

19. Dialogical montage creates interaction and conflict between voices, images, and discourses, but these retain their identity and are not resolved into a third entity or synthesis, as happens with dialectical dynamics. As Brückner affirms, "My films are constructed out of many autonomous particles" (interview with Fischetti, 200). Dialogical montage also militates against a reading of Ursula that would reduce her experiences to an allegorical trope for the German nation.

20. Kosta, *Recasting Autobiography,* 156. Also see Brückner's discussion of the film's segmentation in "Entretien de Sceaux," 20ff.

21. See Caskey, "Interpreting Anorexia Nervosa," 178.

22. Her consumerism is the kind conservatives condoned. See Fehrenbach, *Cinema in Democratizing Germany,* 112.

23. See Koonz, *Mothers in the Fatherland,* 12–13.

24. As Margaret McCarthy notes, Ursula binges here in an unmistakably sexualized fashion: "The manner in which she retrieves the cake . . . is highly sexual: she squats with the [garbage] pail between her legs, running her hands up and down her thighs before reaching in to salvage it. Ursula becomes here, like her father's lover, a deviant body whose unchecked eating signals sexual excess and bodily needs that will not be met" ("Consolidating, Consuming, and Annulling Identity in Jutta Brückner's *Hungerjahre,*" 23).

25. Brückner, "Entretien de Sceaux," 108.

26. This darkly humorous depiction of adolescent voyeurism affords a revealing contrast with and complement to a lighthearted sequence from *Peppermint Peace* in which the as-yet uninhibited, chewing gum–loving children attempt to peer through a keyhole to observe Nilla and Mr. Frieden's illicit amour.

27. In the United States, the first public demonstration staged by the feminist movement born in the 1960s was the "No More Miss America" protest of August 1968, at which a position paper was distributed that outlined how the pageant stood at the crossroads of consumerism, sexism, racism, ageism, and militarism. Brückner's contextualizing of the Miss World footage recalls and extends the politics of that important demonstration.

28. What made this critique of her mother possible, Brückner asserts, was first filming *Do Right and Fear Nobody,* which charts the mother's experiences as a

subject of sociohistorical forces. Brückner explains, "I could never have made [*Hunger Years*] without making the film about my mother first. After my first film I felt I could really begin to 'settle accounts' with my past—now that I had explained how my mother had become how she was, now I'd justified her, I could start to criticise her." Brückner also notes "how my mother broke out of this mould—very late, through a private catastrophe . . . and she tried to become a completely different person, someone strong and brave who speaks her mind" (interview with Harbord, 50, 51).

29. Bordo, for one, theorizes that the denial of appetite, sexual and alimentary, becomes both a way of warding off unwanted advances and a form of self-punishment. The culture faults the female for her own desire and for her provocation of desire in males; internalizing this ideology, the female blames and disciplines herself (*Unbearable Weight*, 8).

30. Bordo wrote in 1983: "In an age when our children regularly have nightmares of nuclear holocaust, that as adults we should . . . most fear 'getting fat'—is far more bizarre than the anorectic's misperceptions of her body image, or the bulimic's compulsive vomiting. The nightmares of nuclear holocaust and our desperate fixation on our bodies as arenas of control—perhaps one of the few areas of control we have left in the twentieth century—are not unconnected, of course. The connection, if explored, could be significant, demystifying, in- structive" (*Unbearable Weight*, 140–141). Also see Brückner's commentary on this sequence ("On Autobiographical Filmmaking," 9).

31. Garber, *Vested Interests*, 11–12.

32. For a discussion of nationalist but still patriarchist revolutionary struggles, see Shohat and Stam, *Unthinking Eurocentrism*, especially 254–255. Also see *Algeria: Women at War* (1992), a videotape produced by Parminder Vir.

33. Brückner, "Entretien de Sceaux," 27.

34. Brückner, "Entretien de Bruxelles," 109. Brückner also explained that she de- stroyed all the photographs of herself from this same period in her life ("En- tretien de Sceaux," 33).

35. Alexander Mitscherlich himself criticizes postwar cinema's problematic fasci- nation with the female body, specifically with large-breasted stars (*Society with- out the Father*, 291). From his viewpoint, however, the cult of these women stars forms an analogue to the cult of the mass leader, Hitler and Marilyn Monroe being seen as parallel icons. His analogy becomes less bizarre in light of Baudry's theory of the mother's breast as a screen onto which men project their desires. Thus, it would seem, even that ultimate fantasy of fathers and sons, Nazi Germany, can be projected and disavowed. The unprecedented valoriza- tion of female thinness in later postwar film—for example, the emaciation recalling women concentration camp inmates in Antonioni's *Blowup* (1966)— may be as much to the point. The eroticized skeletal woman can be seen as an

oblique reference to an event that is "unspeakable" except in the language of projection and connotation, the language of the female body.

36. John Berger, *Ways of Seeing*, 47.
37. Doane, *The Desire to Desire*, 13.
38. Doane, *Femmes Fatales*, 47.
39. Ibid., 48.
40. Irigaray, "Des marchandises entre elles."
41. Riviere, "Womanliness as a Masquerade," 43.
42. For a discussion of Lacan's ideas, see Doane, *Femmes Fatales*, 37–38.
43. Caskey, "Interpreting Anorexia Nervosa," 184. Also see Brumberg, *Fasting Girls*, 271.
44. See Doane, *The Desire to Desire*, 19.
45. Caskey, "Interpreting Anorexia Nervosa," 187.
46. Chernin, *The Hungry Self*, 42.
47. Ibid., 92.
48. Export, "The Real and Its Double," 25.
49. Ibid., 22.
50. Brückner, "Entretien de Sceaux," 44.
51. Wolowitz, "Hysterical Character and Feminine Identity," 313.
52. During her therapy with Breuer, Anna O. discovered the "talking cure" as the method of her own treatment. (Anna O. is the pseudonym for Bertha Pappenheim, who became an active feminist and the first German social worker.)
53. See Bernheimer, Introduction, *In Dora's Case*, 9.
54. Aubenas, "Le cinéma brut ou la brutalité de la biographie," 57.
55. For related perspectives on hysteria as a form of revolt against patriarchy, see Cixous and Clément, *The Newly Born Woman*, 147–160. Clément's discussion of the connections among cinema, hysteria, and the exchange of money also merits attention. See especially 13.
56. Linda Williams, "Film Bodies."
57. Brückner, in fact, speaks of her filmmaking praxis as a "labor of mourning for the cultural paralyzing of our bodies, our eyes, and our time-space relations. The goal: recuperating the means to reconstruct symbolically. . . . I mean recuperating our [women's] capacity to look" ("Recognizing Collective Gestures," 46).
58. Benn used the term "inner emigrant" to describe himself and others who stayed in Germany during the Third Reich but retreated into isolation, not participating but also not actively resisting. Similarly, at one point, the adult narrator in *Hunger Years* asks, "How could one live inside and outside at the same time?"
59. Kosta, *Recasting Autobiography*, 176.
60. Ramas, "Freud's Dora, Dora's Hysteria," 157.
61. Elsaesser, *New German Cinema*, 195.

62. The feeling of entrapment within the body and sense of imprisonment within domestic spaces are visually linked by the similarity between the striped pullover Ursula habitually wears and the striped wallpaper in the home.

63. As Nancy Chodorow observes, a daughter "does not receive the same kind of love from her mother as a boy does, i.e., a mother, rather than confirming her daughter's oppositeness and specialness, experiences her as one with herself; her relationship to her daughter is more 'narcissistic,' that to her son more 'anaclitic'" (*Feminism and Psychoanalytic Theory*, 72). The film shows Ursula's need precisely to have her "oppositeness and specialness" affirmed. For further discussion of Chodorow's relevance to *Hunger Years*, see Mouton, "The Absent Mother Makes an Appearance in the Films of West German Directors," 72–74.

64. For important analyses of the difficulties of this process for adolescent American girls in the 1980s, see Gilligan et al., *Making Connections*.

CHAPTER FOUR

1. Bachmann, as quoted in von Trotta, *Die bleierne Zeit*, 11.

2. To be sure, even as early as 1792, Mary Wollstonecraft had similarly acknowledged that "genteel women are, literally speaking, slaves to their bodies. . . . Taught from their infancy that beauty is woman's scepter, the mind shapes itself to the body, and, roaming round its gilt cage, only seeks to adorn its prison" (*Vindication of the Rights of Woman* [1792; New York: Penguin, 1985], 130–131). It is important to remember that these insights into personal politics and those of the feminists of the 1960s and 1970s predate Michel Foucault's work on disciplined bodies.

3. Jonathan Culler, *On Deconstruction*, 173.

4. Von Trotta disavowed the idea of collaboration on this film: "You can't co-direct. It's a hypocritical term. All I did was work with actors. Volker was in charge of the technique, the artistry, the way the film finally looked. As a director I make the decisions myself. I've watched and collaborated enough" (quoted in Treen, "The Lady behind the Lens").

5. As Paul Coates observes, *Marianne and Juliane* is "profoundly autobiographical. Von Trotta felt no compulsion to be constrained by all the details of the Ensslins' lives, and the image of the fifties as 'a leaden time' is intimately grounded in her own experience. This fusion has caused much confusion among critics prone to mistake the image for the prototype—something von Trotta's concern with mediation warns us against—and then to lacerate the director for putative sensationalism, opportunism, or infidelity. One can indeed argue that Von Trotta is more honest than filmmakers who claim that

resemblances between their characters and living persons are accidental" (*The Gorgon's Gaze*, 223).

6. For further discussion of differences between films by German women and those by men, see Fehervary et al., "From Hitler to Hepburn." An illuminating work that extends and internationalizes this discussion is Teresa de Lauretis's analysis of women's cinema in *Technologies of Gender* (127–148).

7. Morgan, *The Demon Lover*, 180–216.

8. See, for example, Corrigan, *New German Cinema: The Displaced Image;* Franklin, *New German Cinema: From Oberhausen to Hamburg;* Rentschler, *West German Cinema in the Course of Time;* and Sandford, *The New German Cinema.*

9. Elsaesser, *New German Cinema: A History*, 235. Other male scholars who are exceptional in their attention to women filmmakers of the New German Cinema include: Richard W. McCormick (especially *Politics of the Self*); H. B. Moeller ("West German Women's Cinema"); and Silberman ("Women Filmmakers in West Germany" and *German Cinema: Texts in Context*, 198–213). Barbara Koenig Quart provides the most extensive and most laudatory treatment of von Trotta to date, in featuring her as the foremost woman director among the Western Europeans. Yet this critique suffers from a narrow conceptualization of feminism. Quart asserts, "One is grateful that von Trotta is too complex, too ambiguous, to fit into any ideology; that she draws her vision from deeper, wilder places—more paradoxical, irrational, intransigent sources" (*Women Directors*, 94).

10. Delorme, "On the Film *Marianne and Juliane* by Margarethe von Trotta," 47.

11. Ibid., 50.

12. Ward, "Enacting the Different Voice," 54.

13. Seiter, "Women's History, Women's Melodrama: *Deutschland, bleiche Mutter*," 574.

14. Elsaesser, New German Cinema, 237.

15. Delorme, "On the Film *Marianne and Juliane*," 48–49.

16. Kaplan, "Discourses of Terrorism, Feminism and the Family in von Trotta's *Marianne and Juliane*," 67, 66. Among the critics who concur with this reading of the ending is Barton Byg, who summarizes and attempts to extend many of the criticisms leveled against the film; see Byg, "German History and Cinematic Convention Harmonized in Margarethe von Trotta's *Marianne and Juliane*," 259–271.

17. Johnson, *A World of Difference*, 30–31.

18. Kristeva, *Powers of Horror*, 4. For a valuable summary of Kristeva's main ideas, see Creed, "Horror and the Monstrous-Feminine."

19. Sprengnether, *The Spectral Mother*, 9.

20. By the same token, von Trotta's views must be differentiated from Kristeva's. For in *Marianne and Juliane*, which is contemporaneous with *The Powers of*

Horror, von Trotta forcefully contradicts Kristeva's later position urging that matricide—the psychic murder and violent abjection of the mother—is the daughter's only antidote to depression and the only basis for healthy mourning. In Kristeva's theory, the rhetoric of murderous violence against women forms the foundation for conceptualizing the mourning of loss, the successful evasion of melancholy. Remindful of cold-war matrophobia, this position is contrary to the spirit of von Trotta's work. See Schiesari, *The Gendering of Melancholia,* 77–93; and Kristeva, *Black Sun,* especially 28.

21. Von Trotta, interview, New Yorker Films press packet. The look of this color film reinforces the associations of grayness, in both the 1950s and the 1970s segments.

22. Kaplan differs from me on the chronology of the film, seeing the first scene as coinciding with Juliane's discovery "that Marianne could not have hanged herself after all—that her death was murder" ("Discourses of Terrorism," 63). In her view, then, the opening scene precedes Jan's being burned. While I would not rule out this reading, I emphasize the film's resistance to all such efforts to pinpoint the time of the opening scene; the only certainty is that it occurs no earlier than 1980, the latest date on one of Juliane's files.

23. Peter Wollen, *Signs and Meaning in the Cinema,* 124.

24. The black jeans are also a form of rebellion against her father. One recalls here Alexander Mitscherlich's assent to the idea that in America, "Father never knew best," a situation he laments (*Society without the Father,* 147). Many Germans in the 1950s and 1960s were concerned by the American-influenced *Halbstarke* (literally, the half-strong—teenagers, punks, undisciplined, rude young people).

25. On the ethics of sacrificing one's child to an ideology, see the valuable discussions of the story of Abraham and Isaac in Gilligan, *In a Different Voice,* 104–105; and Alice Miller, *The Untouched Key,* 137–145. Their arguments against this kind of sacrifice are informed by an acute awareness of the politics of the personal.

26. Von Trotta, interview press packet.

27. Jan's response to the picture of Marianne is not unlike many West German critics' responses to the picture *Marianne and Juliane.*

28. Quart, *Women Directors,* 113.

29. Kaplan, "Discourses of Terrorism," 64.

30. Kaplan, *Women and Film,* 111.

31. See Seiter, "The Political Is Personal: Margarethe von Trotta's *Marianne and Juliane,*" 112.

32. For a discussion of this type and his role in melodrama, see Byars, "Gazes/Voices/Power," 118–119.

33. Cf. the conclusion of *The Marriage of Maria Braun.*

34. Von Trotta, as quoted in Treen et al., "The Lady behind the Lens."

35. Elsaesser, "Mother Courage and Divided Daughters," 177.

36. Doane, "Women's Stake," 216. The use of terrorism as metaphor in analytical writing is a subject that deserves further study. For example, Fehervary commends Elfi Mikesch's *What Shall We Do Without Death?* because it contrasts with "so much of the avantgardistic literature and film [that] draws a direct line from eroticism and beauty to sado-masochism, violence and death. In this film there is eroticism and beauty, and there is death; but there is no terror. I see this film as rescuing women's bodies from the terrorism of the avant-garde" ("From Hitler to Hepburn," 182). Von Trotta's film also resists the kind of "terrorist" strategies Fehervary describes, strategies which are also present in mainstream cinema. Further, as Barbara Johnson notes, "Deconstruction has sometimes been seen as a terroristic belief in meaninglessness" ("Teaching Deconstructively," 140), and it has been tied to fascism. Von Trotta's film, however, suggests that both terrorist and antiterrorist violence depend on the suppression of contradictory evidence in order to legitimize or morally validate the use of "decisive measures"; the perception of undecidability—or "meaninglessness," as some call it—never motivates violence in the film. What emerges as suspect is not deconstructive thought but the suppression of conflicting evidence and of alternative visions. It is Marianne's refusal to acknowledge the possibility of valid alternatives to her position that prompts Juliane to liken her to the Hitler Youth. To deconstruct politics as usual, to call into question the ideological bases of decisive measures, to refuse the usual terms of terrorist debates—these are the approaches that the film puts forward as its models of resistance.

37. Delorme, "On the Film *Marianne and Juliane,*" 50.

38. Coates suggests that the Grünewald Crucifixion, which is seen in a dream of Juliane's, encapsulates these images. According to this reading, the painting is contextualized to remind us of Jesus' own Jewishness and to emblematize the extreme suffering that the Germans inflicted on the European Jews. For further discussion of the role of the painting in *Marianne and Juliane,* see Coates, *The Gorgon's Gaze,* 209.

39. Kaplan, "Discourses of Terrorism," 66.

40. Coates, *The Gorgon's Gaze,* 208.

41. Ibid., 207. Jan's angry act of tearing the photograph of his mother's face in half, straight down the middle, can thus also be seen as an allusion to Bergman's film, with its violent treatment of the close-up shots of women's faces. Like Brückner, von Trotta protests the cultural practices that determine the cinematic positioning of women through close-ups.

42. Here, Schiesari's words on the daughter's identification with the maternal seem relevant to Juliane's sororal cathexis with Marianne: "But no matter what the precise mode of identification with the mother—whether grief, or guilt, or resentment, or anger—the daughter's identity is necessarily already a communal one to the extent that the other [the maternal imago] is within her. . . . In other words, the mother is not given up as a lost object but is rediscovered through depression and mourning as an object of love and identification. Through depression and mourning, the mother's imago resurfaces from the interstices of the oedipal to assert her desirability as refigured by her identification and solidarity with other women" (*The Gendering of Melancholia,* 76–77).

43. Coates, *The Gorgon's Gaze,* 194.

44. Ibid., 208.

45. Hysteria, according to Freud, stems from the libidinal investment in an object that cannot be relinquished. For Freud, hysteria, like mourning and depression, is a classically feminine condition. For a valuable critique of his views, see Schiesari, *The Gendering of Melancholia,* 44–46 and 66.

46. Moreover, Coates argues that "Von Trotta's film can be read as her separate female contribution to *Germany in Autumn* (*Deutschland in Herbst*), the omnibus film the leading male representatives of the New German Cinema made in meditation on the hysterical West German response to the activities of the Baader-Meinhof group. . . ." (*The Gorgon's Gaze,* 221).

47. See Hirsch, *The Mother/Daughter Plot,* 12–13.

48. This issue comes up in the following four of the first six scenes of the film: 1. Werner's attempt to persuade Juliane to take in Jan; 2. Juliane's meeting with her pediatrician friend, Sabine, who oversees the care of babies up for adoption and who says that potential adoptive parents prefer infants; 3. the abortion-protest scene; and 4. Juliane and Marianne's emotionally charged discussion about Jan's future.

49. Marc Silberman, for one, asserts the latter (*German Cinema,* 211). Coates, on the other hand, suggests that the dark-haired boy's look evokes a Jewish identity. The film's complex contrapuntal relationship to *Persona*'s oedipal discourse, including Bergman's deployment of maternal and filial images, positions us to see a still broader frame of reference, encompassing contemporary Western culture. Simultaneously, like *Peppermint Peace,* with its somewhat similar closing use of a child's direct address, *Marianne and Juliane* allows Jan to retain a historical specificity.

50. Michael Schneider's comments on the postwar fear of mourning as emasculating women's work are worth recalling here ("Fathers and Sons, Retrospectively," 30–31).

CHAPTER FIVE

1. Shklovsky, "Art as Technique," 12.

2. To be sure, according to Rosenbaum, *Peppermint Peace* follows a child's logic of emotion (see Weinberger, "Marianne Rosenbaum and the Aesthetics of *Angst*," 237). But that logic of emotion does not generate the spectator immersion typical of the melodramatic or realist aesthetics. Moreover, this film's humor confirms Henri Bergson's familiar notion that humor requires a certain distance—a "momentary anesthesia of the heart."

3. DuBois, *Sowing the Body*, 7.

4. See, for example, Kaes, *From* Hitler *to* Heimat, 158, and Magee, "Cross Cultural Examination," 64. Barton Byg, in contrast, argues that Meerapfel's films, including *Malou*, typify contemporary German cinema. This construction of German cinema obscures her films' distinctly feminist elements. See Byg, "Extraterritorial Identity in the Films of Jeanine Meerapfel," 229–241.

5. Jenny, "Tango Argentino," 257.

6. Meerapfel, as quoted in Pally, "World of Our Mothers," 15. For a sharply contrasting position, see Monika Treut's remarks on images of women in German cinema, quoted in Knight, *Women and the New German Cinema*, 162–163.

7. Freud's idea of the family romance is that it affords a compensatory fiction for the disappointment one feels in one's actual parents and family. In *Malou*'s case, her fantasies about marriage are extensions of the contradictory, apparently compensatory stories she tells about her childhood and parents, and are constitutive of her family romance.

8. Quoted in Pally, "World of Our Mothers," 15.

9. Hirsch, *The Mother/Daughter Plot*, 11.

10. John Davidson has suggested to me that this zoom out away from the building could have been shot from the roof of Ulrike Ottinger's apartment/office building. The building in the shot is situated near U-Bahnhof Südstern in Kreuzberg.

11. For Benjamin, buildings, urban planning, public regulations, journalism, diaries—texts produced at both higher and lower levels of self-awareness, verbal and nonverbal texts—comprise the language that represents a society as a whole. Juxtapositions of passages from different texts and different eras create the possibility of new levels of speech. As James L. Rolleston asserts, "At perhaps the highest level yet imaginable, a fusion of past texts activates the 'language' of the historian's own epoch. For without such mediation the multiple languages at work in any given present cannot be comprehended; they are ceaselessly subjected to the censuring, masking processes of social and economic power" ("The Politics of Quotation," 16). Also see Benjamin, *Illuminations*, 261.

12. Stewart, *On Longing,* 139.

13. Smith, *A Poetics of Women's Autobiography,* 50.

14. Luce Irigaray's argument that women do not have an adequate signifying economy available to them to give full expression to their melancholias is relevant here.

15. Smith, *A Poetics of Women's Autobiography,* 53.

16. Hannah's appearance recalls that of Mina Harker, the wife in Murnau's *Nosferatu* who, like Dracula himself, is visually coded as Jewish.

17. See Kristeva, *Black Sun,* 78–79.

18. For a relevant discussion of a related myth, see Sichtermann, *Femininity,* 81–90.

19. Stewart, *On Longing,* 135.

20. Further, the psychological separation is not an emptying out of affect, as it is theorized to be in the Freudian paradigm of mourning, but rather a refiguration of the relationship between self and mother that does not depress the mother's value.

21. LaCapra, *Representing the Holocaust,* 205–223.

22. Stewart, *On Longing,* 23.

23. Schiesari is creating a feminist revision of Freud here. See *The Gendering of Melancholia,* 62. Also cf. Juliane's mourning of Marianne in *Marianne and Juliane,* and her quest to verify facts.

24. Stewart, *On Longing,* 61–65. Ibsen's *A Doll's House* is the best-known example.

25. Historicizing psychoanalysis, duBois draws an intriguing analogy between the following: First World economies that produce information and services versus Third World economies that produce commodities in the form of goods; and the Euro-American psychoanalytic shift to the phallus from the penis as the signifier of male supremacy. The dematerialized or abstracted token of exchange is valorized as a product of progress in both cases. See duBois, *Sowing the Body,* 12–15.

26. Fassbinder's work is the best-known illustration of the last.

27. Meerapfel, as quoted in Magee, "Cross Cultural Examination." In poststructuralist terms, the tango did not just speak to her, it *spoke* her.

28. Like Malou, both the word and the genre *melodrama,* according to Peter Brooks, were of specifically French derivation. See *The Melodramatic Imagination,* xii. For an excellent discussion of the term *métissage* in relationship to autobiography, see Lionnet, *Autobiographical Voices,* 1–29.

29. Lopez, "Tears and Desire," 255 and 258. Historically, Argentina itself is distinguished from other comparably industrialized Latin American countries and cultures by its greater conservatism in matters of female purity, sacrifice, and segregation in the domestic sphere. See Radcliffe, "Women's Place," 104–105.

30. Lopez, "Tears and Desire," 258.

31. As John King has documented, Latin American critics, influenced by 1960s critical paradigms, regarded Argentine melodramas of the 1930s and 1940s as politically reactionary—an insufficiently differentiated perspective that is now under scrutiny. King explains, "Film criticism which developed in Latin America in the politicized sixties has too rapidly dismissed the movies of the thirties and early forties. . . . There are signs that this attitude is beginning to change— Garcia Marquez in particular has talked of the need to make progressive *telenovelas*, melodramas of the small screen. There is therefore an awareness that these forms generate pleasure and are not 'in themselves' reactionary or progressive, but can be adapted to both purposes" (*Magical Reels*, 38).

32. The lyrics are:

> [First in German:]
> The little French woman in a strange land,
> she would like to fly homeward,
> but her wings have been burnt off.
> So she wanders through the streets
> that are made up of memories.
> Secretly she weeps in the alleys,
> a little lost child.
> The little French woman keeps on searching for a home,
> But her restless heart keeps on driving her outside.
> At home in Provence when the grapes glow,
> and hanging bunches of lavender blossoms,
> the child wanted to go out, out of the stone house,
> out into the unknown cold world.
> And when she told someone how much she liked to stay,
> her little foot would stumble over luck and love.
> She never put the bag away for long.
> She was used to the night, the wind, the dirt.
> [Then in French:]
> Little French woman, far from home,
> you dream of returning, . . .

33. The first song Malou sings within the diegesis, at the Strasbourg nightclub, is, likewise, about a one-way ticket, a ticket of no return.

34. Lopez, "Tears and Desire," 259–260.

35. The placement of the Chilean flag affords an oblique reference to the Latin American scene of the 1970s, when military governments took over their countries and, in many cases, violated human rights. Argentina was among these. See Radcliffe, "Women's Place," 102ff.

36. Mitscherlich, *Society without the Father*, 145–146.

37. Because Mitscherlich defines Hitler as a maternal figure (*Society without the Father*, 284), thereby splitting off that part of patriarchal history that most thoroughly contradicts his ideal, his lament for the weakening of paternalistic structures does not have to address or fully account for fascist history. In effect, Mitscherlich uses the figure of the mother to suture over the most terrible loss.

38. See de Lauretis, *Technologies of Gender*, 2.

39. Nazism itself is, among other things, a politics of nostalgia, but it would be wrong to reduce all forms of nostalgia—or for that matter, all forms of kitsch—to a fascist common denominator. See Schiesari on fascist nostalgia (*The Gendering of Melancholia*, 68) and Stewart on kitsch (*On Longing*, 168–169).

40. Heilbrun, *Writing a Woman's Life*, 130.

41. It seems likely that this film helped make its successor, *In the Land of Our Fathers*, possible. See Magee, "Cross Cultural Examination," 64.

42. Wim Wenders, as quoted in Dawson, *Wim Wenders*, 17. Also see Covino, "Wim Wenders."

43. Wollstonecraft, *Vindication of the Rights of Woman*, 184–185. Wollstonecraft asks, "What is to be the consequence, if the mother's and husband's opinion should *chance* not to agree?"

44. Huyssen, *After the Great Divide*, 190.

EPILOGUE

1. Elsaesser, *New German Cinema*, 185.

2. Fischer analyzes von Trotta's *Sisters, or The Balance of Happiness* in *Shot/Countershot*; as previously noted, Kaplan discusses *Marianne and Juliane* in *Women and Film*; Judith Mayne assesses Helke Sander's *The All-Round Reduced Personality/Redupers*, and Kaja Silverman comments on that film and on *Hunger Years*, in Erens, *Issues in Feminist Film Criticism*. *Women in German Yearbook* has also accorded the films valuable attention.

3. On *Marianne and Juliane*, see Coates, *The Gorgon's Gaze*, 222; on *Germany, Pale Mother*, see Reimer and Reimer, *Nazi-retro Film*, 203–204. More recently, von Trotta has also gained attention for her film *The Promise* (*Das Versprechen*, 1994). A story about lovers separated by the Berlin Wall, this film was the German entry in the Oscar competition for Best Foreign Film of 1994.

4. A relatively recent example of this neglect is the fall 1993 special issue of *New German Critique*, on German film history. The volume contains a number of excellent articles, but only one—Katie Trumpener's rather negative essay on Ulrike Ottinger—takes a woman director as its central focus. The fall 1994 *New German Critique* is a special issue on Fassbinder. Other important studies and volumes are more inclusive of women's films, but the disproportion remains striking. Worse still, according to Brückner, the current situation in

Germany for feminist films is considerably more neglectful than in the United States. See Brückner, interview with Barbara Kosta and Richard W. McCormick, 345–347, 366–369.

5. "Women who write about mothers," Wagner-Martin continues, "are moving directly into the cross hairs of a number of theoretical issues, many of them feminist" (*Telling Women's Lives*, 94).

6. Ibid., 96–97.

7. See Kaes, *From* Hitler *to* Heimat, 79.

8. Ibid., 79–80.

9. Ibid., 150.

10. Ibid., 145.

11. See, for example, Richard W. McCormick's discussion of this antagonism toward feeling ("Cinematic Form, History, and Gender," especially 39–40).

12. Liebman and Michelson, "After the Fall." In addition to this introduction, the valuable roundtable, "Further Thoughts on Helke Sander's Project," that concludes the volume merits mention. Silvia Kolbowski's insightful comments and Eric Santner's illuminating last words deserve special attention (Michelson et al., "Further Thoughts," 89–113).

13. In fact, after the fall of Berlin, the public rhetoric of gender did identify women as bearing primary responsibility for the national humiliation. See Fehrenbach, *Cinema in Democratizing Germany*, 99.

14. As we have seen, both *Peppermint Peace* and *Germany, Pale Mother* expose the political liabilities of religiously inflected rhetorics and pinpoint their effects on the formation and deformation of representations of female experiences.

15. Freud, "Mourning and Melancholia," 246.

16. Mizejewski, *Divine Decadence*, 236–237.

17. Rentschler, "Remembering Not to Forget," 38. Rentschler cites Syberberg's *Our Hitler* (Hitler—ein Film aus Deutschland, 1977), *Germany, Pale Mother*, Fassbinder's *Lili Marleen* (1980), and Reitz's *Heimat* (1984) as examples. While apparently granting Rentschler's point about the other films and equating *Germany, Pale Mother* with "the woman's point of view," Elsaesser attempts to exculpate Fassbinder by claiming that female protagonists such as Maria in *The Marriage of Maria Braun* "refuse victim thinking" ("Historicizing the Subject," 27–28). This stance begs the questions raised by Maria/Schygulla's aura of innocence and the plot's ultimate positioning of her as a pawn.

18. Rentschler himself does not identify or discuss the allegorical Germania figure in this film.

19. *The Marriage of Maria Braun* pointed to above marks the culmination of this pattern. Tellingly, the Eva Braun/Maria Braun dichotomy that underlies this film is implicitly deconstructed, but once again the film does not follow through by deconstructing per se the rhetorical practice of gendering nations female.

170   Notes to Pages 136–138

20. Fehrenbach, *Cinema in Democratizing Germany*, 116–117.

21. Geyer and Hansen, "German-Jewish Memory and National Consciousness," 178.

22. R. Radhakrishnan poses a number of related questions, worthy of quoting at length for the forceful challenge they provide to the ubiquitous assumption that women's politics must inevitably be subordinated to the politics of national identity: "The conjuncture wherein the women's question meets up with nationalism raises a number of fundamental questions about the very meaning of the term 'politics.' Why is it that the advent of the politics of nationalism signals the subordination if not the demise of women's politics? Why does the politics of the 'one' typically overwhelm the politics of the 'other'? Why could the two not be coordinated within an equal and dialogic relationship of *mutual accountability*? What factors constitute the normative criteria by which a question or issue is deemed 'political'? Why is it that nationalism achieves the ideological effect of an inclusive and putatively macropolitical discourse, whereas the women's question—unable to achieve its own autonomous macropolitical identity—remains ghettoized within its specific and regional space? In other words, by what natural or ideological imperative or historical exigency does the politics of nationalism become the binding and overarching umbrella that subsumes other and different political temporalities?" [italics mine] ("Nationalism, Gender, and the Narrative of Identity," 78).

23. Parker et al., Introduction, *Nationalisms and Sexualities*, 6. Also relevant is Teresa de Lauretis's assertion that "in fact masters are made as we . . . accept their answers or their metaphors" (*Alice Doesn't*, 3), as is her discussion of violence and representation (*Technologies of Gender*, 42–48).

24. Parker et al., Introduction, *Nationalisms and Sexualities*, 6.

25. McClintock, "'No Longer in a Future Heaven,'" 105.

26. The filmmakers' position should also be distinguished from that of Gisela Bock in "Antinatalism, Maternity and Paternity in National Socialist Racism."

27. Though it suffers from a neglect of gender issues, Alice Miller's *For Your Own Good* also sheds light on this violence. The problem has not gone away. In 1991 *Der Spiegel* and *Newsweek* reported on the proposal by the German Parliament for a new child protection law, written in response to severe child-abuse problems. See Michael Meyer's report on *Kinderunfreundlich* Germans, "Be Kinder to Your 'Kinder,'" 43.

28. See von Saldern, "Victims or Perpetrators? Controversies about the Role of Women in the Nazi State," 147–148.

29. Geyer and Hansen, "German-Jewish Memory," 176.

30. "Symbolic capital" is Brückner's phrase. See Brückner, interview with Kosta and McCormick, 219.

31. LaCapra, *Representing the Holocaust*, 213.

Filmography

Brückner, Jutta, director and screenwriter. *Hungerjahre* [*Hunger Years*]. Cinematography by Jörg Jeshel. Edited by Anneliese Krigar. Music by Johannes Schmölling. With Britta Pohland, Sylvia Ulrich, Claus Jurichs. Produced by Jutta Brückner and Zweites Deutsches Fernsehen (ZDF), 1979.

Meerapfel, Jeanine, director and screenwriter. *Malou.* Cinematography by Michael Ballhaus. Edited by Dagmar Hirtz. Music by Peer Raben. With Grischa Huber, Ingrid Caven, Helmut Griem, Ivan Desny. Produced by Regina Ziegler, Berlin, 1980.

Rosenbaum, Marianne S. W., director and screenwriter. *Peppermint Frieden* [*Peppermint Peace*]. Cinematography by Alfred Tichawsky. Edited by Gérard Samaan. Music by Konstantin Wecker. With Peter Fonda, Saskia Tyroller-Hauptmann, Gesine Stremple. Produced by Nourfilm, Munich, 1983.

Sanders-Brahms, Helma, director and screenwriter. *Deutschland, bleiche Mutter* [*Germany, Pale Mother*]. Cinematography by Jürgen Jüges. Edited by Elfi Tillack and Uta Periginelli. Music by Jürgen Knieper. With Eva Mattes, Ernst Jacobi, Elisabeth Stepanek, Anna Sanders, Sonja Lauer, Miriam Lauer. Produced by Helma Sanders-Brahms, Literarisches Colloquium, Berlin, and Westdeutscher Rundfunk (WDR), Cologne, 1979.

von Trotta, Margarethe, director and screenwriter. *Die bleierne Zeit* [*Marianne and Juliane*]. Cinematography by Franz Rath. Edited by Dagmar Hirtz. Music by Nicolas Economou. With Barbara Sukowa, Jutta Lampe, Rüdiger Vogler. Produced by Bioskop-Film (Eberhard Junkersdorf), Munich, 1981.

Bibliography

INTRODUCTION

Seeing Through the "Postwar" Years

Adorno, T. W., Else Frenkel-Brunswik, Daniel J. Levinson, and R. Nevitt Sanford. *The Authoritarian Personality.* New York: Harper and Brothers, 1950.

Aufderheide, Pat. "Good Soldiers." In *Seeing Through Movies,* ed. Mark Crispin Miller, 81–111. New York: Pantheon Books, 1990.

Begley, Louis. *Wartime Lies.* New York: Ivy Books, 1991.

Bordo, Susan. *Unbearable Weight: Feminism, Western Culture, and the Body.* Berkeley: University of California Press, 1993.

Cook, Roger F. "Melodrama or Cinematic Folktale? Story and History in *Deutschland, bleiche Mutter.*" *Germanic Review* 66, no. 3 (Summer 1991): 113–129.

Corber, Robert. *In the Name of National Security: Hitchcock, Homophobia, and the Political Construction of Gender in Postwar America.* Durham, N.C.: Duke University Press, 1993.

Corrigan, Timothy. *A Cinema Without Walls: Movies and Culture after Vietnam.* New Brunswick, N.J.: Rutgers University Press, 1991.

Dinnerstein, Dorothy. *The Mermaid and the Minotaur: Sexual Arrangements and Human Malaise.* New York: Harper and Row, 1976.

Eisler, Riane. *The Chalice and the Blade: Our History, Our Future.* New York: Harper and Row, 1987.

Elsaesser, Thomas. "Historicizing The Subject: A Body of Work?" *New German Critique* 63 (Fall 1994): 11–33.

———. *New German Cinema: A History.* New Brunswick, N.J.: Rutgers University Press, 1989.

———. "Primary Identification and the Historical Subject: Fassbinder and Germany." In *Narrative, Apparatus, Ideology,* ed. Philip Rosen, 535–549. New York: Columbia University Press. Originally published in *Ciné-Tracts* 11 (1980).

Fehrenbach, Heide. *Cinema in Democratizing Germany: Reconstructing National Identity after Hitler.* Chapel Hill: University of North Carolina Press, 1995.

Figge, Susan G. "Fathers, Daughters, and the Nazi Past: Father Literature and Its (Resisting) Readers." In *Gender, Patriarchy and Fascism in the Third Reich: The Response of Women Writers,* ed. Elaine Martin, 274–299. Detroit: Wayne State University Press, 1993.

Flitterman-Lewis, Sandy. *To Desire Differently: Feminism and the French Cinema.* Urbana: University of Illinois Press, 1990.

Freud, Sigmund. "Group Psychology and the Analysis of the Ego." In *The Standard Edition of the Complete Psychological Works.* 24 vols., ed. and trans. James Strachey et al. Vol. 18: 65–143. London: Hogarth Press, 1953–1974.

———. "Mourning and Melancholia." In *The Standard Edition of the Complete Psychological Works.* 24 vols., ed. and trans. James Strachey et al. Vol. 14: 243–258. London: Hogarth Press, 1953–1974.

———. "Three Essays on the Theory of Sexuality." In *The Standard Edition of the Complete Psychological Works.* 24 vols., ed. and trans. James Strachey et al. Vol. 7: 125–245. London: Hogarth Press, 1953–1974.

Friedman, Susan Stanford. "Women's Autobiographical Selves: Theory and Practice." In *The Private Self: Theory and Practice of Women's Autobiographical Writings,* ed. Shari Benstock, 34–62. Chapel Hill: University of North Carolina Press, 1988.

Gilligan, Carol. *In a Different Voice: Psychological Theory and Women's Development.* Cambridge: Harvard University Press, 1982.

Gilligan, Carol, Janie Victoria Ward, and Jill McLean Taylor, with Betty Bardige, eds. *Mapping the Moral Domain.* Cambridge: Harvard University Graduate School of Education, 1988.

Haraway, Donna. *Simians, Cyborgs, and Women: The Reinvention of Nature.* New York: Routledge, 1991.

Huyssen, Andreas. "The Politics of Identification: 'Holocaust' and West German Drama." *New German Critique* 19 (Winter 1980), 117–136. Reprinted in Andreas Huyssen, *After the Great Divide: Modernism, Mass Culture, Postmodernism,* 94–114 (Bloomington: Indiana University Press, 1986).

Jameson, Fredric. "Cognitive Mapping." In *Marxism and the Interpretation of Culture,* ed. Cary Nelson and Lawrence Grossberg, 347–357. Urbana: University of Illinois Press, 1988.

Jay, Martin. "Once More an Inability to Mourn? Reflections on the Left Melancholy of Our Time." *German Politics and Society* 27 (Fall 1992): 75.

Kawin, Bruce. *Mindscreen: Bergman, Godard, and First-Person Film.* Princeton, N.J.: Princeton University Press, 1978.

Knight, Julia. *Women and the New German Cinema.* New York: Verso, 1992.

Kolinsky, Eva. *Women in West Germany: Life, Work and Politics.* New York: Berg, 1989.

Kosta, Barbara. *Recasting Autobiography: Women's Counterfictions in Contemporary German Literature and Film.* Ithaca, N.Y.: Cornell University Press, 1994.

Linville, Susan E. *"Europa, Europa:* A Test Case for German National Cinema," *Wide Angle* 16, no. 3 (February 1995): 39–51.

McCormick, Richard W. "Private Anxieties/Public Projections: 'New Objectivity,' Male Subjectivity, and Weimar Cinema." *Women in German Yearbook* 10 (1994): 1–18.

Miller, Mark Crispin. "Deride and Conquer." In *Watching Television,* ed. Todd Gitlin, 182–228. New York: Pantheon Books, 1986.

Miller, Nancy K. "Representing Others: Gender and the Subject of Autobiography." *Differences* 6, no. 1 (Spring 1994): 1–27.

Mitscherlich, Alexander. *Society without the Father: A Contribution to Social Psychology.* Trans. Eric Mosbacher. New York: Harcourt, Brace and World, 1969.

Mitscherlich, Alexander, and Margarete Mitscherlich. *The Inability to Mourn: Principles of Collective Behavior.* Trans. Beverly R. Placzek. New York: Grove Press, 1975.

Mizejewski, Linda. *Divine Decadence: Fascism, Female Spectacle, and the Makings of Sally Bowles.* Princeton, N.J.: Princeton University Press, 1992.

Modleski, Tania. *The Women Who Knew Too Much: Hitchcock and Feminist Theory.* New York: Methuen, 1988.

Moeller, Robert G. *Protecting Motherhood: Women and the Family in the Politics of Postwar West Germany.* Berkeley: University of California Press, 1993.

Petro, Patrice. *Joyless Streets: Women and Melodramatic Representation in Weimar Germany.* Princeton, N.J.: Princeton University Press, 1989.

Reimer, Robert, and Carol Reimer. *Nazi-Retro Films: How German Narrative Cinema Remembers the Past.* New York: Twayne, 1992.

Rogin, Michael. *Ronald Reagan, the Movie, and Other Episodes in Political Demonology.* Berkeley: University of California Press, 1987.

Rosenbaum, Marianne. "'Frieden' hat für uns Deutsche einen amerikanischen Geschmack. Ein Gespräch mit Marianne S. W. Rosenbaum." With Bion Steinborn and Carola Hilmes. *Filmfaust* 39 (May–June 1984): 27–31.

Sander, Helke. "Nimmt man dir das Schwert, dann greife zum Knüppel." *Frauen und Film* 1 (July 1974): 12–48.

Sanders-Brahms, Helma. "Helma Sanders-Brahms: A Conversation." With Peter Brunette. *Film Quarterly* 44, no. 2 (Winter 1990–1991): 34–42.

Santner, Eric. *Stranded Objects: Mourning, Memory, and Film in Postwar Germany.* Ithaca, N.Y.: Cornell University Press, 1990.

Schiesari, Juliana. *The Gendering of Melancholia: Feminism, Psychoanalysis, and the*

Symbolics of Loss in Renaissance Literature. Ithaca, N.Y.: Cornell University Press, 1992.

Schneider, Michael. "Fathers and Sons, Retrospectively: The Damaged Relationship Between Two Generations." 1982. Trans. Jamie Owen Daniel. *New German Critique* 31 (1984): 3–51.

Silverman, Kaja. *The Subject of Semiotics.* New York: Oxford University Press, 1983.

von Trotta, Margarethe. *Die bleierne Zeit,* ed. Hans Jürgen Weber. Frankfurt: Fischer, 1981.

Wagner-Martin, Linda. *Telling Women's Lives: The New Biography.* New Brunswick, N.J.: Rutgers University Press, 1994.

Ward, Jenifer K. "Enacting the Different Voice: *Christa Klages* and Feminist History." *Women in German Yearbook* 11 (1995): 49–65.

Wrangham, Richard, and Dale Peterson. *Demonic Males: Apes and the Origins of Human Violence.* Boston: Houghton Mifflin, 1996.

CHAPTER ONE

Berger, John. *Ways of Seeing.* London: BBC and Penguin, 1972.

Bettelheim, Bruno. *The Uses of Enchantment: The Meaning and Importance of Fairy Tales.* 1976. New York: Random House, 1989.

Fehrenbach, Heide. *Cinema in Democratizing Germany: Reconstructing National Identity after Hitler.* Chapel Hill: University of North Carolina Press, 1995.

Geist, Kathe. "Mothers and Children in the Films of Wim Wenders." In *Gender and German Cinema,* vol. 1, ed. Sandra Frieden, Richard W. McCormick, Vibeke R. Petersen, and Laurie Melissa Vogelsang, 11–22. Providence, R.I.: Berg, 1993.

Kaschak, Ellyn. *Engendered Lives: A New Psychology of Women's Experience.* New York: Basic Books, 1992.

Koonz, Claudia. *Mothers in the Fatherland: Women, the Family and Nazi Politics.* New York: St. Martin's Press, 1987.

Liebman, Stuart, and Annette Michelson, eds. "Berlin 1945: War and Rape: 'Liberators Take Liberties.'" Special issue of *October* 72 (Spring 1995).

Linville, Susan E. "Agnieszka Holland's *Europa, Europa:* Deconstructive Humor in a Holocaust Film." *Film Criticism* 29, no. 3 (Spring 1995): 44–53.

———. "Fairy Tales and Reflexivity in Marianne Rosenbaum's *Peppermint Peace.*" In *Triangulated Visions: Women in Recent German Cinema,* ed. I. Majer O'Sickey and Ingeborg von Zadow. Albany: SUNY Press, forthcoming.

Malhlmann, Theodor. "Kirche und Wiederbewaffnung." In *Die fünfziger Jahre: Beiträge zu Politik und Kultur,* ed. Dieter Bänsch, 90–107. Tübingen: Gunter Narr Verlag, 1985.

McCormick, Richard W. "Cinematic Form, History, and Gender: Margarethe von Trotta's *Rosa Luxemburg.*" *Seminar* 32, no. 1 (February 1996): 36–41.

———. "Fascism, Film, and Gender: German History and Filmmaking by German Women Directors." Unpublished conference paper for "German Women Writers from Weimar to the Present: Facing Fascism and Confronting the Past," conference at the University of Maryland, February 1993.

———. *The Politics of the Self: Feminism and the Postmodern in West German Literature and Film.* Princeton, N.J.: Princeton University Press, 1991.

Mitscherlich, Alexander. *Society without the Father: A Contribution to Social Psychology.* Trans. Eric Mosbacher. New York: Harcourt, Brace and World, 1969.

Mizejewski, Linda. *Divine Decadence: Fascism, Female Spectacle, and the Makings of Sally Bowles.* Princeton, N.J.: Princeton University Press, 1992.

Modleski, Tania. *Feminism Without Women: Culture and Criticism in a "Postfeminist" Age.* New York: Routledge, 1991.

Moeller, Robert. *Protecting Motherhood: Women and the Family in the Politics of Postwar West Germany.* Berkeley: University of California Press, 1993.

Mulvey, Laura. "Visual Pleasure and Narrative Cinema." *Screen* 16, no. 3 (Autumn 1975): 6–18.

Olivier, Christiane. *Jocasta's Children: The Imprint of the Mother.* 1980. Trans. George Craig. New York: Routledge, 1989.

Owings, Alison. *Frauen: German Women Recall the Third Reich.* New Brunswick, N.J.: Rutgers University Press, 1993.

Rosenbaum, Marianne. "'Frieden' hat für uns Deutsche einen amerikanischen Geschmack. Ein Gespräch mit Marianne S. W. Rosenbaum." With Bion Steinborn and Carola Hilmes. *Filmfaust* 39 (May–June 1984): 31.

Sagan, Eli. *Freud, Women, and Morality: The Psychology of Good and Evil.* New York: Basic Books, 1988.

Schiesari, Juliana. *The Gendering of Melancholia: Feminism, Psychoanalysis, and the Symbolics of Loss in Renaissance Literature.* Ithaca, N.Y.: Cornell University Press, 1992.

Silverman, Kaja. *The Acoustic Mirror: The Female Voice in Psychoanalysis and Cinema.* Bloomington: Indiana Unversity Press, 1988.

Tröger, Annemarie. "German Women's Memories of World War II." In *Behind the Lines: Gender and the Two World Wars,* ed. Margaret Randolph Higonnet, Jane Jenson, Sonya Michel, and Margaret Collins Weitz, 285–299. New Haven, Conn.: Yale University Press, 1987.

Warner, Marina. *Alone of All her Sex: The Myth and Cult of the Virgin Mary.* New York: Knopf, 1976.

Weinberger, Gabriele. "Marianne Rosenbaum and the Aesthetics of *Angst.*" In *Gender and German Cinema: Feminist Interventions,* vol.2, ed. Sandra Frieden,

Richard W. McCormick, Vibeke R. Petersen, and Laurie Melissa Vogelsang, 227–240. Providence, R.I.: Berg, 1993.

———. *Nazi Germany and Its Aftermath in Women Directors' Autobiographical Films of the Late 1970s: In the Murderer's House.* San Francisco: Mellen Research University Press, 1992.

CHAPTER TWO

Bammer, Angelika. "Through a Daughter's Eyes: Helma Sanders-Brahms's *Germany, Pale Mother.*" *New German Critique* 36 (1985): 91–109.

Bettelheim, Bruno. *The Uses of Enchantment: The Meaning and Importance of Fairy Tales.* 1976. New York: Random House, 1989.

Chodorow, Nancy. *The Reproduction of Mothering: Psychoanalysis and the Sociology of Gender.* Berkeley: University of California Press, 1978.

Corber, Robert J. *In the Name of National Security: Hitchcock, Homophobia, and the Political Construction of Gender in Postwar America.* Durham, N.C.: Duke University Press, 1993.

Fischetti, Renate. *Das Neue Kino: Acht Porträts von deutschen Regisseurinnen.* Dülmen-Hiddingsel: Tende, 1992.

Freud, Sigmund. "Female Sexuality." In *The Standard Edition of the Complete Psychological Works,* 24 vols., ed. and trans. James Strachey et al. Vol. 21: 223–243. London: Hogarth Press, 1953–1974.

Goethe, Johann Wolfgang von. *Faust,* vol. I. Trans. David Luke. Oxford: Oxford University Press, 1987.

Hirsch, Marianne. *The Mother/Daughter Plot: Narrative, Psychoanalysis, Feminism.* Bloomington: Indiana University Press, 1989.

Hyams, Barbara. "Is the Apolitical Woman at Peace?: A Reading of the Fairy Tale in *Germany, Pale Mother.*" *Wide Angle* 10, no. 4 (1988): 40–51.

Kaes, Anton. *From Hitler to Heimat: The Return of History as Film.* Cambridge, Mass.: Harvard University Press, 1989.

Kaplan, E. Ann. "The Search for the Mother/Land in Sanders-Brahms's *Germany, Pale Mother.*" In *German Film and Literature: Adaptations and Transformations,* ed. Eric Rentschler, 289–304. New York: Methuen, 1986.

Kosta, Barbara. *Recasting Autobiography: Women's Counterfictions in Contemporary German Literature and Film.* Ithaca, N.Y.: Cornell University Press, 1994.

Liebman, Stuart, and Annette Michelson, eds. "Berlin 1945: War and Rape: 'Liberators Take Liberties.'" Special issue of *October* 72 (Spring 1995).

McCormick, Richard W. "Fascism, Film, and Gender: German History and Filmmaking by German Women Directors." Unpublished conference paper for "German Women Writers from Weimar to the Present: Facing Fascism and Confronting the Past," conference at the University of Maryland, February 1993.

————. *Politics of the Self: Feminism and the Postmodern in West German Literature and Film*. Princeton, N.J.: Princeton University Press, 1991.

Mitscherlich, Alexander, and Margarete Mitscherlich. *The Inability to Mourn: Principles of Collective Behavior*. Trans. Beverly R. Placzek. New York: Grove Press, 1975.

Modleski, Tania. *Feminism Without Women: Culture and Criticism in a "Postfeminist" Age*. New York: Routledge, 1991.

Möhrmann, Renate. "'Germany, Pale Mother': On the Mother Figures in New German Women's Film." *Women in German Yearbook* 11 (1995): 67–80.

Mosse, George. *Nationalism and Sexuality: Middle-Class Morality and Sexual Norms in Modern Europe*. Madison: University of Wisconsin Press, 1985.

Mulvey, Laura. *Visual and Other Pleasures*. Bloomington: Indiana University Press, 1989.

Münzberg, Olav. "'Schaudern vor der *bleichen Mutter*.' Eine sozialpsychologische Analyse der Kritiken zum Film von Helma Sanders-Brahms." *Medium* 7 (July 1980): 34–37.

Sander, Helke. "There Should Be No Scissors in Your Mind: An Interview with Helke Sander," with Stuart Liebman. *Cineaste* 21, nos. 1–2 (1995): 40–42.

————. *Deutschland, bleiche Mutter: Film-Erzählung*. Hamburg: Rowohlt, 1980.

————. "Helma Sanders-Brahms: A Conversation." With Peter Brunette. *Film Quarterly* 44, no. 2 (Winter 1990–1991): 34–42.

Santner, Eric. *Stranded Objects: Mourning, Memory, and Film in Postwar Germany*. Ithaca, N.Y.: Cornell University Press, 1990.

Schiesari, Juliana. *The Gendering of Melancholia: Feminism, Psychoanalysis, and the Symbolics of Loss in Renaissance Literature*. Ithaca, N.Y.: Cornell University Press, 1992.

Schneider, Michael. "Fathers and Sons, Retrospectively: The Damaged Relationship Between Two Generations." Trans. Jamie Owen Daniel. *New German Critique* 31 (1984): 3–51.

Seiter, Ellen E. "Women's History, Women's Melodrama: *Deutschland, bleiche Mutter*." *German Quarterly* 59 (1986): 569–581.

Silverman, Kaja. *The Acoustic Mirror: The Female Voice in Psychoanalysis and Cinema*. Bloomington: Indiana University Press, 1988.

Woolf, Virginia. *Three Guineas*. 1938. Reprint. New York: Harcourt Brace Jovanovich, 1966.

CHAPTER THREE

Aubenas, Jacqueline. "Le cinéma brut ou la brutalité de la biographie." In *Jutta Brückner, Cinéma Regard Violence*, ed. Françoise Collin, 53–59. Brussels: Les Cahiers du Grif, 1982.

Baudrillard, Jean. *La Société de consummation.* Paris: Gallimard, 1970 (as quoted in Maureen Turim, "Gentlemen Consume Blondes," in *Issues in Feminist Film Criticism,* ed. Patricia Erens, 106. Bloomington: Indiana University Press, 1990).

Berger, John. *Ways of Seeing.* London: BBC and Penguin, 1972.

Bernheimer, Charles. Introduction. *In Dora's Case: Freud—Hysteria—Feminism,* 2d ed. Ed. Charles Bernheimer and Claire Kahane. New York: Columbia University Press, 1990.

Bordo, Susan. *Unbearable Weight: Feminism, Western Culture, and the Body.* Berkeley: University of California Press, 1993.

Brückner, Jutta. "On Autobiographical Filmmaking." Trans. Jeannette Clausen. *Women in German Yearbook* 11 (1995): 1–12.

———. "Entretien de Sceaux," with Jacqueline Buet and Françoise Collin. In *Jutta Brückner, Cinéma Regard Violence,* ed. Françoise Collin, 17–51. Brussels: Les Cahiers du Grif, 1982.

———. "Entretien de Bruxelles," with Jacqueline Aubenas, Eliane Boucquey, Jacqueline Buet, Françoise Collin, Marie Denis, Claude Verne, and Christine Graeber. In *Jutta Brückner, Cinéma Regard Violence,* ed. Françoise Collin, 97–111. Brussels: Les Cahiers du Grif, 1982.

———. "Recognizing Collective Gestures," interview with Marc Silberman. *Jump Cut* 27 (1982): 41–53.

———. Interview with Patricia Harbord. *Screen Education* 40 (Autumn/Winter 1981–1982): 48–57.

———. Interview with Renate Fischetti. *Das Neue Kino: Acht Porträts von deutschen Regisseurinnen.* Frankfurt: Tende, 1992.

Brumberg, Joan Jacobs. *Fasting Girls: The History of Anorexia Nervosa.* New York: Penguin, 1988.

Caskey, Noelle. "Interpreting Anorexia Nervosa." In *The Female Body in Western Culture: Contemporary Perspectives,* ed. Susan Rubin Suleiman, 175–189. Cambridge, Mass.: Harvard University Press, 1986.

Chernin, Kim. *The Hungry Self: Women, Eating, and Identity.* New York: Harper and Row, 1985.

Chodorow, Nancy. *Feminism and Psychoanalytic Theory.* New Haven, Conn.: Yale University Press, 1989.

Cixous, Hélène, and Catherine Clément. *The Newly Born Woman.* Trans. Betsy Wing. Minneapolis: University of Minnesota Press, 1986.

Doane, Mary Ann. *The Desire to Desire: The Woman's Film of the 1940s.* Bloomington: Indiana University Press, 1987.

———. *Femmes Fatales: Feminism, Film Theory, Psychoanalysis.* New York: Routledge, 1991.

———. "The Spectatrix." *Camera Obscura* 20–21 (May–Sept. 1989): 144–145.

Elsaesser, Thomas. *"Berlin Alexanderplatz:* Franz Biberkopf'/S/Exchanges." *Wide Angle* 12 (1990): 30–43.

———. *New German Cinema: A History.* New Brunswick, N.J.: Rutgers University Press, 1989.

Export, Valie. "The Real and Its Double: The Body." *Discourse* 11, no. 1 (Fall–Winter 1988–1989): 3–27.

Fehrenbach, Heide. *Cinema in Democratizing Germany: Reconstructing National Identity after Hitler.* Chapel Hill: University of North Carolina Press, 1995.

Freud, Sigmund. "Extracts from the Fliess Papers." In *The Standard Edition of the Complete Psychological Works of Sigmund Freud,* 24 vols., ed. and trans. James Strachey et al. Vol. 1: 175–280. London: Hogarth Press, 1953–1974.

———. "Femininity." In *The Standard Edition of the Complete Psychological Works of Sigmund Freud,* 24 vols., ed. and trans. James Strachey et al. Vol. 22: 112–135. London: Hogarth Press, 1953–1974.

Garber, Marjorie. *Vested Interests: Cross-Dressing and Cultural Anxiety.* New York: Routledge, 1992.

Gilligan, Carol, Nona P. Lyons, and Trudy J. Hanmer, eds. *Making Connections: The Relational World of Adolescent Girls at Emma Willard School.* Cambridge, Mass.: Harvard University Press, 1990.

Irigaray, Luce. "Des marchandises entre elles" [When the goods get together]. Trans. Virginia Hules. In *New French Feminisms,* ed. Elaine Marks and Isabelle de Courtivron, 107–110. New York: Schocken Books, 1980.

Kellner, Douglas. *Jean Baudrillard: From Marxism to Postmodernism and Beyond.* Stanford, Calif.: Stanford University Press, 1989.

Koonz, Claudia. *Mothers in the Fatherland: Women, the Family and Nazi Politics.* New York: St. Martin's Press, 1987.

Kosta, Barbara. *Recasting Autobiography: Women's Counterfictions in Contemporary German Literature and Film.* Ithaca, N.Y.: Cornell University Press, 1994.

McCarthy, Margaret. "Consolidating, Consuming, and Annulling Identity in Jutta Brückner's *Hungerjahre.*" *Women in German Yearbook* 11 (1995): 13–33.

Mintz, Ira. "Self-Destructive Behavior in Anorexia and Bulimia." In *Bulimia: Psychoanalytic Treatment and Theory,* ed. Harvey J. Schwartz, 160–161. Madison, Wisc.: International University Press, 1988.

Mitscherlich, Alexander. *Society without the Father: A Contribution to Social Psychology.* Trans. Eric Mosbacher. New York: Harcourt, Brace and World, 1969.

Mitscherlich, Alexander, and Margarete Mitscherlich. *The Inability to Mourn: Principles of Collective Behavior.* Trans. Beverly R. Placzek. New York: Grove Press, 1975.

Möhrmann, Renate. "Jutta Brückner." In *Jutta Brückner, Cinéma Regard Violence,* ed. Françoise Collin, 9–16. Brussels: Les Cahiers du Grif, 1982. Originally published in Renate Möhrmann, *Die Frau mit der Kamera* (Munich-Vienna: Carl Hanser Verlag, 1980).

Morrison, Susan S. "The Feminization of the German Democratic Republic in Political Cartoons 1989–1990." *Journal of Popular Culture* 25, no. 4 (1992): 35–51.

Mouton, Jan. "The Absent Mother Makes an Appearance in the Films of West German Directors." *Women in German Yearbook* 4 (1988): 69–81.

Ramas, Maria. "Freud's Dora, Dora's Hysteria." In *In Dora's Case: Freud—Hysteria—Feminism*, 2d ed., ed. Charles Bernheimer and Claire Kahane, 149–180. New York: Columbia University Press, 1990.

Riviere, Joan. "Womanliness as a Masquerade." 1929. In *Formations of Fantasy*, ed. Victor Burgin, James Donald, and Cora Kaplan, pp. 35–44. New York: Routledge, 1986.

Sandford, John. *The New German Cinema*. Totowa, N.J.: Barnes and Noble, 1980.

Schiesari, Juliana. *The Gendering of Melancholia: Feminism, Psychoanalysis, and the Symbolics of Loss in Renaissance Literature*. Ithaca, N.Y.: Cornell University Press, 1992.

Shohat, Ella, and Robert Stam. *Unthinking Eurocentrism: Multiculturalism and the Media*. New York: Routledge, 1994.

Weinberger, Gabriele. *Nazi Germany and its Aftermath in Women Directors' Autobiographical Films of the Late 1970s*. San Francisco: Mellen Research University Press, 1992.

Williams, Linda. "Film Bodies: Gender, Genre, and Excess." *Film Quarterly* 44, no. 4 (Summer 1991): 2–13.

———. "'Something Else Besides a Mother': *Stella Dallas* and the Maternal Melodrama." In *Issues in Feminist Film Criticism*, ed. Patricia Erens, 137–162. Bloomington: Indiana University Press, 1990.

Wolowitz, Howard. "Hysterical Character and Feminine Identity." In *Readings on the Psychology of Women*, ed. Judith M. Bardwick, 307–314. New York: Harper and Row, 1972.

CHAPTER FOUR

Byars, Jackie. "Gazes/Voices/Power: Expanding Psychoanalysis for Feminist Film and Television Theory." In *Female Spectators: Looking at Film and Television*, ed. E. Deirdre Pribram, 110–131. New York: Verso, 1988.

Byg, Barton. "German History and Cinematic Convention Harmonized in Margarethe von Trotta's *Marianne and Juliane*." In *Gender and German Cinema: Feminist Interventions*, vol. 2, ed. Sandra Frieden, Richard W. McCormick,

Vibeke R. Petersen, and Laurie Melissa Vogelsang, pp. 259–271. Providence, R.I.: Berg, 1993.

Coates, Paul. *The Gorgon's Gaze: German Cinema, Expressionism, and the Image of Horror.* Cambridge: Cambridge University Press, 1991.

Corrigan, Timothy. *New German Cinema: The Displaced Image.* Austin: University of Texas Press, 1983.

Creed, Barbara. "Horror and the Monstrous-Feminine: An Imaginary Abjection." *Screen* 27 (1986): 45–70.

Culler, Jonathan. *On Deconstruction: Theory and Criticism after Structuralism.* Ithaca, N.Y.: Cornell University Press, 1982.

de Lauretis, Teresa. *Technologies of Gender: Essays on Theory, Film, and Fiction.* Bloomington: Indiana University Press, 1987.

Delorme, Charlotte. "On the Film *Marianne and Juliane* by Margarethe von Trotta." *Journal of Film and Video* 37 (1985): 47–51. Trans. Ellen Seiter. A translation of "Zum Film, *Die bleierne Zeit* von Margarethe von Trotta," *Frauen und Film* 31 (1982): 52–55.

Doane, Mary Ann. "Women's Stake: Filming the Female Body." In *Feminism and Film Theory*, ed. Constance Penley, 216–228. New York: Routledge, 1988.

Elsaesser, Thomas. "Mother Courage and Divided Daughters." *Monthly Film Bulletin* (July 1983): 176–178.

———. *New German Cinema: A History.* New Brunswick, N.J.: Rutgers University Press, 1989.

Fehervary, Helen, Claudia Lenssen, and Judith Mayne. "From Hitler to Hepburn: A Discussion of Women's Film Production and Reception." *New German Critique* 24–25 (1981–1982): 172–185.

Franklin, James. *New German Cinema: From Oberhausen to Hamburg.* Boston: Twayne, 1983.

Gilligan, Carol. *In a Different Voice: Psychological Theory and Women's Development.* Cambridge, Mass.: Harvard University Press, 1982.

Hirsch, Marianne. *The Mother/Daughter Plot: Narrative, Psychoanalysis, Feminism.* Bloomington: Indiana University Press, 1989.

Johnson, Barbara. "Teaching Deconstructively." In *Writing and Reading Differently,* ed. G. Douglas Atkins and Michael L. Johnson, 140–148. Lawrence: University of Kansas Press, 1985.

———. *A World of Difference.* Baltimore: Johns Hopkins University Press, 1987.

Kaplan, E. Ann. "Discourses of Terrorism, Feminism and the Family in von Trotta's *Marianne and Juliane.*" *Persistence of Vision* 2 (1985): 61–68.

———. *Women and Film: Both Sides of the Camera.* New York: Methuen, 1983.

Kristeva, Julia. *Black Sun: Depression and Melancholia.* Trans. Leon S. Roudiez. New York: Columbia University Press, 1989.

———. *Powers of Horror: An Essay on Abjection.* Trans. Leon S. Roudiez. New York: Columbia University Press, 1982.

McCormick, Richard W. *Politics of the Self: Feminism and the Postmodern in West German Literature and Film.* Princeton, N.J.: Princeton University Press, 1991.

Miller, Alice. *The Untouched Key.* New York: Doubleday, 1990.

Mitscherlich, Alexander. *Society without the Father: A Contribution to Social Psychology.* Trans. Eric Mosbacher. New York: Harcourt, Brace and World, 1969.

Moeller, H. B. "West German Women's Cinema: The Case of Margarethe von Trotta." *Film Criticism* 9 (1984–1985): 111–126.

Morgan, Robin. *The Demon Lover: On the Sexuality of Terrorism.* New York: Norton, 1989.

Quart, Barbara Koenig. *Women Directors: The Emergence of a New Cinema.* New York: Praeger, 1988.

Rentschler, Eric. *West German Cinema in the Course of Time.* Bedford Hills: Redgrave, 1984.

Sandford, John. *The New German Cinema.* Totowa, N.J.: Barnes and Noble, 1980.

Schiesari, Juliana. The *Gendering of Melancholia: Feminism, Psychoanalysis, and the Symbolics of Loss in Renaissance Literature.* Ithaca, N.Y.: Cornell University Press, 1992.

Schneider, Michael. "Fathers and Sons, Retrospectively: The Damaged Relationship Between Two Generations." Trans. Jamie Owen Daniel. *New German Critique* 31 (1984): 3–51.

Seiter, Ellen. "The Political Is Personal: Margarethe von Trotta's *Marianne and Juliane.*" In *Films for Women,* ed. Charlotte Brunsdon, 109–116. London: British Film Institute, 1986.

———. "Women's History, Women's Melodrama: *Deutschland, bleiche Mutter,*" *German Quarterly* 59 (1986): 569–581.

Silberman, Marc. *German Cinema: Texts in Context.* Detroit: Wayne State University Press, 1995.

———. "Women Filmmakers in West Germany: A Catalog." *Camera Obscura* 6 (1980): 123–152.

Sprengnether, Madelon. *The Spectral Mother: Freud, Feminism, and Psychoanalysis.* Ithaca, N.Y.: Cornell University Press, 1990.

Treen, Joseph, with Zofia Smardz and Joan Westreich. "The Lady behind the Lens" (review of *Marianne and Juliane*). *Newsweek,* 3 May 1982, intl. ed. Reprinted in the New Yorker Films press packet.

von Trotta, Margarethe. *Die bleierne Zeit,* ed. Hans Jürgen Weber. Frankfurt: Fischer, 1981.

———. Interview, New Yorker Films press packet.

Ward, Jenifer K. "Enacting the Different Voice: *Christa Klages* and Feminist History." *Women in German Yearbook* 11 (1995): 49–65.

Wollen, Peter. *Signs and Meaning in the Cinema.* Bloomington: Indiana University Press, 1971.

Wollstonecraft, Mary. *Vindication of the Rights of Woman.* 1792. Reprint. New York: Penguin, 1985.

CHAPTER FIVE

Benjamin, Walter. *Illuminations.* Ed. Hannah Arendt, trans. Harry Zohn. New York: Schocken Books, 1969.

Brooks, Peter. *The Melodramatic Imagination: Balzac, Henry James, Melodrama, and the Mode of Excess.* New Haven, Conn.: Yale University Press, 1976.

Byg, Barton. "Extraterritorial Identity in the Films of Jeanine Meerapfel." In *"Neue Welt"/"Dritte Welt": Interkulturelle Beziehungen Deutschlands zu Lateinamerika und der Karibik,* ed. Sigrid Bauschinger and Susan Cocalis, 229–241. Tübingen: Franck, 1994.

Coates, Paul. *The Gorgon's Gaze: German Cinema, Expressionism, and the Image of Horror.* Cambridge: Cambridge University Press, 1991.

Covino, Michael. "Wim Wenders: A Worldwide Homesickness." *Film Quarterly* 31 (1977–1978): 9–19.

Dawson, Jan. *Wim Wenders.* New York: Zoetrope, 1976.

de Lauretis, Teresa. *Technologies of Gender: Essays on Theory, Film, and Fiction.* Bloomington: Indiana University Press, 1987.

duBois, Page. *Sowing the Body: Psychoanalysis and Ancient Representations of Women.* Chicago: University of Chicago Press, 1988.

Heilbrun, Carolyn. *Writing a Woman's Life.* New York: W. W. Norton, 1988.

Hirsch, Marianne. *The Mother/Daughter Plot: Narrative, Psychoanalysis, Feminism.* Bloomington: Indiana University Press, 1989.

Huyssen, Andreas. *After the Great Divide: Modernism, Mass Culture, Postmodernism.* Bloomington: Indiana University Press, 1986.

Jenny, Urs. "Tango Argentino." *Der Spiegel,* no. 14 (30 March 1981): 257–258.

Kaes, Anton. *From* Hitler *to* Heimat: *The Return of History as Film.* Cambridge, Mass.: Harvard University Press, 1989.

King, John. *Magical Reels: A History of Cinema in Latin America.* New York: Verso, 1990.

Knight, Julia. *Women and the New German Cinema.* New York: Verso, 1992.

Kristeva, Julia. *Black Sun: Depression and Melancholia.* Trans. Leon S. Roudiez. New York: Columbia University Press, 1989.

LaCapra, Dominick. *Representing the Holocaust: History, Theory, Trauma.* Ithaca, N.Y.: Cornell University Press, 1994.

Lionnet, Françoise. *Autobiographical Voices: Race, Gender, Self-Portraiture.* Ithaca, N.Y.: Cornell University Press, 1989.

Lopez, Ana M. "Tears and Desire: Women and Melodrama in the 'Old' Mexican Cinema." In *Multiple Voices in Feminist Film Criticism*, ed. Diane Carson, Linda Dittmar, and Janice R. Welsch, 254–270. Minneapolis: University of Minnesota Press, 1994.

Magee, Shawn S. "Cross Cultural Examination." *Jump Cut* 30 (March 1985): 63–64.

Mitscherlich, Alexander. *Society without the Father: A Contribution to Social Psychology*. Trans. Eric Mosbacher. New York: Harcourt, Brace and World, 1969.

Pally, Marcia. "World of Our Mothers." *Film Comment* (March–April 1984): 11–17.

Radcliffe, Sarah A. "Women's Place: Latin America and the Politics of Gender Identity." In *Place and the Politics of Identity*, ed. Michael Keith and Steve Pile, 102–116. New York: Routledge, 1993.

Rolleston, James L. "The Politics of Quotation: Walter Benjamin's Arcades Project." *PMLA* 104, no. 1 (January 1989): 13–27.

Schiesari, Juliana. *The Gendering of Melancholia: Feminism, Psychoanalysis, and the Symbolics of Loss in Renaissance Literature*. Ithaca, N.Y.: Cornell University Press, 1992.

Shklovsky, Victor. "Art as Technique." In *Russian Formalist Criticism: Four Essays*, ed. and trans. Lee T. Lemon and Marion J. Reis, 3–57. Lincoln: University of Nebraska Press, 1965.

Sichtermann, Barbara. *Femininity: The Politics of the Personal*. Trans. John Whitlam. Minneapolis: University of Minnesota Press, 1986.

Smith, Sidonie. *A Poetics of Women's Autobiography: Marginality and the Fictions of Self-Representation*. Bloomington: Indiana University Press, 1987.

Stewart, Susan. *On Longing: Narratives of the Miniature, the Gigantic, the Souvenir, the Collection*. Durham, N.C.: Duke University Press, 1993.

Weinberger, Gabriele. "Marianne Rosenbaum and the Aesthetics of *Angst*." In *Gender and German Cinema: Feminist Interventions*, vol.2, ed. Sandra Frieden, Richard W. McCormick, Vibeke R. Petersen, and Laurie Melissa Vogelsang, 226–240. Providence, R.I.: Berg, 1993.

Wollstonecraft, Mary. *Vindication of the Rights of Woman*. 1792. Reprint. New York: Penguin, 1985.

EPILOGUE

Bock, Gisela. "Antinatalism, Maternity and Paternity in National Socialist Racism." In *Nazism and German Society, 1933–1945*, ed. David F. Crew, 110–140. New York: Routledge, 1994.

Brückner, Jutta. Interview with Barbara Kosta and Richard W. McCormick. *Signs* 21, no. 2 (Winter 1996): 343–373.

Coates, Paul. *The Gorgon's Gaze: German Cinema, Expressionism, and the Image of Horror.* Cambridge: Cambridge University Press, 1991.

de Lauretis, Teresa. *Alice Doesn't: Feminism, Semiotics, Cinema.* Bloomington: Indiana University Press, 1984.

———. *Technologies of Gender: Essays on Theory, Film, and Fiction.* Bloomington: Indiana University Press, 1987.

Elsaesser, Thomas. "Historicizing the Subject: A Body of Work?" *New German Critique* 63 (Fall 1994): 11–33.

———. *New German Cinema: A History.* New Brunswick, N.J.: Rutgers University Press, 1989.

Erens, Patricia, ed. *Issues in Feminist Film Criticism.* Bloomington: Indiana University Press, 1990.

Fischer, Lucy. *Shot/Countershot: Film Tradition and Women's Cinema.* Princeton, N.J.: Princeton University Press, 1989.

Fehrenbach, Heide. *Cinema in Democratizing Germany: Reconstructing National Identity after Hitler.* Chapel Hill: University of North Carolina Press, 1995.

Freud, Sigmund. "Mourning and Melancholia." In *The Standard Edition of the Complete Psychological Works,* 24 vols., ed. and trans. James Strachey et al. Vol. 14: 243–258. London: Hogarth Press, 1953–1974.

Geyer, Michael, and Miriam Hansen. "German-Jewish Memory and National Consciousness." In *Holocaust Remembrance: The Shapes of Memory,* ed. Geoffrey Hartman, 175–190. Cambridge, Mass.: Basil Blackwell, 1994.

Kaes, Anton. *From Hitler to Heimat: The Return of History as Film.* Cambridge, Mass.: Harvard University Press, 1989.

Kaplan, E. Ann. *Women and Film: Both Sides of the Camera.* New York: Methuen, 1983.

LaCapra, Dominick. *Representing the Holocaust: History, Theory, Trauma.* Ithaca, N.Y.: Cornell University Press, 1994.

Liebman, Stuart, and Annette Michelson. "After the Fall: Women in the House of the Hangman." *October* 72 (Spring 1995): 5–14.

Mayne, Judith. "Female Narration, Women's Cinema: Helke Sander's *The All-Round Reduced Personality/Redupers.*" In *Issues in Feminist Film Criticism,* ed. Patricia Erens, 380–394. Bloomington: Indiana University Press, 1990.

McClintock, Anne. "'No Longer a Future in Heaven': Women and Nationalism in South Africa." *Transition* 51 (1991): 104–123.

McCormick, Richard W. "Cinematic Form, History, and Gender: Margarethe von Trotta's *Rosa Luxemburg.*" *Seminar* 32, no. 1 (February 1996): 36–41.

Meyer, Michael. "Be Kinder to Your 'Kinder.'" *Newsweek* 16 December 1991: 41.

Michelson, Annette, Andreas Huyssen, Stuart Liebman, Eric Santner, and Silvia Kolbowski. Roundtable, "Further Thoughts on Helke Sander's Project." *October* 72 (Spring 1995): 89–113.

Miller, Alice. *For Your Own Good: Hidden Cruelty in Child-Rearing and the Roots of Violence.* Trans. Hildegarde and Hunter Hannum. New York: Farrar, Straus, Giroux, 1983.

Mizejewski, Linda. *Divine Decadence: Fascism, Female Spectacle, and the Makings of Sally Bowles.* Princeton, N.J.: Princeton University Press, 1992.

Parker, Andrew, Mary Russo, Doris Sommer, and Patricia Yaeger. Introduction. *Nationalisms and Sexualities.* Ed. Andrew Parker et al., 1–18. New York: Routledge, 1992.

Radhakrishnan, R. "Nationalism, Gender, and the Narrative of Identity." In *Nationalisms and Sexualities*, ed. Andrew Parker, Mary Russo, Doris Sommer, and Patricia Yaeger, 77–95. New York: Routledge, 1992.

Reimer, Robert, and Carol Reimer. *Nazi-Retro Film: How German Narrative Cinema Remembers the Past.* New York: Twayne, 1992.

Rentschler, Eric. "Remembering Not to Forget: A Retrospective Reading of Alexander Kluge's *Brutality in Stone.*" *New German Critique* 49 (Winter 1990): 23–41.

Silverman, Kaja. "Dis-embodying the Female Voice." In *Issues in Feminist Film Criticism,* ed. Patricia Erens, 309–327. Bloomington: Indiana University Press, 1990.

von Saldern, Adelheid. "Victims or Perpetrators? Controversies about the Role of Women in the Nazi State." In *Nazism and German Society, 1933–1945,* ed. David F. Crew, 141–165. New York: Routledge, 1994.

Wagner-Martin, Linda. *Telling Women's Lives: The New Biography.* New Brunswick, N.J.: Rutgers University Press, 1994.

Index

Liebman, Stuart, and Annette Michelson, 169 n.12
Lopez, Ana M., 122, 123

Malou. See Meerapfel, Jeanine: *Malou*
Marianne and Juliane. See von Trotta,
    Margarethe: *Marianne and Juliane*
Marriage of Maria Braun, The. See
    Fassbinder, Rainer Werner: *The*
    Marriage of Maria Braun
matrophobia. *See* authoritarianism,
    postwar theories of: matrophobia
    in; Hitchcock, Alfred, matrophobia
    in *The Man Who Knew Too Much*
    and *Notorious*
McCarthy, Margaret, 157 n.24
McCormick, Richard W., 57, 141 n.15,
    146 n.2, 150 n.30, 153 n.28, 154 n.42,
    161 n.9
Meerapfel, Jeanine: *In the Land of Our*
    Fathers, 168 n.41; *Malou,* 15–16, 109–
    128, 136–137
melancholy: and European Renais-
    sance Humanism, 4–5; vs. female
    depression, 4, 132, 141 n.9; and fe-
    male identity formation, 45, 166 n.14;
    vs. female mourning, 118; masculin-
    ist mythos of, 4–5, 6, 38–39, 118–119,
    132–134. *See also* Freud, Sigmund:
    "Mourning and Melancholia"
melodrama: in *Germany, Pale Mother,*
    41, 56, 89, 154 n.42; in *Hunger Years,*
    69, 81; in *Malou,* 112, 121–125, 127; in
    Marianne and Juliane, 85–86, 89–
    90, 91, 99, 102; multicultural, 122.
    See also Argentine melodrama
Metz, Christian, 3, 81–82
Mikesch, Elfi: *What Shall We Do*
    Without Death?, 163 n.36
Miller, Alice, 162 n.25, 170 n.27
Miller, Mark Crispin, 146 n.59

Miller, Nancy K., 17
mindscreen, 15; in *Hunger Years,* 81; in
    Malou, 112–113, 117, 123; in *Marianne*
    and Juliane, 88, 94; in *Peppermint*
    Peace, 25
Mitscherlich, Alexander: *Society with-*
    out the Father, 3–13, 63, 125, 134,
    144 n.38, 158 n.35
Mitscherlich, Alexander and Mar-
    garete: *The Inability to Mourn,* 3–
    9, 27, 29, 42–43, 64, 66, 105, 132,
    151 n.5, 152 n.23
Mizejewski, Linda, 134, 146 n.1
Modleski, Tania, 141 n.15, 148 n.19,
    149 n.21
Morgan, Robin, 87
mother-daughter dyad, 14, 29–31, 42–
    50, 52–55, 62, 71, 76. *See also* Antig-
    one phase; mourning, feminist con-
    cepts of; Oedipus complex, negative
mother-son paradigms, 38, 48–49, 60,
    152 n.23. *See also* Mitscherlich; Mit-
    scherlich and Mitscherlich; oedipal
    paradigms
mourning, 82–83, 85, 90–91, 119, 138–
    139; devaluation of women's, 5, 92,
    113, 119; feminist concepts of, 91,
    104–105, 107–108, 118–119, 159 n.57,
    164 n.42, 166 n.20; German incapac-
    ity for, 7–9, 22, 27, 32–34, 37, 51–52,
    65; work of, in *Germany, Pale Mother,*
    42, 87, 154–155 n.48; work of, in *Hun-*
    ger Years, 14, 65–66, 82–83; work
    of, in *Malou,* 15–16, 117–120; work
    of, in *Marianne and Juliane,* 15, 85–
    87, 90–92, 104–108; work of, in
    Peppermint Peace, 38–40. *See also*
    Freud: "Mourning and Melancho-
    lia"; Holocaust; Mitscherlich and
    Mitscherlich
Mühlhiasl, 26

Sanders-Brahms, Helma: *Germany,*
Pale Mother, 14, 41–63, 68, 72, 129,
130–131, 133–137, 149 n.24, 169 nn.14,17
Santner, Eric, 42–44, 142 n.20, 153 n.33,
169 n.12
Schelsky, Helmut, 12
Schiesari, Juliana, 4–8, 37, 44, 118,
141 n.9, 142 n.19, 164 n.42
Schlöndorff, Volker, and Margarethe
von Trotta: *Germany in Autumn,*
107, 164 n.46; *The Lost Honor of*
Katharina Blum, 86–87, 160 n.4
Schmölling, Johannes, 69
Schneider, Michael, 7–8, 51, 63
Schneider, Peter, 99
Seiter, Ellen, 89
self-reflexivity, 19, 146 n.59; in *Ger-*
many, Pale Mother, 55, 58–59; in
Hunger Years, 77, 80–81; in *Malou,*
144; in *Marianne and Juliane,* 87, 89,
94; in *Peppermint Peace,* 31, 34–35, 38
sexuality, repression of: in *Hunger*
Years, 65, 69–72, 79, 81–82; in *Pep-*
permint Peace, 13, 25–26, 35–38
Shklovsky, Victor, 109–110
Sierck, Detlev. *See* Sirk, Douglas
Silberman, Marc, 161 n.9, 164 n.49
Silverman, Kaja, 34, 42, 44–46, 55–56,
152 n.23, 154 n.40
Sirk, Douglas (Detlev Sierck), 127; *All*
that Heaven Allows, 99, 127; *La Ha-*
bañera, 121
Smith, Sidonie, 116
social gender hierarchy, 3, 5, 9–11; and
Hunger Years, 83; and *Peppermint*
Peace, 27–29, 35–36, 150 n.32
social imaginary, 141 n.6
spectatorship, female: in *Hunger Years,*
66–68, 77–78, 82–83; in *Peppermint*
Peace, 28–31, 35. *See also* gaze; surveillance; voyeurism

speech disorder, 80
Spiegelman, Art: *Maus,* 17–18
Sprengnether, Madelon, 91
Stella Dallas, 112
Stewart, Susan, 115, 117
surveillance, 31, 34–37, 39, 77, 102–104,
150 n.33
Syberberg, Hans Jürgen: *Our Hitler,*
169 n.17

tango melodrama. *See* Argentine
melodrama
terrorism, 37, 86, 89, 98, 101–102,
163 n.36. *See also* Baader-Meinhof
group
Theweleit, Klaus, 148 n.19
Trauerarbeit (work of mourning). *See*
mourning
Tröger, Annemarie, 22, 38

Varda, Agnès, 53
Vaterliteratur (Father Literature), 7–8,
142 n.23
Verhoeven, Michael: *The Nasty Girl,*
146 n.1
Vietnam War, 16, 84, 87, 142–143 n.27
violence: aestheticization and specularization of women as, 68, 78–79,
102, 157 n.16; domestic, 100, 102,
137–138; fascist, 35, 57, 102, 111, 137–
138; in Hollywood film, 102; and the
male gaze, 78; origins of, 11; politics
and, 87, 91, 100–101
voice-over narration, 54–56, 68–69,
74, 76
von Trotta, Margarethe: *Marianne and*
Juliane, 15, 34, 84–108, 117, 126–127,
129, 150 n.34; *The Promise,* 168 n.3;
The Second Awakening of Christa
Klages, 92, 98; *Sheer Madness,* 92;